VIOLENCE AND CONFLICT

Understanding the issues and consequences

Karl Schonborn, Ph. D.

KENDALL/HUNT PUBLISHING COMPANY
4050 Westmark Drive   Dubuque, Iowa 52002

Copyright ©1998 Kendall/Hunt Publishing Company

Library of Congress Catalog Card Number 97-75522

ISBN 0-7872-4599-2

Printed in the United States of America
10 9 8 7 6 5 4 3 2

DEDICATION

To my wife, Leslie
and to my children, John-Scott and Lindsay,
for whom I wish a world of nonviolence

CONTENTS IN BRIEF

CONTENTS

PART III
GROUPS, VIOLENCE & CONFLICT 89

PART IV
ORGANIZATIONS, VIOLENCE & CONFLICT 129

PREFACE

The primary focus of this book is domestic violence, street gang violence, bloody encounters with cults and militias, and the riots and disorders that have plagued several American cities of late. The focus, then, is not on rape, robbery, assault, and conventional murder, but rather on the less conventional kinds of violence along with the conflicts that underlie them.

Moreover, the book looks at so-called legitimate violence in our society such as the use of deadly force by the police. The book tries to make sense of the factors that cause legitimate violence to sometimes turn illegitimate as it does, say, in cases of police brutality. The objective of the book, then, is to make readers aware of the issues and consequences of some of the unconventional violence in America.

The book is designed for general-interest readers and not just for students of violence and conflict. While the book comfortably ranges over much social science turf, it is grounded in pragmatism and should be appealing to future or present-day teachers, researchers, social workers, law enforcers, correctional officers, etc.

The author has spent his professional career studying and researching violence. However, because the topics examined in the book are vast and wide-ranging, he has brought in a few outside authors to help out. Most of the contributing authors are nationally-regarded authorities or experts at the big picture. Thus, the book has the advantages of a solely-authored book as well as the advantages of a multiple-authored book.

Special features of the book

— a systems-level approach that distinguishes the book from the usual approaches by institution (school, prison, workplace), by causal factors (drugs, parenting, the media, the economy), etc.

— an easy-to-learn framework which gets rid of some of the confusion about violence and conflict

— introductions to each part of the book, setting the stage for what is to come in upcoming chapters

— concepts and themes that recur throughout the book, reinforcing what has been presented earlier

— appropriateness for courses, from junior colleges to graduate schools

Instructors will find the range of topics covered—and the concepts and theory presented—quite suitable for courses in criminology, juvenile delinquency, deviant behavior, abnormal psychology, and the like. The book is also ideal for courses in the increasingly important areas of mediation, conflict resolution, and violence management. The book can be used as a reference source, a supplement, or a main text in quarter or semester courses. A study guide is available which contains, among other things, well thought-out student exercises together with some interesting class projects and field assignments. It also contains a list of resources, including an annotated list of videos suitable for classroom use.

Students will appreciate the wealth of information in the book, including its interesting case studies. The book is well-organized—with five parts that tie together nicely—and it has a clear, straightforward writing style. The student guide has a list of relevant internet sites in its Resources section.

INTRODUCTION

We live in a violent world and a violent society. Whether it is a murderous family fight, a drive-by gang shooting, or a terrorist explosion that kills scores of people, violence gets our attention and often troubles us to the core.

Every day we hear about violence striking somewhere new, and sometimes violence seems as unpredictable as lightening. But, there is some predictability and sense to what seems mysterious and senseless sometimes.

One of the goals of this book is to introduce readers to the length and breadth of the knowledge available today about violence. Embarking on a study of violence and conflict can not only open our eyes to what is currently known, but it can also empower us. It is hoped that this new-found knowledge and understanding might motivate readers to tackle a piece of the violence problem—through research, intervention, prevention, or some other activity.

PART I—THE NATURE OF VIOLENCE & CONFLICT

This book is divided into five parts with the first part devoted to presenting some basic terms, concepts and theories which will help the reader understand the issues and consequences of violence and conflict.

Important terms and concepts throughout the book are printed in **boldface** type. These are defined in the glossary as well as in the book. Items of lesser importance are *italicized*. The companion study guide for the book helps readers both learn and make use of many terms and concepts. All these features are intended to facilitate study and comprehension of the material.

The book presents a framework, too, which will allow readers to be creative and see similarities between, say, interpersonal conflicts they are embroiled in and other, larger conflicts in society. The systems theory framework that is offered gives readers the tools to find similarities or parallels among other seemingly unrelated kinds of violence and conflict. An additional plus to the framework is that it allows one to sort out and understand a large number of the many types of violent conflicts that occur.

The system characteristics of the four kinds of conflict and the four kinds of parties (participants) that engage in them are defined in Part I. Incidentally, while readers may certainly read chapters out of order, one gets a better sense of the increasing complexity of violent conflict by reading chapters sequentially.

Since much important violence and conflict occurs at each of the four levels dealt with in this book—ranging from the individual to the communal level—a brief review of each of the levels is in order now. The review will also provide an opportunity to introduce some of the features of the book. Each part of the book is devoted to a different system level.

PART II—INDIVIDUALS, VIOLENCE & CONFLICT

Because of the heightened public awareness of domestic violence due to the O.J. Simpson trial, the book examines in detail the nature and scope of the problem of family violence. Victims of homicidal family violence are the most likely of all victims to be subjected to excessive violence: that is, more than one stab wound or gunshot wound. Often the family intimate stabs the victim countless times or empties the gun into him or her, reloads, and empties it again! In addition to the traditional victims of domestic violence—battered women—the book examines child abuse, elder abuse, marital rape, and battered men.

In focusing on the individual, Part I also deals with the *fear of violence*. People are often asked by researchers, "Do you feel safer today than you did ten years ago?" In survey after survey, the answer, clearly, is "No." It is ironic, however, that much of the fear people feel concerns being victimized by total strangers when in fact, most of us are statistically more likely to be brutalized by our loved ones, by family intimates.

The issue of guns and gun control is also discussed. Regarding guns, in some areas of this country guns come close to being household appliances. They are used almost as casually as a toaster! Mindful of this, Part I includes an examination of various statutes and efforts to control guns in America.

PART III—GROUPS, VIOLENCE & CONFLICT

Most youths find little reason to become involved in law-violating activities. But others— with needs frustrated and no where else to find hope—become attracted to street gangs. These gangs become quasi-families and offer acceptance, status, and esteem.

However, the relatively innocuous street gangs of the 1950s have become the gun-wielding, drug-trafficking gangs of the 1990s. With some of the most lethal weapons available, many street gangs are terrorizing and terrifying citizens. They are also spreading from metropolitan areas outward to other communities in America.

Police gang units seem to be helpless to defuse gang violence or prevent its spread. Grassroots community groups have had *some* success, though, with gang members, but gang reduction ultimately depends on providing children of the underclass with more positive options than they have today. Youths derive meaning and have their needs met or ignored in their social contacts with family members, peers, teachers, and community leaders. Important in this regard is getting young people involved in groups at their churches, in community sports teams, or in groups involved in legitimate school activities.

PART IV—ORGANIZATIONS, VIOLENCE & CONFLICT

Experts believe that there are an unusually large number of millenarian cults active today, each prophesying death and Apocalyptic doom. How should these cults be handled? And how should law enforcement organizations deal with the myriad extremist political organizations that dot the American landscape and occasionally make trouble? One popular tactic has been to use a massive display of force and intense psychological pressure to negotiate a settlement. Unfortunately, this has not worked of late, as Waco and the following incident in Philadelphia indicate.

During a confrontation in 1985 with an anarchistic, anti-technology cult called MOVE, police engaged in a 90 minute firefight—firing 7,000 rounds—after their water cannon barrage failed to get the cult to surrender. So, following an unsuccessful SWAT assault, the mayor and police chief decided to drop an explosive on the cult's rooftop bunker. Sixty surrounding homes were almost instantly destroyed by the raging inferno that resulted. Eleven bodies (including those of 4 children) were pulled from the rubble of the cult's house; and hundreds of innocent residents in the leveled two city blocks were left homeless. The city had confronted MOVE once before in 1978, and at that time a fierce shoot-out ended in the death of a policeman.

Besides troubles with religious, cult-like organizations, Part IV includes discussion of violence issues with regard to political organizations such as militias. Militias have troubled officials of late, from the 80-day standoff with the Freeman "Justus township" in eastern Montana to the arrest of 12 middle-class, suburban "Viper Militia" members who allegedly plotted to blow up government buildings in Phoenix, Arizona. The chapters in Part IV deal with, among other things, the various complexities regarding the confrontations at Waco and Ruby Ridge.

PART V—COMMUNITIES, VIOLENCE & CONFLICT

Whether they are villages, towns, or sections of a city, most communities over history have tended to be similar or homogeneous in racial or ethnic makeup. As a result, communities have been involved in much conflict because of the seemingly intractable problems of racism and ethnocentrism.

In Part V, it becomes painfully clear that different ethnic and racial communities have used collective violence for a variety of reasons throughout American history. A while back, the famous Swedish social scientist Gunnar Myrdal concluded after an exhaustive examination of American race relations that race is America's dilemma. This conclusion would certainly not surprise anyone today.

There is an extensive investigation and analysis of race riots, civil disorders and other communal conflict in Part V. It might be concluded after the analyses of the various 1990s riots in Miami as well as the deadliest riot in America this century (the Rodney King riot in South Central Los Angeles) that *violence* is also America's dilemma.

Terrorism also has important communal violence aspects to it. Part V deals with a variety of issues regarding this most complex, frightening, and potentially devastating form of violence. Fear of international terrorism has inhibited many Americans from traveling abroad. Of late there has been legislation in the U.S. to implement profile systems at airports and programs that "match" travelers meeting the profile with their luggage.

While *international* terrorism has existed for years, it is only in recent years that Americans in general have become concerned about *domestic* terrorism. The World Trade Center bombing, the long reign of the Unabomber, and—without a doubt—the Oklahoma City bombing have brought terrorism to the forefront of America's collective mind.

In recent times, terrorist acts have become more political, more common, and more violent—especially in terms of damage and deaths and injuries inflicted on innocent bystanders. Thus, it behooves Americans to understand terrorism; and perhaps the information in Part V about the objectives, strategies, and tactics of terrorism will facilitate this.

PART 1

The Nature of Violence & Conflict

1

TOOLS FOR THE STUDY OF VIOLENCE AND CONFLICT

The three chapters in this first part of the book provide important tools for the study of violent conflict. These tools include terms and concepts defining the very essence of violence and conflict. The chapters also deal with conflict management, including violence intervention and prevention. As such, the chapters provide an important introduction to the issues dealt with throughout the book.

Definitions, concepts, and system levels

In Chapter 2, the author presents a widely-accepted definition of violence as being behavior that is intended to inflict physical injury on people or property. Violence usually consists of physical force, delivered with passion and intensity. The author distinguishes between legitimate and illegitimate kinds of violence. Legitimate violence is that violence where a majority of people feel the violence is justified. (The legitimacy question is a common theme that appears again in Henslin's Chapter 3.) The author states there are other important distinctions regarding violence, i.e., the difference between lawful and unlawful violence, and between rightful or wrongful violence. These are respectively legal and moral distinctions.

Conflict is defined in Chapter 2 as occurring when the goals, values, conditions or practices of various parties are incompatible. Conflict often causes parties to try to neutralize, harm, injure, or destroy one another at some point. Children's scuffles over toys, partners arguing, and gangs fighting over turf are common examples of social conflicts.

A term often confused with conflict, competition, is also defined. Competition involves the pursuit of goals by parties where goal-attainment by one precludes identical goal attainment by the other. In competition, parties seek the same goals whereas parties do not necessarily do so in conflict.

Chapter 2 goes on, then, to differentiate between realistic and nonrealistic conflict, as well as to distinguish among first, second and third parties (participants) in conflicts. The author explains that conflict parties are usually social units, that is collections of people who are conscious of sharing membership in a social aggregate of some sort.

A systems theory framework is then presented which simplifies and expedites the study of violence and conflict. The framework facilitates, among other things, the discovery of similarities in how violence and conflict are conducted across different system levels. The author defines the four key levels of conflict which respectively involve individuals, groups, organizations, and communities. He then presents some system level hypotheses and generalizations, and discusses the important processes of *polarization* and *conflict escalation*.

Continuing on, Chapter 2 tackles the issue of the management of violence and conflict. The differences among domination, compromise and integration are spelled out in a discussion of conflict outcomes. The chapter concludes with an explanation of the conflict-management roles and tasks of peace*keeping* and peace*making*. The differences among conciliation, arbitration, and mediation are specified.

Power, authority and coercion

In Chapter 3, Henslin points out that the state is a political entity that claims a monopoly on violence over a particular territory. If enough people consider a state's power and violence to be illegitimate, revolution is possible.

The essential nature of politics is power and behind that power lurks violence. Henslin uses the term micropolitics to refer to the exercise of power in everyday life. By contrast, macropolitics is large-scale power such as that wielded by a state or government.

Chapter 3 continues with an exposition of how authority and coercion are related to power. Basically, authority is power that people consider to be legitimately exercised over them while coercion is power they consider unjust.

Henslin then engages in a discussion of Max Weber's three types of authority. Power in *traditional authority* derives from custom—that is, patterns set down in the past create the rules for the present. Power in *rational-legal authority*, on the other hand, is based on law and written procedures. (This type of power is also called bureaucratic authority). Lastly, in *charismatic authority*, power is based on loyalty to an individual to whom people are attracted and give allegiance. Charismatic authority, which undermines traditional and rational-legal authority, has built-in problems with respect to the transfer of authority to a new leader.

As with Chapter 2, Chapter 3 deals with *ideal types*. Henslin presents the three types of authority as ideal types. Schonborn notes that an *ideal type* does not refer to what is ideal or desirable, but to a composite of characteristics found in many real-life examples, classes or categories. In fact, any specific, real person, event or phenomenon may be difficult to classify because of showing a combination of characteristics. For instance, ideal-typic textbook cases of a disease are rarely found in real life. People only have some of the symptoms.

Understanding, intervening, and preventing

In Chapter 4, Roth provides an important micro to macro perspective on violence. He also presents a wealth of specific information about the who, what, where, and why of violence and violent crime. Roth opens his chapter by describing patterns of violence in the U.S. and trends. It is a sobering account of some of the consequences of violence in American society, and it is not a pretty picture.

Important trend graphs of violent crime cases per 100,000 (the usual unit used) from 1930 to 1990 are exhibited. Also pie charts showing the various relationships offenders had to their male and female homicide victims are presented. The "stranger percentage" might surprise some people, and the percentage is significantly different for males and for females.

The two stories presented also provide food for thought—as well as anchoring interpersonal violence in some concrete real-life details. The good news from these troublesome stories is that Roth feels there are several places in episodes like these where intervention could take place, preventing the serious violence from occurring.

Roth adds another *framework* to the main one presented by Schonborn in Chapter 2: namely, a framework for organizing risk factors which coincide with the standard theory strata of biological, psychological, social psychological (microsocial) and sociological (macrosocial). In this framework, Roth has provisions for individuals, gangs, families, and community organizations. (These are essentially the same levels as presented in Schonborn's chapter.) Roth uses his framework to analyze the two stories he presents earlier.

Throughout his chapter, Roth reports on the findings of the National Academy of Sciences panel on violence that he directed. The key findings of the panel, according to Roth, can be summarized thus:

— Regarding long-term prevention, it should include strategies directed toward children and their caregivers and biomedical strategies in such areas as substance abuse by pregnant women.

— Regarding intervention undertaken at the social and community level, the most immediate effects may be obtainable by intervening in:

— situations where violent events cluster such as illegal drug markets,

— certain places where alcohol and firearms are readily available,

— certain physical locations conducive to crime, and

— schools, using anger-management and anti-bullying programs.

In concluding his chapter, Roth talks about three needed research initiatives:

— better systems to measure violence,

— inquiry into neglected topic areas, and

— a long-term study of individual as well as social factors that cause a small percentage of children to have high potential for violent behavior as adults, while most do not.

He also calls for research into certain neglected areas, especially

— the nature of neurological responses that indicate elevated potentials for violent behavior, and

— the nature of violence by "custodians"—be they police officers, prison guards, day care workers or anyone else who may be authorized to use violence, that is, "legitimate violence."

In sum, Roth suggests that violence is worse in the U.S. than in the rest of the industrialized world. However, violence is not a totally unyielding or unsolvable problem. There are promising intervention strategies. But, most importantly, there are important prevention strategies. These will require comprehensive problem-solving by not only criminal justice agencies, but schools, social service agencies, and public health organizations.

2

VIOLENCE AND CONFLICT: TERMS, CONCEPTS, AND FRAMEWORKS

What does one have to do to begin to understand and make sense of the "bloomin', buzzin' confusion" that is violence and conflict? To start with, there are some basic terms, concepts and frameworks that need to be mastered at the outset. Let us begin with the meaning of the term "violence."

VIOLENCE

First, try your hand at recognizing examples of violence. Which of the following do you consider to be examples of violence?

— A family homicide

— A fatal automobile accident.

— A suicide.

— A forcible rape

— An earthquake or hurricane that destroys and kills.

— The arson of a building known to be uninhabited

— An industrial accident which kills thousands (as happened at the Union Carbide plant in Bhopal, India in 1984)

— The ineptness of a leader which causes donated food to be late getting to a famine-stricken area, resulting in hundreds of people starving to death.

Keep your answers in mind as you read on.

There is a good deal of consensus that **violence** is any behavior that is designed to inflict injury— especially physical injury—on people or property. It usually consists of physical force, delivered with passion and intensity. Many scholars, experts, and researchers define violence in this way,[*] including most of those involved with the prestigious National Commission on the Causes and Prevention of Violence.[1]

One of the advantages of this definition is that it allows one to measure violence across many different cultures and subcultures. The consequences of an injury like a broken arm or a cut that requires five stitches are pretty well understood in France, Iran and China as well as in the U.S. Thus, our definition of violence deals primarily with behavior and consequences that are comparable and equivalent across cultures.

Some other definitions of violence that embrace all forms of *harm* as well as *injury* can lead to measurement and cross-cultural difficulties.[2] Regarding measurement, harm requires us to measure nonphysical pain and emotional distress. And regarding cross-cultural comparativeness, harm (along with other words similar to "injury" like damage, hurt, or impairment) has slightly different connotations in different cultures and subcultures. In effect, injury—which implies the marring of the appearance, health, or soundness—is easier to discern and measure.

A disadvantage of our definition is that it excludes *institutional* violence. Think of the difference between, say, racism and institutional racism. The former is overt, easy to measure. The latter is subtle, long term and hard to measure. The same can be said for violence and *institutional* violence. Our definition suggests there must be a quickness and intensity to violence. If it is long and drawn out, it is best to call it institutional violence or as some call it, structural violence. Institutional violence is a good description of the last example given in the list just presented.

Moreover, in our definition of violence there must be an *intention* or a design to inflict injury. Therefore, hurricanes, earthquakes, auto accidents and other disasters that result in injury are technically not violent. Since an industrial accident is devoid of intention, it is not an example of violence. It may be a case, though, of institutional violence if poor maintenance or safety violations caused the accident.

Some scholars believe a definition of violence should not include injury and damage to *property*. They feel that violence must be directed at humans, and that people who bomb or torch buildings known to be empty are no different than those who burn a flag or tear up a hated document. Other scholars feel that property, especially real (estate) property and possessions—especially weapons—are integral to the sense of security people have. If you trespass or invade my home, you are that much closer to being able to injure me. Property is also important in a culture such as ours which values material possessions. Remember, Elvis sang, "You can do anything you want, just don't step on my blue suede shoes."

When we think of violence, mostly we are dealing with illegitimate or unsanctioned violence. *Illegitimate* violence is what everyday citizens do and includes the common four felonious crimes against *persons* as well as various other acts such as engaging in arson or mayhem during a riot or terrorist attack. The common violent crimes include homicide, rape, robbery, and aggravated assault. Crimes against *property* are considered to be nonviolent crimes.

---

*Most of the definitions presented here are *operational* definitions. Such definitions are designed to allow real world measurement of behavior or phenomena. *Theoretical* definitions, by contrast, are broader and can run several paragraphs in length. A *gut* definition has its place, too. Many people, including most children, would define violence by saying "Violence hurts and is scary. I don't like it."

But what if the police or some law enforcement agency engage in violence, as they sometimes do? What do we call it? Generally, people label law enforcement violence and other state-sponsored violence (such as executions and acts of war) *legitimate* violence. But there are clearly times when law enforcers and the state engage in questionable violence, and people label it illegitimate violence. The L.A.P.D.'s beating of Rodney King and the government's assault on the Branch Davidian cult in Waco are examples, though not everyone perceives these cases to be illegitimate.

It is important to note that these assessments are social. There are *moral* as well as *legal* assessments, too; and they are all made according to different criteria. *Legitimacy* or *illegitimacy* is usually determined by whether a majority of the people concerned feel that a given course of action is justifiable or desirable. (Revolutionary violence directed against the British by American colonists in the 1770's was considered legitimate by Americans, but illegitimate by Britishers.)

Whether violence is *right* or *wrong* is determined in approximately the same way, except that much more good-bad evaluation and moral judgment are involved. (Americans decided that political assassination attempts were rightful in the case of Adolf Hitler but wrongful in the case of Franklin Roosevelt.)

Lastly, whether violence is *lawful* or *unlawful* is determined by traditional procedures (a ritualistic decree by a king or a committee of elites) or by legislative or parliamentary procedures. (The killing of a national enemy in wartime is lawful while the killing of a personal enemy in peacetime is unlawful.)

To be sure, in an imperfect social order some acts may be regarded as legitimate even though they are unlawful (the killing of a deviant criminal by vigilantes). Conversely, other acts may be seen as illegitimate even though they are lawful (the execution of a person guilty of committing a capital crime while a juvenile).

CONFLICT

Much violence grows out of circumstances in which people are in conflict with others. To use the "When there's smoke, there's fire" analogy, one might say "When there's violence, there's conflict." There are, of course, exceptions to both these statements. In the case of violence, there are seemingly random and senseless killings of strangers. However, in even these cases, the killer is probably in conflict with someone, but is either purposely displacing it onto a complete stranger or is totally unconscious of it. Many anger-motivated rapists hate "significant" women in their lives, but randomly choose women who are strangers to prey on. (Incidentally, such rapists usually brutalize their victims more than is ever necessary to get them to comply.)

Because of the intrinsic relationship between violence and conflict, it is important in any study of violence to learn as much as possible about the phenomenon of conflict.[†] Conflict is

---

†The focus of this chapter is violent conflict, but it must be remembered that there is infinitely more *non*violent conflict in human affairs.

a phenomenon of immense variety and complexity. The word "conflict" derives from the Latin *confligere* which means to clash or to strike together. It has sociological aspects since it involves scarcities of status, power, and resources. And it has psychological aspects because it involves feelings of hate, fear, and distrust. Conflict can cause death, disorder, and social disorganization. But it can also have positive effects, as sociologists Georg Simmel and Lewis Coser have shown.‡

There are several basic types of conflict. *Emotional* conflict occurs as a state of tension caused by discrepant tendencies active within a person's mind. *Social* **conflict** by comparison occurs when the goals, values, or practices of various parties are incompatible—or are perceived to be so. In serious conflicts, this causes parties to try to neutralize, injure, or destroy each other. (Conflicting parties may derive from wholly different social units or from the same one, as in a civil war or any other *intra*unit conflict.) The incompatible goals, values, or practices involved in conflicts may be rational, instrumental, and tangible (*realisitc* conflict); or they may be irrational, expressive, and symbolic (*non-realistic* conflict). To quote conflict theorists Raymond Mack and Richard Snyder:

> Realistic conflict is characterized by opposed means and ends, by incompatibility of values and interests. Non-realisitc conflict arises from the need for tension release, from deflected hostility, from historical tradition, and from ignorance or error. The two types differ in origin and in the ultimate motivation behind opposed action.[3]

While most conflicts are *realistic* (e.g., arising from a fear of a weakened economy) or *non-realistic* (e.g., arising from a fear of sinister forces), some conflicts are both. For instance, Nazi Germany's conflicts with others were fueled by a realistic fear that certain countries were trying to weaken her economy combined with a non-realisitc fear that "sinister" internal forces were gaining undue influence in Germany.

Quite complex definitions of social conflict have been proposed from time to time. In their definition, Mack and Snyder set forth the properties which, taken together, definie and identify conflict:

1. Conflict requires at least two parties or two analytically distince units or entities. . . .

2. Conflict arises from "position scarcity" and "resource scarcity". . . .

---

‡Simmel and Coser have pointed out that conflict and violence have positive functions under certain circumstances.[4] Conflict, for example, can create loyalty, and cohesion *within* social units. Jealousy and petty differences are submerged—even if momentarily—while members of a social unit prepare for and then do battle. Conflict can also organize and strengthen previously weak social units. Many groups, communities, and nations become more efficient and gain identity when they are engaged in conflict. (In fact international conflict created many of today's nations and continues to sustain a good number of them.)

In addition, violent conflict can serve as a signal that needs are not being met or that social systems are not functioning properly.[5] No matter if it involves two spouses or two nations, violence is a signal that change may be in order. In some cases, it may even serve as a vehicle for that change. Finally, conflict can serve still other positive functions such as ventilation, articulation, motivation (as a catalyst for change), and innovation (as a type of achievement).[6]

3. Conflictful behaviors are those designed to destroy, injure, thwart, or otherwise control another party or other parties, and a conflict relationship is one in which the parties can gain (relatively) only at each other's expense. . . .

4. Conflict requires interaction among parties in which actions and counteractions are mutually opposed. . . .

5. Conflict relations always involve attempts to gain control of scarce resources and positions or to influence behavior in certain directions; hence a conflict relationship always involves the attempt of the actual acquisition or exercise of power. . . .[7]

While unwieldly, this definition is useful in determining what is and is not genuine conflict in the sociological sense. This is important if one wishes to distinguish conflict from closely related phenomena such as competition, opposition, rivalry, hostility, or antagonism. Of these, competition is the one most frequently confused with conflict.

Competition is a milder form of social interaction than conflict. It consists of "simultaneous pursuit of goals by two or more persons . . . where goal-achievement by one person . . . precludes identical goal-achievement by the other."[8] The rules and norms surrounding competition forbid physical attacks on fellow competitors, and allow only single-minded concentration on goals. Businesses compete for the same customers; universities compete for the same athletes; and nations compete for the same "firsts" in outer space. Competition is sometimes totally impersonal; parties are often not aware that they are competing with each other. If the rules governing competition break down, then it turns into conflict. Thus, football competition is transformed into conflict if players—motivated by a fear of losing—start grabbing facemasks, committing penalty offenses, and generally breaking the rules that prohibit physical assault.

Another distinction between conflict and competition is that conflict usually involves awareness of the opposition.[**] Competition often does not. Cotton farmers in one part of the world are often unaware of all the other farmers with whom they are competing, but since the advent of global communication, this may be less and less true.

Conflict parties

Before using the term **party** any further, a definition is in order. A party is a person or aggregate of people involved in a social activity or process. In the study of conflict, parties refer to the social units—regardless of how many people they include—involved in a given conflict.[††] Besides *first* and *second* parties (e.g., a husband and wife; African Americans and

---

[**]In addition to conflict and competition, there is one other major "social process" which is present in all societies: cooperation. (The analysis of social processes has been an important concern in sociology ever since they were popularized in Robert Park and Ernest Burgess' influential textbook, *An Introduction to the Science of Sociology.*) *Cooperation* occurs when parties work together in situations where goal-achievement by one facilitates goal-achievement by another. Parties that cooperate usually share the same values, beliefs, and sentiments.

[††]A social unit is a collection of people who are conscious of sharing membership in a social aggregate of some sort.

Korean Americans in South Central, L.A.), there may be *third* parties (neutral participants such as family-fight police or national guardsmen trying to keep hostile communities from each other). More about impartial third parties as peacekeepers and peacemakers later in this chapter.

Much important violence and conflict occurs at four different social levels, ranging from the individual level (e.g., violence among intimates) to the communal level (e.g., violence between communities). Thus, first and second parties embroiled in conflicts may consist of individuals, groups, organizations or communities. Before examining the specific system characteristics of the four levels, let us look at the rationale for using a systems framework when studying conflict.

THE *SYSTEMS THEORY* FRAMEWORK

A systems theory framework has long been a favored approach of scholars and researchers studying conflict.[9] Systems theory tries to understand social behavior by focusing on systems. It attempts to identify patterns, mechanisms and regularities in *conflict* which exist regardless of the size of the social units involved. It also attempts to discover patterns and regularities in *conflict resolution* across different-sized conflicts. This allows social scientists to extend the scope and exactitude of their understanding.

Systems are composed of parts or elements that are interrelated in a certain way. It is assumed that there is a relatively organized or orderly arrangement of these parts and elements. It is also assumed that systems operate in a somewhat harmonious way and that there is integration in their structure.[10] Systems are essentially an aggregate of related activities and interests.

System level units

As noted earlier, much violence and conflict occurs between parties at each of the four system levels. The characteristics of the four social units or parties are as follows:

Individuals are the building blocks of all social aggregates, be they groups, organizations, or communities. Unlike such aggregates, individuals have no division of labor or complex social structure. Therefore interpersonal conflicts between individuals are relatively simple in comparison to those between groups, between organizations, and between communities. Exhibit 1 itemizes the main characteristics of the four system levels.

Social scientists do not use the word group to refer to just any collectivity. They may occasionally use the vernacular, and use group in the broad generic sense to include almost any social aggregate. In the systems-theory framework, however, **group** refers to social aggregates of three to thirty people. These aggregates are characterized by closeness, social pressure, and flexibility in meeting member's needs. Common examples of groups are extended families, street gangs, and school social cliques.

The next social unit is the organization or association as some researchers like to call it. An **organization** is an aggregate which ranges in size from approximately 30 to 5,000 people.

The size of most organizations makes full communication among all members difficult to achieve. Therefore rules are created which spell out the communication channels that members must use, from leaders down to the rank and file. Sometimes rules are formalized and written down. Elaborate hierarchies of rank (authority) are often developed to coordinate all the roles, subunits, and communication channels that exist within an organization. There are political, religious, industrial, criminal, and law enforcement organizations, to name just a few types.

A **community** is similar, yet more complex than an organization. A community is composed of a localized population that provides for most of its daily needs. These needs range from simple food and shelter to education, government, and protection from certain deviants such as criminals. Communities are often homogeneous in terms of race, ethnicity, or national origin. This is true whether they are villages, towns, or sections of a city. And communities share many characteristics with organizations: written rules, formal roles and extensive division of labor, for example.

The formerly clear territorial boundaries between communities in the U.S. have broken down somewhat by the extreme economic interdependence people share, by swift transportation, and by television, radio and magazines that socialize people to increasing degrees of sameness. However, the concept of community is still an important one in systems theory and sociological research.

How system levels aid understanding

There are good reasons for categorizing conflicts in terms of the levels of the parties involved rather than in terms of something else. One is that the levels tell a great deal about the factors that come into play in each type of conflict. The nature of the disputing parties or aggregates determines the nature of the conflict. For example, different numbers of people, communication channels, and rules for behavior may cause different amounts of violence, different degrees of intractability, and so forth during a conflict. All these factors—social structural factors—help determine not only the intensity but also the possible outcomes of conflicts. In short, to fully understand a given conflict (or violent incident), one must be aware of the structural factors of the social aggregates involved.

This is also true if one wishes to understand a given person's behavior during conflict or violence. In fact, all people's behavior—whether it is conflict behavior or not—is affected by social structural factors. It is a basic tenet of sociology, moreover, that "the way men behave is largely determined by their relations with each other and by their membership in groups."[11]

The pressures exerted and the rewards offered by various social units account for much of the behavior that occurs during conflicts. However, members of social units or aggregates engaged in conflict belong to other aggregates which also influence them. Luckily for conflict analysts, though, people respond first and foremost to the social aggregate that is the most important, involving, and proximate to them. In this regard, sociologists Leonard Broom and Philip Selznick have written:

A member of a street gang . . . is also a member of groups that touch him less closely, but in his everyday life it is the proximate membership that has the greatest effect.[12]

———— EXHIBIT 1 ————

Characteristics of Conflict Units (parties)

	Individual	Group	Organiza-tion	Community
Number of members (usual range)	1	3 to 30	30 to 5,000	5,000 to 500,000
Communication among all members (interaction)	Instanta-neous	Easy	Difficult	Very difficult
Rules for behavior (norms)	Not applica-ble	Informal and unwrit-ten	Informal and unwrit-ten, plus for-mal and written	Formal and written
Agreement on values (consensus)	Not applica-ble	Very high	High	Low
Division of labor (role differentia-tion)	Nonexistent	Very low	Low	High
Cohesive-ness (pres-sure to conform)	Not applica-ble	Very high	High	Low

---

Much can be learned from structural analyses of conflicting parties. The information in the exhibit suggests that conflicts between increasingly larger sized parties are characterized by increasing *complexity*, *destructiveness*, and *impersonality*. This is due partly to the fact that the social units at higher and higher levels have more and more rules, members, rank-hierarchies, communication channels, and the like.

The enhanced complexity and destructiveness of larger-sized conflict and violence are obvious. The enhanced impersonality may be less so. However, a look at the lowest and highest of the four levels makes this clear. Fights between individuals are usually characterized by intimacy and intense self-involvement. This is because individuals act primarily on their own behalf, and are motivated by irritations, ego-slights, and love-hate emotions that they personally feel.

Fights between communities, on the other hand, are characterized by anonymity and detachedness. People act on behalf of large social entities whose goals, beliefs, and values may not be the same as their own. Impersonalization in intercommunal conflict is epitomized by the practice of throwing fire bombs from a hundred feet away, engaging in, say, looting where the store owner is unknown but thought to be an oppressive enemy.

One of the advantages of using the four levels to categorize conflict is that there is a large body of theory and research associated with each of the four. Entire courses are taught on the sociology of the group, the sociology of the organization, and so on. Hence students of conflict and violence can build on an immense amount of work already done. (Cumulativeness is important in the social sciences, and it is especially so in a fledgling field like violence and conflict studies.)

System level hypotheses and generalizations

A few representative hypotheses from each of the four levels serve to suggest the scope and nature of the research literature on conflict. (No assumption is made as to the relative worth or correctness of the hypotheses quoted here.)

Interpersonal conflict

Hypothesis:

Tensions increase in the relations between people if either, or both, has a set of expectations which are mutually inconsistent, so that the satisfaction of one expectation leads to a violation of the other.[13]

Intergroup conflict

Hypothesis:

Conflict with other groups contributes to the establishment and reaffirmation of the identity of the group and maintains its boundaries against the surrounding social world.[14]

Hypothesis:

Mild power disparity between the parties to collective bargaining is functional in maintaining stability of the industrial institution because it serves to reduce the amount of total conflict between them.[15]

Intercommunal conflict

Hypothesis:

The higher the level of prosperity, the less intense the conflict between ethnic and racial majorities and minorities.[16]

A caution about ideal types

Keep in mind that the social units presented here are ideal types, and that not all characteristics need be present in any one case.[17] Absolutely "pure" examples of a category would display all the elements noted. **Ideal types** are used to identify members of a category or class, and carry no connotations of "goodness" or desirability. They are non-normative.

Also, keep in mind the interconnectedness of social units. As Kriesberg notes in this regard,

> [A] major variation in the types of [social] units that may be in conflict is their systemic relations to each other. The conflict units may be independent of each other and of any unit superordinate to them; or both units may be within a larger entity, or one unit may be a part of the other unit which claims jurisdiction over it.[18]

What this means is that conflict units are often intricately interrelated. Social units may both be part of a larger, integrating unit (e.g., two organizations disagreeing about abortion may be part of the same community). All may be independent systems and yet subsystems, too, of a larger societal system. Or one unit may actually be in conflict and rebelling against a larger unit of which it is a part (e.g., a street gang at war with the community in which it operates.)

Polarization and conflict escalation

An additional advantage in using the four levels for categorizing conflict is that they help stimulate theoretical insights into conflict processes. To illustrate how they do this, the four levels will be interrelated with two sociological concepts, *polarization* and *escalation*, which will be discussed at this point in some detail.

The amount of polarization that exists in the social environment where a conflict is being waged affects the seriousness of the conflict and the chances of it escalating. Polarization occurs when different ideas, values, or interests become strongly opposed. (These things may eventually become opposite rallying points for great numbers of people if they are embodied in symbols and ideologies.) In such situations, the sentiments of most people do not converge and consensus does not grow. Instead, sentiments diverge into opposing camps. The identities and allegiances of people keep referring back to the same two poles (e.g., black or white, establishment or anti-establishsment). As a consequence, even the most trivial conflicts become identified with these poles or people. Conflicts tend to reinforce rather than neutralize each other under such circumstances. The result is that polarized environments are more likely to be host to conflicts that grow and escalate until they explode in full-scale violence.

In *non*polarized environments, by contrast, identities and allegiances refer back to numerous ideas, values, and interests. Here conflicts do not reinforce one another; rather they neutralize and cancel each other out over the long run. That is, at one moment Joe will be a laborer, in conflict with managers. The next moment he will be a Catholic, siding with Catholic managers against all Protestant laborers and managers. And at yet another moment, he will side with both Catholic and Protestant whites against both Catholic and Protestant blacks. (The United States can be regarded as fairly nonpolarized, at least in comparison with most other societies.)

A piece of paper can be used to show how polarization and nonpolarization affect the escalation potential of conflicts. If the paper is *folded* repeatedly in the same pattern, the crease (conflict) lines reinforce each other with every refolding. (This illustrates the polarized situation.) Sooner or later the paper will rip apart ("explode") along the crease lines because the repeated folding has weakened the paper. However, if the paper is *crumpled* repeatedly, the crease (conflict) lines run every which way, neutralizing one another. (This represents the nonpolarized situation.) The paper is not likely to ever rip apart ("explode") because the criss-crossing creases have not weakened it.

What causes polarization that leads to conflict escalation? Isolation, among other things. For example labor-management conflicts have been most serious and most frequent over the decades in those industries which are geographically isolated (mining, lumber) or socially isolated (shipping, fishing).[19] Conversely, they have been least severe and least frequent in industries such as hotels, clothing, restaurants, construction, food processing, and general manufacturing—none of which is particularly isolated from society.

How does isolation polarize people? Laborers—as well as managers—in the coal patch or the logging camp tend to create their own myths, heroes, and codes of conduct. They develop their own subcultures and world views. (With respect to laborers, because they all experience the exact same situations and grievances it is easy for them to unite in anger over wages, hours, and job-related issues.)‡‡ But most important, there are very few neutrals or diversions in these isolated places to dilute the solidarity of each party and moderate their conflict. (In nonpolarized, less-isolated industries, laborers and managers have many other

---

‡‡The isolation and limited skills of laborers often prevent them from changing jobs to resolve their dissatisfactions. Also loggers, miners, and others accustomed to hard physical work may be more disposed to physical or violent solutions to their problems than less-active, less-isolated waiters, sales clerks, or assemblyline workers.

outside interests and concerns. Their countless cross-cutting allegiances tend to mitigate their conflicts.)

In general, polarized social environments tend to produce people who would rather not deal with conflicts, even conflicts of their own making. Instead of shouldering some of the responsibility and endeavoring to work things out, they prefer to pass the buck. This can cause conflicts to escalate. To show how this might happen, racial friction, say between two *persons* might be used as an illustration. The people involved might refuse to face their problem or be unwilling to change, compromise, or accommodate. They might then pass their problem off—unresolved—to two *groups* that they belong to, causing the groups to become hostile towards each other. These groups might then try to resolve the conflict, absorbing some of the burden; or they might in turn let two *organizations* pick up the respective causes. These organizations might also refuse to deal with the issues and tension. The conflict might then be passed on to two opposing racial *communities*. These two might eventually explode into violence, which would be far greater than any violence the smaller social units would have engaged in. Such violence would also be far more difficult to manage since the larger the conflict, the harder it is to deal with as a rule. (This illustration is intended to show how the people produced in polarized environments can cause conflicts to escalate. It is not intended to suggest that conflicts at any level can always be traced to a problem at the interpersonal level. This would be sheer reductionism.)

By comparison, in *non*polarized environments, people are less likely to pass the buck. Small amounts of tension are more apt to be absorbed at each level. Trouble is not shunted aside only to burst forth at a higher level. This is one reason why nonpolarized societies can tolerate much more conflict than polarized ones.

Sometimes escalation occurs *naturally*, without any conscious buck passing. When this happens, the initial parties to a conflict may be completely forgotten. During the Civil Rights period of the 1950s and 1960s, the first persons or groups to be involved in an incident were often dwarfed by organizations (black churches, white citizens' councils, chapters of SCLC, SNCC, KKK) which subsequently entered the conflict. These organizations themselves were often forgotten when even larger organizations (the Alabama State Legislature, the U.S. Department of Justice) came upon the scene. In effect, when large social units enter conflicts to go to bat for smaller ones, the latter frequently get lost in the shuffle. Ironically, the antagonistic small ones sometimes make peace on their own, while their respective champions keep on battling.

Another natural process that commonly occurs at all levels of conflict is the escalation of *issues*. The original issue which triggers the clash usually brings other ones to mind. These other issues may have come up before and were suppressed, perhaps because they were not worth pursuing. Now, however, the pressures of the conflict may cause disputing parties to dredge them up.

Stress, emotion, and escalation processes encourage each party to see the other as entirely bad. (The ambivalence of normal interaction—where good and bad are balanced and in-betweens tolerated—gives way to black-white thinking during conflict interaction.) This in turn causes opponents to dig even deeper for issues and differences that divide them. Often the initial issue is totally forgotten or abandoned for bigger bones of contention.

The flow diagram below shows how the two natural escalation processes operate during conflicts at all levels, from interpersonal to intercommunal.[20]

| Original issue causes conflict between original parties | ⇨ | Previously sup- pressed issues arise as do new issues. | ⇨ | Parties come to view each other as all bad. Per- sonal attacks begin. | ⇨ | Addi- tional par- ties (invited and unin- vited) enter the conflict. | ⇨ | Conflict becomes indepen- dent of original issues and original parties. |

The next-to-last stage deserves further comment. The urge to win may cause the original conflicting parties to solicit support not only from larger-sized social units, but also from equal-sized ones (i.e. peers). When this happens outsiders may have a hard time staying neutral, regardless of whether the plea is for real or symbolic support. This situation is particularly apparent when married couples begin to split up. Each spouse asks mutual friends to take sides. Neutrality is discouraged, causing a dilemma which is notably agonizing for friends who like both spouses. Eventually, true neutrals may be distrusted and even excluded by conflicting parties. Similar pressures are put on neutrals during other conflicts, especially racial ones. Phrases such as "You're either for us or against us," and "If you're not part of the solution, you're part of the problem" epitomize these pressures.

MANAGEMENT OF VIOLENCE AND CONFLICT

Violence and conflict management involve intervening in conflicts so that violence and other destructive behavior exact as little toll as possible. There are other goals besides the important one of minimizing casualties (injuries, deaths, destruction). The *permanence* of the conflict outcome is critical as is the *quality* of the conflict outcome. What follows is an elaboration of three types of conflict resolution outcome, progressing from the lowest to the highest quality outcome:

Domination. "A victory of one side over the other. This is the easiest way of dealing with conflict, the easiest for the moment but not usually successful in the long run."[21] Since one side wins everything and the other loses everything, domination means that one party commands, controls, or prevails over the other at will. This mastery allows the dominant party to determine much of the subordinate's future behavior.

Compromise. "That mode of resolving conflicts in which all parties agree to renounce or reduce some of their demand. A compromise in contrast to a dictated solution such as is involved in domination and conformity, implies some degree of equality or bargaining power. . . . The agreement involved in compromise is also to be distinguished from that involved in integration. In the former case, each party is able to identify the precise extent of his losses and gains; in the latter new alternatives are accepted of such a kind as to render it extremely difficult to discern the balance between concessions made and concessions received."[22]***

Integration. "The true integration of two desires—in contrast to a compromise—signifies 'that a solution has been found in which both desires have found a place, that neither side has had to sacrifice anything. . . .' It is assumed, under such circumstances, that neither side ever gives in but that there often comes a moment when interests on both sides are suddenly perceived in a new perspective and 'unity precipitates itself.' So it frequently comes about, once an integration is effected, that the compatible, even cooperative, effort compels a change in the whole motivation of the two parties, and a new relationship emerges. In this fashion true integration becomes a kind of 'flowing together,' a merging of purpose, which makes it possible for the interests of the parties to dovetail, 'to fit into each other,' so that all participants find some place in the final solution."[23]

Managers of violence and conflict are fortunate in that there are several internal and external factors that encourage the moderation of violence. These factors include, among others: (a) the functional interdependence of the conflicting parties (husband and wife must cooperate to some extent to run a household; blacks and whites must communicate to some degree to run a city); (b) the human inclination to cut short the physical, emotional, or financial suffering which parties are inflicting on each other; and (c) the inevitable exhaustion of energy and resources such as supplies, ammunition, and mangerial efficiency.

These and other factors can cause some serious conflicts to become institutionalized. ("Institutionalization" means that specific procedures are followed—sometimes ritualistically—every time a certain type of conflict arises.) Conflict between labor and management organizations in the United States is an example of institutionalized conflict. Complex Taft-Hartley protocols are followed whenever serious industrial conflict threatens (whether annually, biennially, etc.); all sides are saddled with legal and contractual red tape. Special provisions are built into the ritualized protocols to deal with changes in the goals and strength of different parties over time. Usually, the more stable and evenly matched the strength of the parties, the higher the degree of institutionalization. Successful institutionalization of conflicts requires that the regulating procedures be internalized (believed in) by all parties, be stated in writing, and be backed up by firm sanctions.[24] Mack and Synder note:

> Out of institutionalized conflict come new social policies. As conflict is partially resolved at various stages through time, certain issues disappear, and a common law governing formerly disputed matters is built up. Ways of measuring power relations and correcting imbalances without aggressive conflict or violence are developed. Institutionalization requires the combination of conflict and cooperation, since rules and procedures cannot function in the absence of voluntary obedience or enforcement through sanctions. . . ..[25]

***Similar, yet different concepts are worth noting here: *accommodation* resembles compromise and *assimilation* resembles integration. *Accommodation* takes place when antagonists agree to disagree. A kind of low-level truce obtains; differences are not resolved, but there is a mutual adjustment while both sides continue to seek their former goals. *Assimilation* occurs when more than just mutual adjustment takes place. It is the process by which differences between parties disappear, usually through acculturation and incremental change over time.

Peace*keeping* and peace*making* are the two major approaches to managing violence and conflict. A third approach, peace*building*, involves working to eliminate the root causes of violence and conflict. Peacebuilding will not be addressed here, although in the long run, remedying the factors that cause conflict is the best approach.

Peace*keeping*

Peace*keeping* is usually more active and dangerous than peacemaking because it involves third parties such as police or riot control troops going to the scene of a conflict and interposing themselves. Peacekeepers include law enforcement personnel of all sorts: campus police, transit police, municipal police, private security guards, state national guardsmen, federal police agents (ATF, FBI, etc.), and special US military units earmarked for riot control. Included, too, are Guardian Angels, gay patrols, senior citizen monitors, and marshals for special events. In addition, peacekeepers may include *some* of the following depending on their work environment or work assignment: school teachers, corrections officers, mental health personnel, social workers (parole, probation), and rescue personnel (paramedics, firefighters).

Here are some things peacekeepers do regardless of the level of conflict with which they are dealing:

Peacekeepers

— take safety precautions before intervening or interposing,

— protect innocent parties from violence,

— secure vital facilities, and

— bring violence under control and terminate it if possible.

In the process of doing the above, peacekeepers

— disarm disputants,

— allow parties to express their hostilities nonviolently (e.g., verbally),

— separate parties,

— keep new participants and new weapons out of the conflict, and

— gain as much control over the conflict situation as is necessary.

Peace*making*

Peace*making* generally consists of efforts to moderate violence and conflict by means of impartial negotiation, mediation, or arbitration. It is less active than peacekeeping because it generally involves having first and second parties come to third parties rather than having third parties go to conflicting first and second parties.

Peacemakers skilled at conflict resolution take to heart the literal definition of "resolution:" to break into constituent parts or elements. They break down large, complex conflicts into smaller, simpler ones which can be dealt with more easily; and thus they reduce the chance of dangerous deadlocks occurring. Legal scholar Roger Fisher calls this process conflict "fractionation."[26] He believes that *issue* control is just as important as *arms* control in managing conflict. For this reason, Fisher recommends that peacemakers get parties to talk in terms of specific issues ("We got a bad deal *this* time") rather than general ones ("We get a bad deal *all* the time"). He likewise recommends that peacemakers get parties to argue over the application of a principle, rather than over the principle itself. (Conflict fractionation can also involve fragmenting parties themselves into smaller social units—i.e. breaking disputing communities into disputing organizations, or quarrelling groups into quarrelling individuals.)

There are numerous kinds of peacemakers: negotiators, facilitators, overseers, and ombudspersons. What follows is a discussion of the roles enacted by the three most important types of peacemakers: namely, conciliators, arbitrators, and mediators.

Conciliators

Conciliators try to bring seriously antagonistic parties together by means of meetings, conferences, and gatherings where demonstrations of goodwill can take place. Conciliators encourage antagonists to adhere to standards of fairness, integrity, and justice. They help parties think through possible courses of action and alternative conflict outcomes; and they attempt to win over the hostile and placate the angry. (When conciliators fail, arbitrators or mediators usually try their hand.)

Arbitrators

Arbitrators have been around since time immemorial. Tribal priests arbitrated disputes among primitive men, and a while later ecclesiastical authorities performed similar duties. Arbitrators were used extensively to resolve conflicts among the Greek city states.

Arbitrators are frequently brought in to deal with conflicts which have reached an impasse. They carefully assess the issues and then pass judgment by formulating a solution. Disputing parties are then compelled—often by their own prior consent—to accept the decision of the arbitrators as final and binding. Thus, arbitrators resemble judges (or juries if there are several of them) who hear all sides of a dispute and then reach a verdict. (In fact arbitration is often used in place of court litigation; it saves time, money, and effort.)

There are two major ways arbitrators get involved in conflicts. They may be asked to intervene—over the objections of the parties—by some local, state, or federal statutory authority. Or they may be invited to intervene by the parties themselves. When invited, especially if an arbitration panel is needed, they are commonly chosen as follows. Each party to the conflict selects an arbitrator. Then the two arbitrators that are selected get together and choose a third, thereby ensuring a truly impartial panel. Depending on the size and importance of the conflict, the arbitrators selected may be *amateurs* (common citizens), *professionals* (members of the American Arbitration Association), or *agencies* (courts of justice).

0436 0

Arbitrators play a major role in today's industrial conflicts. Because most U.S. courts are not equipped to deal with such conflicts, both labor and management use arbitrators to resolve their disputes over wages, working conditions, and interpretation of contracts. State or federal arbitrators listen to each party and then formulate decisions, called awards, which are binding. Advisory and non-binding forms of arbitration—sometimes called fact-finding—are occasionally used in industrial peacemaking. (Arbitrators are made available to labor and management because the general public has a stake in obtaining swift resolution of most industrial conflicts.)

Mediators

Like arbitrators, mediators have had a long and important history. They help disputing parties settle their differences, often by suggesting solutions to them. But these solutions are not binding or compulsory because mediators rarely have the power necessary to enforce them. As a consequence, mediators are not as threatening—nor as rigid and formal—as arbitrators. Also, unlike arbitrators, mediators are usually invited to intervene in conflicts. (Mediation, therefore, is a diplomatic approach to the resolution of conflict whereas arbitration is a judicial approach. This is why mediation is often more successful at achieving permanent, high-quality resolutions.)

Mediators sound out all sides to a dispute to learn what outcomes and arrangements each one prefers. They help disputing parties work out solutions, compromises, and graceful retreats. In addition mediators try

— to inform parties of their relative strength so that faulty assessments of strength do not lead to unnecessary bloodshed.[28]

— to establish norms for rationality, mutual respect, open communication, and the use of persuasion rather than coercion.[29]

— to change the value or factual premises of one or more parties, so that workable solutions acceptable to all will result.[30]

— to make agreed-upon solutions appear attractive and prestigeful to all parties and to interested audiences as well.[31]

Peacekeeper and peacemaker tasks

Peacekeeping and peacemaking roles overlap in some cases. (The same persons or parties sometimes play both roles.) Since there is some overlap, one can summarize some of the tasks peacekeepers and peacemakers perform when managing violence and conflict.[27] Interestingly, these task summaries are examples of generalizations that can be made across different levels using the systems theory approach.

Peacekeepers and peacemakers

— point out to disputing parties the dangers—e.g., increasing bloodshed—they face if their conflict is not resolved (The larger the conflict, the more important this task is).

- influence disputants' notions of what is acceptable conflict behavior, encouraging them to be at least minimally civil to one another

- keep channels of communication open between disputants and serve as go-betweens when necessary

- provide information and clear up confusion during conflict

- help disputing parties find and identify salient conflict outcomes. These outcomes are solutions toward which the expectations of disputants naturally converge: i.e., they are natural focal points or areas of agreement in the resolution of a conflict.

- facilitate face-saving maneuvers on the part of disputants. For example, they allow disputants to declare that they are "retreating" because of third-party pressure, not because of weakness or softness.

In conclusion, violent conflict—no matter at what system level it is exhibited—is as complex as it is troublesome. Nevertheless, armed with the terms, concepts, and systems-theory framework presented here, one should be well on one's way towards understanding some of the "bloomin', buzzin' confusion" of violence and conflict.

CHAPTER 2—ENDNOTES

[1] National Commission on the Causes and Prevention of Violence, *To Establish Justice, To Insure Domestic Tranquillity* (New York: Bantam, 1970). See also Donald Mulvihill and Melvin Tumin, eds., *Crimes of Violence* (National Commission on the Causes and Prevention of Violence, US Government Printing Office, 1969).

[2] Felice Levine and Katherine Rosich, *Social Causes of Violence: Crafting a Science Agenda* (Washington, DC: American Sociological Association, 1996).

[3] Raymond Mack and Richard C. Snyder, "The Analysis of Social Conflict: Toward an Overview and Synthesis," *Journal of Conflict Resolution* 1 (1957): 219.

[4] G. Simmel, *The Sociology of George Simmel*, trans. Wolff (New York: Free Press, 1950), *passim*; and L. Coser, *The Function of Social Conflict* (New York: Free Press, 1956), *passim*.

[5] *Ibid*.

[6] L. Coser, *Continuities in the Study of Social Conflict* (New York: Free Press, 1970), 78-92.

[7] Mack and Snyder, 218-219.

[8] O.N. Larsen and W.R. Catton, Jr., *Conceptual Sociology* (New York: Harper & Row, 1971), 119.

[9] Robert Angell, "The Sociology of Human Conflict," in E. McNeil, ed., *The Nature of Human Conflict* (Englewood Cliffs, NJ: Prentice-Hall, 1965). See also Murray Straus, "A General Systems Theory Approach to a Theory of Violence between Family Members," *Social Science Information* 12 (1973): 105-125; and Karl Schonborn, *Dealing with Violence: The Challenge Faced by Police and Other Peacekeepers* (Springfield, IL: Charles C. Thomas, 1975), *passim*.

[10] H.P. Fairchild, ed., *Dictionary of Sociology and Related Sciences* (Totowa, NJ: Littlefield, Adams, 1969), 315.

[11] L. Broom and P. Selznick, *Sociology* (New York: Harper & Row, 1968), 17.

[12] *Ibid*.

[13] A. Gouldner, *Wildcat Strike* (New York: Harper & Row, 1954), 133.

[14] L. Coser, *The Functions of Social Conflict* (New York: Free Press, 1956), 38.

[15] R. Dubin, "A Theory of Conflict and Power in Union-Management Relations," *Industrial & Labor Relation Review* 13 (1960): 514.

[16] Mack and Snyder, 237.

[17] Fairchild, 147.

[18]Louis Kriesberg, *The Sociology of Social Conflict* (Englewood Cliffs, NJ: Prentice-Hall, 1973), 16.

[19]Based on H.L. Sheppard, "Approaches to Conflict in American Industrial Society," *British Journal of Sociology* 5 (1954): 337; and A. Siegel, "The Interindustry Propensity to Strike: An International Comparison," in Kornhauser et al., eds, *Industrial Conflict* (New York: McGraw-Hill, 1954), 190-191.

[20]Some of these ideas come from J.S. Coleman, *Community Conflict* (Glencoe: Free Press, 1957), 11.

[21]M.P. Follet, *Dynamic Administration* (Bath: Management Press, 1941), 31.

[22]H.D. Lasswell, "Compromise," *Encyclopedia of the Social Sciences*, vol. 4 (New York: Macmillan, 1954), 147-149.

[23]R. North, H. Koch, and D. Zinnes, "The Integrative Functions of Conflict," *Journal of Conflict Resolution* 4 (1960): 364-365.

[24]Paraphrase of L. Kriesberg, The Sociology of Social Conflicts (Englewood Cliffs, NJ: Prentice-Hall, 1973), 9.

[25]Mack and Snyder, 243.

[26]R. Fisher, "Fractionating Conflict," in R. Fisher, ed., *International Conflict and Behavioral Sciences: The Craigville Papers* (New York: Basic Books, 1964), 91-110.

[27]Karl Schonborn, "Police and Social Workers as Members of New Crisis Management Teams," *Journal of Sociology and Social Welfare* 3, no. 6 (July 1976): *passim.*

[28]Adapted from L. Coser, "The Termination of Conflict," *Journal of Conflict Resolution* 5 (1961), 347-353.

[29]After M. Deutsch, in C. Smith, ed., *Conflict Resolution* (South Bend, IN: University of Notre Dame, 1971), 47.

[30]*Ibid.*

[31]*Ibid.*

POLITICS: POWER AND AUTHORITY—

HENSLIN

MICROPOLITICS AND MACROPOLITICS

Although the images that come to mind when we think of politics are those of government—kings, queens, coups, dictatorships, running for office, voting—politics in the sense of power relations, is also an inevitable part of everyday life (Schwartz 1990).[1] As Weber (1968) said, **power** is the ability to carry out your will in spite of resistance, and in every group, large or small, some individuals have power over others.[2] Symbolic interactionists use the term **micropolitics** to refer to the exercise of power in everyday life. Routine situations in which people jockey for power include employees' attempts to make a good impression on the new boss—who will decide which one of them will be promoted to manager—as well as an argument between a couple over which movie to see or efforts by parents to enforce their curfew on a reluctant daughter or son. *Every group, then, is political, for in every group there is a power struggle of some sort.*

In contrast, **macropolitics**—the focus of this chapter—refers to the exercise of large-scale power over a broad group. Governments, whether the dictatorship faced by Iraquis or the elected forms in the United States, Canada, and Germany, are examples of macropolitics. Let us turn, then, to macropolitics, considering first the matter of authority.

POWER, AUTHORITY, AND COERCION

For a society to exist, it must have a system of leadership. Some people will have to have power over others. As Max Weber (1947) pointed out, however, people can perceive power as legitimate or illegitimate.[3] Weber used the term **authority** to refer to legitimate power—that is, power that people accept as right. In contrast, illegitimate power—**coercion**—is power that people do not accept as just.

Suppose that you are on your way to buy a CD player on sale for $250. As you approach the store, a man jumps out of the alley, throws an arm around your neck, and shoves a gun in your back. He demands your money. Frightened for your life, you hand it over. Now suppose instead that before you go to the CD sale first you have a final examination. As you drive there, traffic makes you late. Afraid you might miss the test, you step on the gas. As the needle hits eighty-five just a mile from campus, you see flashing blue and red lights in your rear-view mirror. Your explanation about the final examination doesn't faze the officer—nor the judge before whom you appear a few weeks later. She first lectures you on safety and then orders you to pay $50 court costs plus $10 for every mile an hour over sixty-five. You pay the $250.

The mugger, the police officer and the judge all have power. The end result is also the same; in each case you part with $250 and go home minus a CD player. The difference is that the mugger has no authority. You don't consider him as having the *right* to do what he did. In contrast, you acknowledge that the officer has the right to stop you and that the judge has the right to fine you.

Authority and legitimate violence

As sociologist Peter Berger observed, however, it makes little difference whether you pay the fine that the judge levies against you willingly or refuse. The court will get its money one way or the another.

> There may be innumerable steps before its application (violence), in the way of warnings and reprimands. But if all the warnings are disregarded, even in so slight a matter as paying a traffic ticket, the last thing that will happen is that a couple of cops show up at the door with handcuffs and a Black Maria. Even the moderately courteous cop who hands out the initial traffic ticket is likely to wear a gun—just in case (Berger 1963).[4]

The **state**, then—a term synonymous with government—is the source of legitimate force in society. This point, made by Max Weber (1946, 1968)—that the state claims exclusive right to use violence and the right to punish everyone else who does—is critical to our understanding of macropolitics. If someone owes you a debt, you cannot imprison them or even forcibly take money from them. The state can. The ultimate proof of the state's authority is that you cannot kill someone because he or she has done something that you consider absolutely horrible—but the state can. As Berger (1963) summarized this matter, *"Violence is the ultimate foundation of any political order."*[5]

Below, we shall explore the origins of the modern state, but first let us look at a situation in which the state loses legitimacy.

The collapse of authority. Sometimes the state oppresses its people, and they resist their government just as they do a mugger. The people cooperate reluctantly—but with a smile if that is what is required—while they eye the gun in the hand of the government's representatives. When the people get a chance, however, they work against the system. And, as they do with a mugger, if they are able they even take up arms to free themselves.

What some see as coercion, however, others may see as authority. Consequently, some people will remain loyal to a government, willingly defend it, perhaps even die for it, although others are ready to take up arms against it. In the absence of outside forces such as a defeat in war, *the more a government is seen as legitimate, the more stable it is.*

As a government loses its legitimacy—that is, as the people reject its right to rule over them—it becomes unstable. As public order breaks down, the government may compound the situation by becoming even more oppressive to try to reassert its control. The people, or a group of them, might then take up arms and try to overthrow the government. **Revolution,** armed resistance with the intension to overthrow a government, is not only a people's rejection of a government's claim to rule over them but also a rejection of its monopoly on violence. In a revolution, the people claim that right for themselves and if successful, they will establish a new state in which they have the right to monopolize violence.

If leadership is more stable when people accept its authority, it is worth examining the sources of that authority. Just why do people accept power as legitimate? Max Weber (1968) identified three sources of authority: traditional, rational-legal, and charismatic. Let us examine each in turn.

Traditional authority

Throughout the world's history, the most common form of authority has been traditional. **Traditional authority,** which is based on custom, is the hallmark of preliterate groups. In these societies, custom dictates basic relationships. For example, because of birth a particular individual becomes chief, king, or queen. As far as members of that society are concerned, this is the right way to determine a ruler because "that is the way it has always been done."

Gender relations in preliterate groups are also based on traditional authority. The divisions between men and women are based on the past, with custom determining that a gulf should be maintained between them. Custom also dictates the specifics of their relationships. For example, in small villages in southern Spain and in a large part of Portugal, widows are expected to wear black only until they remarry—which generally means that they wear black for the rest of their lives. By law, a widow is free to wear any color she wishes, but not by tradition. Tradition decrees black, and she—along with her community—accepts the legitimacy of the authority. The force of tradition is so strong that if a widow were to violate the dress code, she would create a scandal. She would be seen as having profaned the memory of her deceased husband and would be ostracized by the "respectable" members of the community.

When traditional society changes, traditional authority is undermined. As a society industrializes, for example, new perspectives on life open up, and no longer does traditional authority go unchallenged. Thus, in contemporary southern Spain and other parts of Portugal, you can see old women dressed in black from head toe—and you immediately know their marital status. Younger widows, however, are likely to be indistinguishable from other women. Because large sections of these countries have industrialized, the more recently widowed find alternatives to the custom that ruled their ancestors for centuries.

Even in industrial and postindustrial societies, however, traditional authority never totally dies out (Schwartz 1990).[6] Parental authority provides an excellent example. Parents exercise authority over their children *because* they have always had such authority. From generations past, we inherit the idea that parents are not only responsible for providing their children with food, shelter, and discipline, but also that they have the right to choose their children's doctors and schools, and to teach them religion and morality.

This traditional authority of parents over their children—unquestioned in most places of the world—has not gone completely unchallenged, however. Just as for the widows of Spain and Portugal, matters are no longer as clear-cut as they once were, and some Western societies debate the right of parents to spank their children. Sweden has even passed laws that forbid spanking, and Swedish authorities arrest parents who lay a hand on their children.

Rational-legal authority

The second type of authority identified by Weber, **rational-legal authority**, is not based on custom but on written rules. "Rational" means reasonable, and "legal" means part of law. Thus "rational-legal" refers to matters agreed to by reasonable people and written into law (or regulations of some sort). The matters agreed to may be as broad as a constitution that specifies the rights of all members of the group, or as narrow as a contract between two individuals. The bureaucracies in Chapter 7 are based on rational-legal authority. Consequently, rational-legal authority is also called *bureaucratic authority*.

Rational-legal authority derives from the position that an individual holds, not from the person who holds the position. In a democracy, for example, the president's authority comes from the office, as specified in a written constitution, not from his or her reputation or personal characteristics. Similarly, rational-legal authority subjects everyone—no matter how high the office—to the organization's written rules. In governments based on traditional authority the ruler's word may be law, but in those based on rational-legal authority the ruler's word is subject to the law.

Charismatic authority

Over five hundred years ago, a farmer's daughter heard a voice urging her to go to war. Her king, Charles VII, had been prevented by the English from ascending to the French throne. The voice told her that God had a special assignment for her and that she should put on male clothing and recruit an army to fight on Charles' behalf. In 1429, Joan of Arc obeyed. She recruited an army, and her leadership had phenomenal results. She conquered cities and routed the English. Later that year, her visions were fulfilled as she stood next to Charles while he was crowned king of France (Bridgwater 1953).[7]

Joan of Arc is an example of **charismatic authority**, the third type of authority Weber identified. *Charisma* is a Greek word that means a gift freely and graciously given (Arndt and Gingrich 1957).[8] A charismatic individual is someone to whom people are drawn because they see the individual as exceptionally gifted. Note that the armies did not follow Joan of Arc because it was the custom to do so, as in traditional authority. Nor did they risk their lives alongside her because she held a position defined by written rules, as in rational-legal authority. Instead, people followed her because they were drawn to her outstanding traits. They saw her as a messenger of God, fighting on the side of justice, and accepted her leadership because of these attractive qualities.

The threat posed by charismatic authority. Charismatic leaders work outside the established political system. Because they rule neither by custom nor law, but by their personal ability to attract followers, they pose a threat to the established political order. Whereas a king owes allegiance to tradition and a president to the system of law, to what does a charismatic leader owe allegiance? Independent of the political structure, he or she can direct followers according to personal preference—which can include the overthrow of traditional and rational-legal authorities.

Because charismatic leaders pose a threat to the established order, traditional and rational-legal authorities are often quick to oppose them. If they are not careful, however, they can create a martyr, arousing even higher sentiment in favor of the charismatic leader and in opposition to themselves. Occasionally, the Roman Catholic church faces such a threat when a priest claims miraculous powers, a claim perhaps accompanied by amazing healings. As people flock to this individual, they bypass parish priests and the formal ecclesiastical structure. The transfer of allegiance to an individual in this way threatens the church bureaucracy. Consequently, the church hierarchy may encourage the priest to withdraw from the public eye, perhaps to a monastery to rethink matters. Thus the threat is defused, rational-legal authority reasserted, and the stability of the organization maintained.

Authority as ideal type

Weber's classifications—traditional, rational-legal, and charismatic—represent ideal types of authority. **Ideal type** does not refer to what is ideal or desirable, but to a composite of characteristics found in many real-life examples. In fact, then, a particular leader may be difficult to classify, as he or she may show a combination of characteristics.

A remarkable example occurred after World War I, when Germany, still suffering the stinging humiliation of national defeat, was ravaged by high unemployment and hyperinflation. Many Germans of that period saw Adolf Hitler as a type of savior, destined to create a new Germany. At first, Hitler could attract only few radicals. As his vision of a new Germany spread, however, it eventually encompassed the middle classes. Coming to see Hitler as having the ability to restore prosperity and pride to Germany, businessmen contributed to his campaign. After Hitler was elected, he used his power to suspend elections and have his decrees made law. As an elected official, Hitler was a rational-legal leader. But he was also charismatic, his speeches mesmerizing masses of Germans. He was able to instill such devotion in thousands of followers that they were willing to endure hardships, even to lay down their lives for him.

Another example is John F. Kennedy. As the elected head of the United States government, Kennedy, too, represented rational-legal authority. Yet his mass appeal was so great that his public speeches aroused large numbers of people to action. When in his inaugural address Kennedy said, "Ask not what your country can do for you, but what you can do for your country," millions of Americans were touched. When Kennedy proposed a Peace Corps to help poorer countries, thousands of idealistic young people volunteered for challenging foreign service.

Charismatic and traditional authority can also overlap, as illustrated by the case of the Ayatollah Khomeini of Iran. Khomeini was a religious leader, holding the traditional position of ayatollah. His embodiment of Iranian people's dreams, however, as well as his austere life and devotion to principles of the Koran, gave him such mass appeal that he was also a charismatic leader. Khomeini's followers were convinced that he had been given a gift from God, and his speeches could arouse tens of thousands of followers to action. In rare instances, then, traditional and rational-legal leaders possess charismatic traits. Instances of this are unusual, however, and most authority is clearly one type or another.

Note also that charismatic leaders can be good or evil. As mentioned, Hitler, the Ayatollah Khomeini, and John F. Kennedy can be classified at least partially as charismatic leaders. Joan of Arc, as well as Moses, Jesus Christ, and Muhammad, are pure charismatic leaders, for they held no office, either traditional or rational-legal, and yet each recruited ardent followers. Following the symbolic interactionists, we can see that people impute goodness or badness to a charismatic leader. Most Americans, for example, perceived Khomeini as bad, while Iranians saw him in a different light. In the case of Joan of Arc, the English and French had quite different views, the Egyptians certainly didn't see Moses in the same light as the Israelites did, and so on.

The transfer of authority

The orderly transfer of authority at the death, resignation, or incapacitation of a leader is critical for social stability. Under traditional authority, people know who is next in line. Under rational-legal authority, people may not know who the next leader will be, but they do know *how* that person will be selected. In both traditional and rational-legal systems of authority, the rules of succession are established.

Charismatic authority, however, poses a problem of succession, which makes it inherently less stable than either traditional or rational-legal authority. Because charismatic authority relies neither on custom nor law, but is built around a single individual, the death or incapacitation of a charismatic leader can mean a bitter struggle for succession. Consequently, some charismatic leaders make arrangements for an orderly transition of power by appointing a successor. This does not guarantee orderly succession, of course, for the followers may not perceive the designated heir in the same way as they did the charismatic leader. A second strategy is for the charismatic leader to construct an organization, which then perpetuates itself with a rational-legal leadership. Weber used the term the **routinization of charisma** to refer to the transfer of authority from a charismatic leader to either traditional or rational-legal authority.

CHAPTER 3—ENDNOTES

[1]Mildred A. Schwartz, *A Sociological Perspective on Politics* (Englewood Cliffs, NJ: Prentice-Hall, 1990).

[2]Max Weber, *Economy and Society,* trans. Ephraim Fischoff (New York: Bedminster Press, 1968); first published in 1922.

[3]Max Weber, *The Theory of Social and Economic Organization*, trans. A.M. Henderson and Talcott Parsons (Glencoe, IL: Free Press, 1947); first published in 1904-1905.

[4]Peter L. Berger, *Invitation to Sociology: A Humanistic Perspective* (New York: Doubleday, 1963), 3-7.

[5]*Ibid.*

[6](not clear: Berger or Schwartz? check with AU)

[7]William Bridgwater, ed., *The Columbia Viking Desk Encyclopedia* (New York: Viking, 1953).

[8]William F. Arndt and F. Wilbur Gingrich, *A Greek-English Lexicon of the New Testament and Other Early Christian Literature* (Chicago: University of Chicago Press, 1957).

UNDERSTANDING AND PREVENTING VIOLENCE—ROTH

The National Academy of Sciences Panel on the Understanding and Control of Violent Behavior was established to review existing knowledge about violence, with a view toward controlling it in the United States. The panel, set up at the request of three Federal agencies—the National Institute of Justice, the National Science Foundation, and the Centers for Disease Control and Prevention—reached the following fundamental conclusions:

— While present murder and other violent crime rates per capita are not unprecedented for the United States in the century, they are among the highest in the industrialized world.

— While sentencing for violent crimes grew substantially harsher between 1975 and 1989, the number of violent crimes failed to decrease. This happened apparently because the violence prevented by longer and more common prison sentences was offset by increases due to other factors and suggests a need for greater emphasis on preventing violent events before they occur.

— Although findings of research and program evaluations suggest promising directions for violence prevention strategies, developing effective prevention tactics will require long-term collaborations between criminal justice and juvenile justice practitioners, other social service agencies, and evaluation researchers.

— More research and better measurement are needed to identify the causes of violence and opportunities for preventing it—in situations where violence occurs, in communities, and in psychosocial and biological facets of individual human behavior.

This Research in Brief more fully explains these conclusions and their implications.

Issues and Findings

Key issues: The extent and nature of violence in this country; promising opportunities for prevention; and areas in which further research and better measures are needed, particularly to identify causes and additional opportunities for prevention.

Key findings:

— The level of violent crime in this country has reached high, though not unprecedented levels.

— Between 1975 and 1989, harsher prison sentencing prevented some violent crimes through incapacitation and deterrence, but crimes by persons still in the community offset those preventive effects.

— In addition to an effective criminal justice response, the strategy for violence reduction should include preventive interventions directed at the multiple factors affecting the risk of violence.

— Recognizing the full range of risk factors expands the list of promising, though often untested, opportunities for violence prevention.

— Long-term prevention should include strategies directed toward children and their caregivers; interventions undertaken at the social and community level; and biomedical strategies in such areas as substance abuse by pregnant women. More immediate effects may be obtainable by intervening in situations where violent events cluster, such as illegal drug markets, certain places where alcohol and firearms are readily available and physical locations conducive to crime.

— Because evaluations are not yet conclusive enough to warrant a commitment to any single strategy, violence control policy should proceed through a problem-solving strategy in which many tactics are tested, evaluated, and refined. This approach requires sustained, integrated efforts by criminal justice, social service, and community-based organizations.

— The knowledge base needs to be increased by developing better systems to measure violence, expanding research support in certain neglected areas, and through long-term study of the factors that give rise to violent behavior.

PATTERNS AND TRENDS IN VIOLENCE

Violence is a serious social problem. In 1990, 23,438 Americans were murdered—a rate of 9.4 for every 100,000 people. In the latest years for which comparative data are available, this rate was nearly double that of Spain, which had the second highest rate in the industrialized world. The murder rate in the United States in 1988 was four times that of Canada.

Violent crime short of murder is also a frequent occurrence in this country. An estimated 2.9 million serious nonfatal violent victimizations—rapes, personal robberies, and aggravated assaults—occurred in 1990, according to the National Crime Victimization Survey (NCVS). The rates per 100,000 population for these crimes were also among the world's highest. In addition, the NCVS reported more than 3.1 million simple assaults—less serious crimes that neither involved a weapon nor injured the victim. National reporting systems do not include many other violent acts, especially those committed in families, between friends and inti-mates, by caregivers, by law enforcement officers, in prisons, and in schools. And no statis-tics fully capture the devastating effects of violence on local communities—their economies, neighborhoods, and quality of life.

Violence falls most heavily on ethnic minority males and occurs most often in urban areas. The lifetime risk of being murdered is about 42 per 1,000 for black males and 18 per 1,000 for Native American males. By contrast, it is only 6 per 1,000 for white males and and 3 per 1,000 for white females. Except for forcible rape, serious violent crime reported through the FBI's Uniform Crime Reporting Program is highest in our largest cities. The violent crime rate is 2,243 per 100,00 population in cities with populations greater than 1 million. This is three times the rate for the country as a whole. Since 1980, however, serious violent crime rates in the third population tier (cities between 250,000 and 499,999) have exceeded those in the sec-ond tier (cities between 500,000 and 999,999).

Violence in America today is not unprecedented. Nor, despite the statistics above and some news media portrayals, is it limited predominantly to young men, or common in all areas of large cities, or primarily a matter of attacks by strangers, as the following panel findings attest:

— Murder rates have been as high as they are now twice before in this century—around 1931–34 and again in 1979–81. Because the U.S. population today is higher than ever, however, these per capita *rates* are producing unprecedented *numbers* of deaths.

— The 1990 count of serious violent crimes (2.9 million) is at about its 1975 level, follow-ing a peak around 1980, a decrease during the early 1980's, and an increase that began in 1986.

— Blacks' murder victimization rates have generally exceeded those of whites through-out this century. However, the trends for the two races do not always move together over time. Between 1970 and 1980, for example, the rate at which white males became murder victims rose from 7.3 to 10.9 per 100,000 population, while the rate for black males fell from 82.1 to 71.9. (See exhibit 2.)

— The black/white difference in murder victimization rates appears primarily to reflect conditions in low-income neighborhoods and tends to disappear altogether in high-income neighborhoods (according to the four available studies of this topic).

— Although teenagers and young adults are more likely than older adults to be murdered in any given year, three-fourths of all murder victims are killed after age 24, regardless of ethnicity. Minority murder rates are higher than white rates at all ages.

— Not all types of violent victimization rates move together over time. After 1973, aggravated assault and rape increased fairly steadily in cities of all sizes, but murder increases were greatest in large cities, and robbery rose during some periods and fell during others.

— Variations in violent crime rates by neighborhood in large cities are comparable to the variations in rates between large and small cities, and only a small percentage of all street addresses may account for a substantial share of a city's violent crimes.

— In nearly 40 percent of all murders, the relationship between victims and their killers is unknown to police at the time the statistics are reported. Among the remaining murders, strangers account for only 2 of every 10, while intimate partners or family members account for 3 of every 10, and other acquaintances for 5 of every 10.

— Women face only about one-third the murder risk faced by men. However, among murder victims, women are more than four times as likely as men to have been killed by spouses or other intimate partners. Male victims are nearly twice as likely as female victims to be killed by friends, acquaintances, or strangers. (See exhibits 3 and 4.)

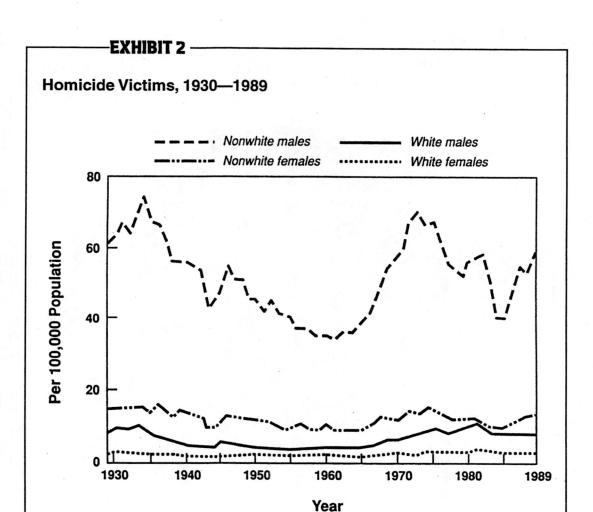

EXHIBIT 2

Homicide Victims, 1930—1989

Legend:
- – – – Nonwhite males
- —— White males
- –·–·– Nonwhite females
- ·········· White females

Y-axis: Per 100,000 Population (0, 20, 40, 60, 80)

X-axis: Year (1930, 1940, 1950, 1960, 1970, 1980, 1989)

Source: Adapted from Reiss, Albert J., Jr. and Jeffrey A. Roth, eds., *Understanding and Preventing Violence*, Washington, D.C.: National Academy Press, 1993, p. 51.

Homicide Distributions by Victim Relationship to Offender for *Male* Victims, 1987. Includes only murders with known victim-offender relationships.

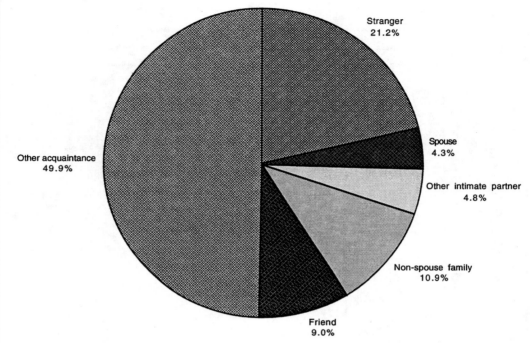

Stranger
21.2%

Spouse
4.3%

Other intimate partner
4.8%

Non-spouse family
10.9%

Friend
9.0%

Other acquaintance
49.9%

Source: Adapted from Reiss, Albert J., Jr., and Jeffrey A. Roth, eds., *Understanding and Preventing Violence*, Washington, D.C.: National Academy Press, 1993, p.80.

Homicide Distributions by Victim Relationship to Offender for _Female Victims, 1987._ Includes only murders with known victim-offender relationships.

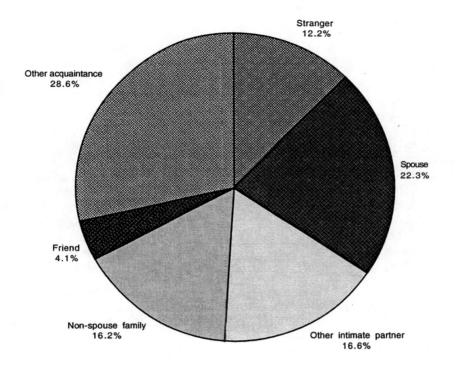

Stranger
12.2%

Other acquaintance
28.6%

Spouse
22.3%

Friend
4.1%

Non-spouse family
16.2%

Other intimate partner
16.6%

Source: Adapted from Reiss, Albert J., Jr., and Jeffrey A. Roth, eds., _Understanding and Preventing Violence_, Washington, D.C.: National Academy Press, 1993, p. 80.

Jason's and His Father's Story

Dave, Evelyn, and their 10-month-old son Jason were struggling. Jason was born just a few weeks after Evelyn's 20th birthday and 4 months before Dave was laid off from his job as a day laborer.

Things had clearly gone wrong since the layoff. Dave had become moody. They argued more frequently, mostly about money. During several of the arguments, Dave had slapped Evelyn, but begged for forgiveness each time and promised never to hit her again. Worst of all, Dave seemed to have begun resenting Jason. He had never quite mastered feeding and changing and had stopped trying to learn. He has almost stopped playing with the baby, and what playing he did struck Evelyn as too rough.

Evelyn finally figured out a solution: she'd get back her old job as a waitress. Even though she would hate being away from Jason, they needed the money. Less financial pressure might relieve the psychological pressures that, she believed, were making Dave more abusive.

Dave didn't fight her idea, but Evelyn had mixed feelings about leaving Jason in his care. He was no model babysitter, but perhaps time alone together would build his bonds with Jason and take his attention off his joblessness. Anyway, there was no choice. She knew none of their neighbors, especially none whom she would trust with Jason, and the local day-care center had a 3-month waiting list.

As Evelyn left for her first day at work, Dave "hit bottom." All the humiliation—over the layoff, the rejections, loan's from Evelyn's parents, and his new status as babysitter—descended at once. He heard Jason's bawling as yet another insult, not a cry for mother. Whatever Jason's problem was, Dave couldn't fix it. The more he tried, the louder the bawling, and the deeper his own despair and frustration.

Dave's self-control finally broke when Jason wet him. He turned on the "hot" tap, filled the bathtub with scalding water, and held Jason in the tub by his arm and leg. Jason's crying eventually stopped, but not until third-degree burns covered 35 percent of his body, according to the medical examiner's report.

THE NEED FOR PREVENTION

Usually the criminal justice system responds *after* a violent event occurs. The event must be reported to, or observed by, the police. Then an arrest may be made, the arrestee convicted, and the offender punished. Between 1975 and 1989, the probability of clearing a violent crime by arrest remained roughly constant. However, sentencing policy became much harsher. Increases in both a convicted violent offender's chance of being imprisoned and the average prison time served if imprisoned at all combined to cause a near tripling of the expected prison time served per violent crime.

The criminal justice system's increased use of prison reduced violent crime levels in two ways. First, it prevented 10 to 15 percent of potential violent crimes through incapacitation—the isolation that presents prisoners from committing crimes in the community. Second, it prevented additional violent crimes through deterrence, by discouraging people in the community from committing them.

There is no reliable means of estimating the size of the deterrence effect and the total number of violent crimes the harsher sentencing policy averted. Whatever the number, however, those potential crimes must have been "replaced" by others, because the actual number of serious violent crimes was about the same in 1989 as in 1975—2.9 million. This suggests that by itself the criminal justice response to violence could accomplish no more than running in place. An effective control strategy must also include preventing violent events before they happen.

RISK FACTORS AND VIOLENCE PROTECTION

Every violent event is a chance occurrence, in the sense that no human characteristic, set of circumstances, or chain of events makes violence inevitable. It seems reasonable to assume that some intervention might have prevented each violent event, but the correct intervention cannot be know in advance for every individual case. As starting points for exploring prevention, there are well-documented risk factors, which increase the odds that violence will occur. Some risk factors can be modified to reduce those odds. There is always a chance, however, that violence will occur in a low-risk setting or fail to occur in a very high-risk setting.

As shown in exhibit 7, risk factors for violence can be classified in a framework that has two dimensions. The first is temporal proximity—how close in time the factor is to the violent event. Furthest removed in time are predisposing risk factors, which increase the probability of violent events months or even years ahead. Situational risk factors are circumstances that surround an encounter between people and that increase either the chance that violence will occur or the harm that will take place if it does. Activating events are those that immediately lead to a violent act.

The second dimension of the framework is the level at which the risk factor is most directly observed. The panel thought in terms of four levels:

— Macrosocial: Characteristics of large social units such as countries and communities. Examples are social values that promote or discourage violence against women, the structures of economic rewards and penalties for violent and nonviolent behavior, and catalytic events such as the 1992 announcement of the Rodney King beating trial verdicts.

—EXHIBIT 6—

Andy's and Bob's Story

Wrightstown had long been known as a tough blue-collar suburb. Residents rarely ventured downtown, with its open-air drug markets and drive-by shootings. Still "men were men," and their reputations depended on toughness, sexual and beer-drinking prowess, and family honor. Big Sunday-afternoon beer parties were a local ritual, and everyone knew that some of the biggest and wildest happened at Andy's house.

In a tough town, Andy's friend Bob was one of the toughest. Like his father before him, Bob had begun drinking heavily as a teenager and had accumulated records of school fights and simple assaults. He nearly always won the fights, but had recently lost his job for missing work—he had been in jail after a bar brawl that got out of hand.

Late one Sunday afternoon, on a run to replenish the beer supply, Andy ran into his out-of-luck friend and invited him back to join the party. Once there, Bob quickly drank up a six-pack and began making passes at Andy's sister Charlene. Charlene had never liked Bob. The more she resisted his advances, the more aggressive he became, until she slapped him hard across the mouth. Bob stepped back and tripped over a coffee table. As he picked himself up, half the crowd was laughing at him. The other half was yelling at Charlene to "make it up to him like a good girl," but Andy saw his sister's honor at stake.

Andy came at Bob. The two fought in the living room until Andy's older brother told them to "take it outside" after they broke the coffee table. As the crowd moved out to the porch to watch and cheer, Bob yanked a tire iron out of his trunk and used it to knock Andy to the ground, unconscious. The crowd fell silent only after Bob jumped into his car, ran over Andy twice, and roared away. After what seemed like forever, an ambulance responded and took Andy to the hospital emergency room, where he died 4 hours later of massive internal injuries.

— Microsocial: Characteristics of encounters among people. Examples are whether insults are exchanged, whether weapons are easily accessible, and how bystanders respond to an escalating confrontation.

— Psychosocial: Individuals' characteristics or temporary states that influence patters of interaction with others. Examples are individuals' customary ways of expressing anger, or of behaving under the temporary influence of alcohol or stress.

— Biological: Chemical, electrical, and hormonal interaction, primarily in the brain, which underlie all human behavior.

Exhibit 8 illustrates the framework with two descriptions of murders, which were adapted from actual murder cases adjudicated during 1988 and recorded for other purposes. Just these two cases are sufficient to illustrate three principles about understanding and preventing violence:

— The diversity of these two events demonstrates the inadequacy of broad legal and statistical categories such as "murder" for understanding and preventing violent events. The risk factors and associated prevention strategies in just these two murders are quite different, and they represent only a small slice of the diversity in murder.

— It is important for prevention purposes to view a violent event as the outcome of a long term chain of preceding events, which might have been broken at any several links, rather than as the product of a set of factors that can be ranked in order of importance. To device a strategy that might have prevented Jason's death, one need not designate either Dave's accumulated humiliations or Jason's crying as the more "important" cause; rather, one must search for interventions that might have broken some link in a chain of events.

— Encouragingly, the two murders described here suggest a broad set of intervention points for preventing violent deaths before they occur.

It is useful to speculate about strategies that might have prevented Jason's and Andy's deaths. Conceivably, Jason's death might have been prevented if Dave had been raised to have higher self-esteem, if Evelyn had sought to help when Dave first slapped her, if a nurse or social worker making regular home visits had noticed the inadequate family functioning or Dave's poor parenting skills and shown Dave how to deal with problems more constructively, or if the neighborhood were characterized by more active social networks or more accessible child care services. Andy's death might have been avoided if Bob's early adolescent patterns of drinking and fighting had led to a referral for successful alcohol abuse treatment, if someone had thought of a recreational alternative to the usual Sunday beer party, if Andy's older brother had used his influence to stop the escalating fight instead of moving it outside, or if emergency medical services had been more accessible. The point is not that any single strategy will eliminate all violence, but that violence levels can be reduced by a variety of individual decisions and nonintrusive public policies.

EXHIBIT 7

Matrix for Organizing Risk Ractors for Violent Behavior

Units of Obser-vation and Explanation	Proximity to Violent Events and Their Consequences		
	Predisposing	Situational	Activating
SOCIAL Macrosocial	Concentration of poverty Opportunity structures Decline of social capital Oppositional cultures Sex role socialization	Physical structure Routine activities Access: weapons, emergency medi-cal services	Catalytic social event
Microsocial	Community organizations Illegal markets Gangs Family disorganization Pre-existing structures	Proximity of responsi-ble monitors Participants' social relationships Bystanders' activities Temporary communi-cation impairments Weapons: carrying, displaying	Participants' commu-nication exchange
INDIVIDUAL Psychosocial	Temperament Learned social responses Perceptions of rewards/penalties for violence Violent deviant sexual preferences Social, communication skills Self-identification in social hierarchy	Accumulated emo-tion Alcohol/drug con-sumption Sexual arousal Premeditation	Impulse Opportunity recogni-tion
Biological	Neurobehavioral "traits" Genetically mediated traits Chronic use of psychoac-tive substances or exposure to neurotoxins	Transient neurobe-havioral* states Acute effects of psy-choactive sub-stances	Sensory signal pro-cessing errors

*Includes neuroanatomical, neurophysiological, neurochemical, and neuroendocrine. "Traits" describe capacity as determined by status at birth, trauma, and aging processes such as puberty. "States" describe tem-porary conditions associated with emotions, external stressors, etc.

Source: Adapted from Reiss, Albert J., Jr., and Jeffrey A. Roth, eds., *Understanding and Preventing Violence*, Washington, D.C.: National Academy Press, 1993, p. 297.

COMPREHENSIVE VIOLENCE PREVENTION

Murder was only one of many types of violence explored by the panel. Research and evaluation findings concerning all forms of interpersonal violence suggest a variety of strategies that merit consideration and testing in any comprehensive violence prevention effort.

During child development. Promising violence prevention strategies include:

— Programs and material to encourage and teach parents to be nonviolent role models, provide consistent discipline, and limit children's exposure to violent entertainment.

— Regular postpartum visits by public health nurses to provide health information, teach parenting skills, and give well-baby care, while taking the opportunity to detect signs of possible child abuse.

— Programs such as Head Start preschool enrichment and early-grade tutoring to reduce the risk of early-grade school failure, a well-known precursor of violent behavior.

— Social learning programs for parents, teachers, and children to teach children social skills for avoiding violence, ways to view television critically, and nonviolent means to express anger and meet other needs.

— School-based anti-bullying programs.

Neurological and genetic processes. All human behavior, including aggression and violence, is the outcome of complex processes in the brain. Because of ethical constraints on research involving human subjects, the most firmly established knowledge about these processes concerns aggressive behavior by animals. Its applicability to violent behavior is still speculative.

Available research suggests that violent behavior may be associated with certain relatively permanent conditions and temporary states of the nervous system. These possibilities relate to the following processes: the functioning in the brain of certain hormones and other body chemicals called neurotransmitters; certain physical abnormalities in the brain, which could be present at birth or develop as a result of brain injuries or maturation; certain abnormal brain wave responses to outside stress; brain dysfunctions that, by interfering with communication and thought processes, lead to school failure and other childhood problems that are well-known precursors of violent behavior; and temporary effects of drinking alcohol, perhaps heightened by hypoglycemia or other health problems.

EXHIBIT 8

Examples of Possible Risk Factors in Two Murders

Units of Observation and Explanation	Proximity to Violent Events and their Consequences		
	Predisposing	Situational	Activating
SOCIAL Macrosocial	1. Low neighborhood social interaction. 2. Neighborhood culture values fighting, drinking, sexual prowess.	1. No child care providers in the neighborhood. 2. No local emergency medical services.	
Microsocial	1. Dave began hitting Evelyn months ago. 2. Widespread expectations of wild drinking parties at Andy's house.	1. Baby cries, Dave unable to cope. 2. Charlene humiliates Bob by resisting his advances.	1. Baby wets Dave. 2. Older brother says "take it outside," crowd goes outside to watch and cheer.
INDIVIDUAL Psychosocial	1. Dave has low self-esteem. 2. Bob develops adolescent pattern of drinking and violent behavior.	1. Dave humiliated by Evelyn's new job, his own lack of parenting skills. 2. Threats to Andy's family status, Bob's personal status.	
Biological	2. Possible familial traits of alcoholism and anti-social behavior in Bob's family.	2. Andy, Bob, and bystanders under alcohol influence.	

Murder 1: 10-month-old baby scalded to death by father; no witnesses.

Murder 2: 20-year-old male beaten and intentionally run over by automobile; many witnesses.

Note: This is an illustration of the Exhibit 7 framework.

The roles of these processes in human behavior are far too uncertain to specify any neurological "markers" for violence or to warrant any wholesale biomedical interventions solely to prevent violent behavior. However, they do suggest that violence prevention may be a positive side-effect of certain interventions intended to achieve other goals. Based on its review of available evidence, the panel concluded that potentially useful biomedical violence prevention strategies include:

— Programs to reduce maternal substance abuse during pregnancy, children's exposure to lead in the environment, and head injuries.

— Intensive alcohol abuse treatment and counseling programs for those in their early adolescent years whose behavior patterns include both conduct disorder and alcohol abuse, especially if alcohol dependence runs in their families.

— Developing pharmacological therapies to reduce craving for nonopiate illegal drugs, much as methadone reduces demand for heroin.

— Completing the development of medicines that reduce potentials for violent behavior during withdrawal from opiate addiction.

In statistical studies of twins, adoptees, and their families, researchers have found correlations suggesting that genetic and social processes interact as influences on the probabilities of many human behaviors, including alcoholism, antisocial behavior, and juvenile delinquency. However, the few available studies of human violent behavior have produced mixed results, suggesting at most a weak genetic influence on the chance of violent behavior. The statistical patterns make clear that, even if eventually discovered, any such influence would involve many genes rather then any single "violence gene" and would involve interactions with social conditions and life events.

Social and community-level interventions. Research on social and community-level influences on violence is difficult to carry out, and evaluations of interventions at these levels are scarce. As a result, the knowledge base for formulating violence prevention strategies at these levels is not as strong as it should be. Research conducted thus far highlights the need for further development in the following areas:

— Housing policies to reverse the geographic concentration of low-income families.

— Programs to strengthen community organizations, social networks, and families that promote strong prosocial values.

— Economic revitalization in urban neighborhoods to restore opportunities for economic self-advancement through prosocial, nonviolent activities.

— Stronger community policing programs as a means of improving police responsiveness to community needs, stronger community-based violence prevention initiatives, reinforcement of prosocial values, and increased certainty of arrest and punishment for violent crimes.

— Strategies to reduce the violence-promoting effects of community transitions that occur in the course of new construction, gentrification, and other disruptions.

— Programs to reduce violence associated with prejudice and with the activities of some gangs.

Situational approaches. The strategies outlined above are long-range approaches rather than immediate means to prevent violence. Time is needed to change the pathways through which a few aggressive children develop into violent adults and to change the communities in which they live.

Shorter-term strategies for violence prevention require altering or eliminating situations that present immediate opportunities for violent events. One approach involves cooperation between police and business proprietors to diagnose and remove the risk factors in "hot spots"—addresses or telephone locations that generate unexpectedly high volumes of "911" calls for emergency police assistance to deal with violence.

The diversity of violence means that different "hot spots" will require different remedies. However, a large body of research points directly to three commodities that should often be considered in situational violence prevention:

— Alcohol: Use of prevention education, laws and law enforcement, taxes, and social pressure, among other measures to deal with underage drinking. Such measures appear to reduce teenagers' involvement in automobile crashes and may therefore reduce their excessive involvement in violence.

— Illegal drugs: Reducing the demand that fuels violence-ridden illegal drug markets; and using drug abuse prevention, drug treatment, coordination of in-prison drug treatment with post-release treatment, and (in the near future) methadone equivalents for drugs other than heroin.

— Firearms: Better enforcement of laws that regulate the allocation and uses of guns, and especially reducing juveniles' access to guns by enforcing laws prohibiting gun sales to minors and by disrupting illegal gun markets.

DIVERSIFIED PROBLEM-SOLVING IN VIOLENCE PREVENTION

The strategies discussed above constitute a portfolio of promising violence prevention opportunities. The findings of program evaluations are not yet conclusive enough to warrant a national commitment to any single strategy. Therefore, violence control policy should be diversified through small investments in testing many strategies rather than a major commitment to nationwide implementation of one or two. Interventions that succeed in one setting sometimes fail in another because of the unintended consequences of interactions that are poorly understood. Even when the potential effectiveness of a specific strategy is fairly clear, the choice of implementation tactics may not be. Strategies aimed at predisposing risk factors, even when they are effective, require time to demonstrate that they will work. And while some strategies will doubtless prove more effective than others, the diversity of violent events guarantees that no single strategy will prevent more than a small fraction of them.

For these reasons, "diversified investments" in many small-scale but sustained problem-solving initiatives are needed.

Like initiatives to develop vaccines for preventing single disease, each problem-solving initiative should focus on a specific source of violence. Each initiative involves five steps:

1. Diagnose the problem, using criminological and epidemiological techniques to document its importance and identify risk factors that suggest a preventive strategy.

2. Develop prototypes of several tactics for strategy implementation that show promise based on theory, research findings, or experience.

3. Compare the effectiveness of the alternative tactics through rigorous evaluations that use randomized assignment wherever feasible.

4. Refine the tactic for implementation, using the evaluation findings as the basis.

5. Replicate the evaluation and refinement steps to sharpen the effectiveness of the interventions and adapt them to local community characteristics.

The panel called for problem-solving initiatives aimed at sources of violence in several areas: childhood development; "hot spot" locations, routine activities, and situations; illegal markets, especially for drugs, guns, and prostitution; firearms, alcohol, and drugs; bias crimes, gang activities, and community transitions; and relationships between intimate partners.

Over time, this problem-solving approach may reduce the levels of different types of violence in large enough numbers to make a significant "dent" in the overall problem. Such progress in prevention is especially likely when the chances of early success can be maximized by focusing on certain categories of problems and interventions: those for which the risk factors are most firmly established, those for which evaluation findings are most positive, and those for which tactics are most easily marshaled. Progress in prevention also requires treating initial evaluation failures (which are inevitable) as indicators of the need for tactical refinements rather than as signals to abandon a strategy entirely. Simultaneously, progress in understanding violence will be made to the extent social scientists make greater use of findings from well-controlled outcome evaluations as evidence of the causes of violent events.

The preventive, problem-solving approach to violence is not intended to replace arrest and other traditional criminal justice responses. But it would involve integrating criminal justice responses with a broad range of preventive interventions, which are often administered by other public and private agencies. For example, arrest at the crime scene has been found to break the cycle of spouse assault/intervention under some conditions. However, arrest has never been systematically compared to, or integrated with, such interventions as referring battered women to shelters, teaching batterers nonviolent ways to deal with anger, or requiring batterers to participate in alcohol abuse treatment. Coordinating and evaluating all these elements of a spouse assault prevention initiative would require cooperation between police departments and the agencies that provide the other services.

More generally, violence problem-solving will require long-term collaboration and new organizational arrangements among local law enforcement, criminal justice, schools, and public health, emergency medicine, and social service agencies, all working with program evaluators and other researchers. Developing these arrangements will also require new leadership approaches by administrators of all agencies involved.

BUILDING KNOWLEDGE FOR FUTURE USE

To strengthen the knowledge base for developing the next generation of violence prevention strategies, three research initiatives are needed: better systems to measure violence, research in neglected topics, and a long-term study of the factors operating in communities and in individual development that cause a small percentage of children to have high potential for violent behavior as adults, while most do not.

Measurement systems. Because of certain basic limitations in systems for gathering information on violence, many important questions in policy and science cannot be answered today, and emerging violence problems are sometimes slow to be discovered. For these reasons relevant information systems should be modified and expanded to provide:

— Better counts of intrafamily violence, robberies committed in commercial establishments, violent bias crimes, and violence in schools and correctional facilities.

— More comprehensive recording of sexual violence, especially events involving intimates, and acts (for example, serial killings) in which the sexual component may not be immediately apparent.

— Baseline measures of the prevalence and incidence of risk factors for violence (for example, arguments between intoxicated spouses or intimates, drug transactions, and situations in which employees handle cash alone, especially at night).

— Links between the systems that measure all aspects of a violent event—the consequences, the treatment of victims, and the circumstances precipitating the event.

— Better systems for measuring violence levels in small geographic areas, to facilitate evaluating the effects of intervention.

— More detail about the attributes of violent events and their participants, to facilitate better studies of risk factors.

Neglected research areas. Certain research areas are of special concern because, having been largely devoid of resources, they could make rapid progress with relatively small-scale infusion of funds. These areas include:

— The effects of weapon type death rates in assaults and robberies.

— Interactions among demographic, situational, and spatial risk factors for violent events and violent deaths.

— Comparisons of how individuals' potentials for violent behavior develop in ethnically and socioeconomically different communities.

- The nature of neurological responses that indicate elevated potentials for violent behavior.

- Development of medications that prevent violent behavior without the debilitating side effects of "chemical restraint."

- Interactions among cultural, developmental, and neuropsychological causes of sexual violence against strangers, intimate partners, and other family members.

- Violent behavior of custodians (for example, caretakers, correctional officers) against wards (for example, children in daycare and prison inmates).

Multicommunity longitudinal studies. To lay the specific groundwork for the next generation of preventive interventions, a multicommunity program of developmental studies of aggressive, violent, and antisocial behaviors is needed. By tracing the influences of the community, the family, and other individuals on children as they grow up, this program should improve the understanding of causes and lead to improved medical, developmental, and social interventions. The program should include randomized experiments that will identify developmental and social interventions for preventing high potentials for violent behavior in children. With support from the National Institute of Justice and the John D. and Catherine T. MacArthur Foundation, implementation of this recommendation has begun through a Program on Human Development and Criminal Behavior. Additional support is being solicited from a consortium of private and public sources.

CONCLUSION AND IMPLICATIONS

Violence is a pervasive national problem, more serious in the United States than in the rest of the industrialized world, and especially serious for males who belong to demographic and ethnic minorities. However, the problem is neither unprecedented nor intractable. Existing knowledge reveals a number of promising prevention strategies involving factors at work in communities, in individuals, and in hazardous situations that present special risks of violence.

Implementing effective prevention strategies requires recognizing that the criminal justice response is not enough to reduce violence levels. Rather, prevention requires comprehensive problem-solving strategies that involve criminal justice agencies, schools, and public health, emergency medicine, and social service agencies. Cooperation among these agencies and community-based organizations is needed in specific problem-solving initiatives to systematically test and refine promising violence prevention tactics. At the same time, to lay groundwork for the next generation of approaches to violence prevention, research should be carried out to improve the measurement of violence, to study certain topics neglected in recent years, and to learn more about what causes a small proportion of all children to commit violent acts as adults.

PART II

Individuals, Violence & Conflict

INDIVIDUALS, VIOLENCE AND CONFLICT

Interpersonal conflict and violence occur between people acting as individuals rather than as members of social aggregates or units. Unlike social aggregates, individuals have no division of labor or complex social structure. Therefore, conflicts between individuals are relatively simple in comparison to those between other social aggregates. Be aware that serious *inter*personal conflicts often start as *intra*personal ones—that is, they may originate in the frustration, neurosis or psychoses of an individual. By entangling others in their own troubles—through projection, scapegoating, and so on—some individuals transform their intrapersonal conflicts into interpersonal ones.

NONVIOLENT INTERPERSONAL CONFLICT

Before dealing with violent interpersonal conflict, a few words about the many kinds of nonviolent conflict between individuals, especially between those in intimate relationships. Intimacy has always involved a degree of conflict, and few would dispute this fact. Even people revered for their wisdom, such as Socrates, Abraham Lincoln, and Robert Frost, have had stormy marital relationships, marked by constant strife.

Given that intimacy tends to be conflictful, the main issue then is how can this conflict be managed and resolved by intimates. While there are no easy guidelines, the key requirement is that it be handled constructively and not destructively. In fact, avoiding conflict completely in intimacy is destructive. It sets people up for boredom, difficulties and often a failed relationship. The trick is to harness the energy of conflict to keep a relationship from getting boring. This is the challenge of nonviolent conflict. To do this requires that parties be assertive, but not aggressive in handling their anger. This statement contains three important terms that are similar and related to "violence," and so these terms will be defined here.

First, the anger people feel in relationships is altogether natural. **Anger** is an emotion of sudden and strong displeasure, usually directed at the cause of an assumed wrong or injury. It is an explosive feeling of wrath or ire.[1] Intimates can use anger—as they use conflict—to improve the quality of their communication. This ultimately helps relationships.

One way to constructively use anger is to be assertive. **Assertion** is behavior that enables a person to exercise his or her rights without denying the rights of others. Examples of assertion are: refusing to do more than one's share of housework, or insisting on a fair division of mutually earned income. Assertion is not the same as aggression, however. **Aggression** is an act of physical or verbal abuse that one person directs at another. When aggression entails physical abuse, it is violence. However, when aggression involves only verbal abuse (even if it is emotional or psychological abuse), it is not violence. To use mathematical set theory: all violence is an act of aggression, but not all aggression is an act of violence.[2]

VIOLENT INTERPERSONAL CONFLICT

In her chapter on domestic violence, Sue Titus Reid covers the gamut of violent conflict that one finds in intimate settings: child abuse, elder abuse, marital rape and male/female battering. She begins with a definition of domestic violence which is violence within the family or within other close associations. Thus, it includes violence against spouses, lovers, housemates, children, and parents.

Reid gives a brief overview of the problems of collecting and analyzing domestic violence data. To add another illustration to those Reid gives of the difficulty of getting reliable data: when O.J. Simpson's history of wife-battery came to light after his arrest, *Time* magazine said four million women are assaulted by domestic partners each year and *Newsweek* said the number was two million! These are quite different numbers. One would have thought the numbers would have been closer together, especially given that both magazines consulted national experts for their figures.

Domestic violence

Reid then proceeds in Chapter 6 with a discussion of each of the major types of domestic violence. She talks about child abuse which she defines as physical and emotional abuse of children, including sexual abuse and child pornography. Reid goes into some detail regarding the findings about one form of sexual abuse: namely, incest which involves sexual relations between members of an immediate family (other than husband and wife) such as sex between brother and sister, or between a parent and child. Reid elucidates social process and social structural theories used to explain child abuse, and elucidates the *cycle of violence* concept.

The author then examines elder abuse which entails the mistreatment of elderly persons who are usually the parents of the offender. Reid devotes the rest of the chapter to female battery which is the most frequently occurring form of domestic violence. She deals with the history of the problem and highlights the social scientific efforts to study and explain female battering as well as the psyche of the male batterer. She also deals with myths and stereotypes about battered women.

Next, Reid addresses the *battered person syndrome*. This is a syndrome arising from a cycle of abuse by a special person—often a parent or a spouse—which leads the battered person to perceive that violence against the offender is the only way to end the abuse. In some cases, the battered person murders the batterer. Reid concludes her chapter with discourses on marital rape (a type of forcible rape where the victim of coerced intercourse is a spouse) and male battery (a relatively rare event in heterosexual relationships).

After reading Reid's chapter, one is still left wondering why so much domestic violence occurs in families, in a domestic setting? There are a few factors worth noting.[3]

For one thing, there is a good deal of intimacy in the family setting. And the intimacy of the family predisposes it to conflict: the closer people get to one another emotionally, the greater chance they will fail to live up to each other's expectations. In addition, the more people are around each other, the greater the chance they will get on each other's nerves.

Family settings also involve love, and love can easily turn to hate because love often leads to feelings of jealousy and exclusiveness. Families are thus vulnerable to conflict-generating possessiveness and territoriality, as well as to violence that can come from the interpersonal power and control that are frequently a part of love.

Another reason families are the locus of so much violent conflict is that they entail compulsion and pressure. Parents, children, and various relatives are often involuntary members of families, and blood relationships make it difficult for them to leave when the going gets rough. Thus, conflict grows because incompatible family members, like the characters in Jean Paul Sartre's *No Exit*, are trapped in a situation which requires them to keep interacting with each other.

The constant change implicit in family life also causes conflict. The needs of each member continually change as family size increases; and as members grow older their roles change as well. Thus as each set of problems is surmounted, new ones threaten to disturb family equilibrium.

Finally, social pressures often come home to roost within the family unit. The frustrations of overcrowding, unemployment, low incomes, inferior housing, and inadequate education all strain domestic relationships and can lead to violence.

VIOLENCE, FEAR AND FIREARMS

In Chapter 7, Reid examines issues closely related to the domestic violence problem: namely, guns, gun regulation, and the fear of crime.

Fear of crime

In her section on the fear of crime, Reid notes that people's fear of violent crime is dependent on who they are, where they live, and the kind of lifestyle and social interaction they engage in. As a consequence of their fear of violence, people change their behavior and so do businesses and even cities (e.g., Orlando, Florida).

Significantly, there are many inconsistencies and contradictions with respect to people's fear of violence. Often people's fear does *not* reflect reality. For most people, the probability of dying from natural causes is still greater than it is from dying from violence.

To cite another inconsistency: many middle-class males are fearful of violence while many poor males profess to have no fear of it. In fact, well-off males are significantly less likely to be homicide victims than poor males are. (As noted in the chapter on street gangs, some gang members feel they must display fearlessness, part of the desired **locura** state of mind.)

Another inconsistency regarding fear of violence: even though official statistics show crime is beginning to decline, many people still feel they have substantial risk of being a victim of random, violent crime.

As Reid suggests, some of this inconsistency may be illuminated by the analysis of *fear spots* in terms of the visibility and escape potential such fear spots offer. Also useful in explaining inconsistencies is the analysis of the role the mass media play in creating fear. Studies show that the people who watch the most TV are often the ones most afraid of random violence, especially by strangers. In this regard deBecker states:

> The local news has a financial investment in making us believe in the randomness of violence. We live in a country in which only 20 percent of the homicides are committed by strangers, and yet look at the news-media coverage. The phrase 'random and senseless' is [a distortion;...W]e are focused on unusual fears [because] we aren't interested in hearing about the risks posed by the people in our lives."[4]

Whenever the fear of violence is out of synch with the reality of violence, perhaps we should create programs for reducing that fear. Why? As Reid notes, many elderly have died from heat stroke in their apartments out of fear that they might be attacked on the streets during hot weather.

Guns and gun control

The second section of Chapter 7 deals with gun control and violent crime. Unfortunately in her opening remarks, Reid intermixes statements about guns and gun control. Let us keep them separate. First, let us take a look at guns and the problems they create.

America's motto might be Guns 'R' Us, given the Department of Health and Human Services projection that—if recent trends hold—more deaths will be caused by guns than by automobiles by the year 2003! This should not be surprising: guns have played a big role in America's history. They are so much a part of us that we unconsciously use words and phrases that refer to guns—like "shoot," "high caliber," "blown away," and "half-cocked." We constantly use gun imagery in much of our daily vocabulary.

As is clear throughout this book, guns repeatedly come up as a factor in most types of violence in contemporary America. We know guns are a factor in interpersonal conflict, and obviously they make street gang life dangerous: there are no drive-by stabbings, just drive-by shootings. And guns come into play with organizations, whether with cults and militias stockpiling arms or police organizations with trigger-happy cops.

A few facts to add to those Reid presents regarding guns[5]:

— For every gun death, there are 4 to 10 gunfire injuries.

— The *New England Journal of Medicine* reports that for every justifiable, self-defense homicide in a home, there are 1.3 accidental deaths, 4.6 homicides, and 37 suicides involving guns.

— Art Kellerman at the University of Washington found that a gun in the home is 43 times more likely to kill its owner, a family member, or a friend than an intruder.

— Guns have caused the loss of "childhood innocence" for many children:

  — Many children "play "with real guns and hurt themselves or others.

  — Children in some inner city "war zones" witness so much gun violence that they "play funeral" rather than traditional kids games.

  — More and more children every year have aimed a gun at someone or had one aimed at them.

  — Children have jumped out of a closet, shouting "boo," and been shot dead by a startled parent.

— In some neighborhoods, guns come close to being household appliances. They seem to be used as casually as a toaster!

— People allege that gun shows attract felons, that the shows are turning into "Tupperware" parties for criminals, militia members and the like. In the process, billions of dollars worth of weapons are changing hands. This compounds an already difficult problem of stolen guns.

— The fastest growth in gun ownership lately has been among women. Gun boutiques have sprung up all over, and ads blatantly tout the need for "feminine protection."

Assault weapons

In her discussion, Reid says almost nothing about assault weapons or the efficacy of assault weapon control efforts. Unfortunately, bans have made legislators "feel good" about doing something, but the effectiveness of bans is questionable. Part of the problem is the definition of assault weapons, and the ease with which guns can be modified to avoid legal definitions. Essentially, assault weapons are semi-automatics with an additional handle so that they can be gripped with both hands. Assault weapons were originally designed for military or commando-style assaults. Such weapons have been used in all too many mass-murders.

The gun regulation debate

Some Americans have been concerned about guns and violence for decades. However, the National Rifle Association has been an extraordinarily effective lobby for the status quo over the years. Slowly, though, research findings are making the issues and consequences clear: for instance, Henry Sloan's seven-year study of two very similar cities with vastly different gun laws—Seattle and its neighbor Vancouver, British Columbia. His study found eight times more gun assaults and five times more gun murders in Seattle as compared to Vancouver.

Also, the "medicalization" of the gun problem is bearing fruit. Treating death by gunfire as if it were a disease has been successful. Many emergency room doctors used their prestige a few years ago to publicize the problem. The cost for treating a gun wound is about $14,000—enough for that victim to go to college. The annual hospital cost in the U.S. for treating gun injuries hit the $1 billion mark long ago.

And finally, local efforts and grass roots movements seem to be paying off. In many areas, people have been encouraged to trade their guns in—no questions asked—for money, computers, pro game tickets, etc. And legislators have been moved by activist groups that have placed tennis shoes on capitol steps—or displayed a Quilt of Tears—where each shoe or each quilt panel represents a child who has died from gun violence.

Of course, the Brady Group, Handgun Control Inc., and the Center to Prevent Handgun Violence have squared off with the National Rifle Association (with its millions of members), The Second Amendment Foundation, and the American Hunter. Essentially at issue is the interpretation of constitutional rights, and the battle can be reduced to the following:

"A well-regulated militia being necessary to the security of a free State, the right of the people to keep and bear arms shall not be infringed."

versus

"Someone's right to have a gun took away my right to have a child."

Gun control

What have all of the above efforts wrought in terms of gun control and regulation? Reid starts her gun control discussion with a review of the vicissitudes of various gun control legislation. Different level courts have made pronouncements on the Gun-Free School Zones Act and the Brady Act.

Reid brings up the issue of the Brady Act's five-day waiting period. Though she does not spell it out, the assumption behind the waiting period is that it prevents crimes of passion. Enraged, cuckolded mates cannot then go to a nearby store, buy a cheap Saturday night special, and return home to kill the unfaithful mate and his or her lover. Likewise, a battered person in a platonic domestic setting is prevented from doing the same.

Reid then addresses the debate over the effectiveness of the Brady bill. While some feel the Brady bill has been a success, others cite the lack of funding for enforcement, the burden background checks place on small rural police agencies, and the ages-old issue of false-identities: to wit, many prospective purchasers are "Joe Smiths" staying at local motels. Reid notes the tracking efforts using the FBI's NCIC database, but many feel that ultimately a nationwide system is needed which would allow any police agency to easily tap into a centralized list of convicted felons and others who are prohibited from possessing firearms.

CHAPTER 5—ENDNOTES

[1]Redford Williams and Virginia Williams, *Anger Kills* (New York: Harper Perennial, 1993), *passim*.

[2]Harry Kaufman, *Aggression and Altruism: A Psychological Analysis* (New York: Holt, Rinehart and Winston 1970), *passim*.

[3]Based in part on "Family Crises and Their Management" in Karl Schonborn, *To Keep the Peace: Crisis Management in Law Enforcement* (San Francisco: National Institute of Law Enforcement and Criminal Justice, 1976), 15-16.

[4]Gavin De Becker, *The Gift of Fear: Survival Signals that Protect Us from Violence* (New York: Little, Brown 1997), *passim*.

[5]Based on a variety of newspaper and newsmagazine sources as well as Robert Regoli and John Hewitt, *Delinquency in Society*, (New York: McGraw-Hill, 1997) 460-467; the National Commission on the Causes and Prevention of Violence, *Firearms & Violence in American Life*, *vol 7* (Washington, DC.: U.S. Government Printing Office, 1969); and Philip Cook and Mark Moore, "Gun Control," in James Q. Wilson and Joan Petersilia, eds., *Crime* (San Francisco: Institute for Contemporary Studies, 1995).

6

DOMESTIC VIOLENCE—REID

Although the *UCR's* list of serious crimes does not include **domestic violence** as a separate category, a discussion of violent crime is not complete without an analysis of this type of violence. Domestic violence is an example of behavior that historically has not been considered as a serious violent crime. It occurs within the setting where people can and should expect warmth, reinforcement, support, trust, and love. Domestic violence has been considered a personal, domestic problem, not an act of violence. In early Roman and English law, parents had almost exclusive rights to discipline their children. These rights permitted physical punishment and death. The Bible said that a stubborn and rebellious child could be taken by the parents into the city and there stoned to death by the elders. The death sentence was permitted for children who cursed or killed their parents. Historically, wives were the property of their fathers and, later, their husbands, who were allowed to discipline them virtually without penalty.

Even after the abuse of family members was no longer sanctioned as proper, little attention was paid to these actions. They were considered to be domestic matters and of little or no concern to the rest of society. Thus, although we have known about family violence for a long time, it has been only recently that these long-known facts have been pulled together into a general analysis of violence in the home.

The seriousness of domestic violence was emphasized by the Task Force on Victims in its 1982 report. The commission reported that domestic violence is more complex than violence against strangers. The task force recommended that the government appoint a new task force to study family violence. On 19 September 1983, the U.S. attorney general announced the formation of the Task Force on Family Violence, but it was not until 1994 that Congress enacted the Violence Against Women Act (VAWA) as part of the Violent Crime Control and Law Enforcement Act of 1994. The act makes gender-based violence a violation of civil rights, giving victims a civil cause of action that, if successful, entitles them to attorney fees as well as compensatory and punitive damages. By the spring of 1995, a new journal, *Violence against Women*, signaled the importance of a significant increase in scholarly research on domestic violence.

Republicans threatened to scale back the programs approved by the VAWA, but in March 1995 President Clinton announced the availability of $26 million in grants as a beginning for funding the act's provisions, which include programs to assist sexual assault victims as well as to work toward prevention of domestic violence against women and children. The president named Bonnie Campbell, author of one of the first antistalking laws, the first director of the newly created VAWA, but there are problems. For example, it is expected that the law may have a negative impact on divorce, child custody battles, and alimony; it will increase the caseload of already crowded court dockets. There are evidentiary regulations that may impinge on defendants' rights, and in an August 1996 decision one court held part of the act unconstitutional. The measure covering evidence has not gone into effect yet as there is a clause providing for judicial feedback before the measure is implemented.

Despite these advances in research and attitudes toward domestic violence crimes, some historical feeling remained. In October 1994 a defendant who pleaded guilty to killing his wife after finding her in bed with another man was sentenced to eighteen months in jail. The sentencing judge stated, "I seriously wonder how many men married five, four years would have the strength to walk away without inflicting some corporal punishment." The judge stated he imposed this sentence only to keep the system honest; he preferred not to send the defendant to prison at all. In late October 1995 the defendant was released from prison after serving one year rather than eighteen months because of his good-time credits for good behavior. Judge Robert E. Cahill Sr. was investigated for possible violations of the Code of Judicial Conduct. He was cleared of all charges. On the other hand, many people reacted negatively to the acquittal of O.J. Simpson, charged with the brutal murders of his ex-wife Nicole Brown Simpson and her friend, Ron Goldman. During the trial the prosecution introduced evidence that O.J. engaged in domestic violence against Nicole while they were married.

Nature and scope of domestic violence

In his announcement of federal grants, President Clinton called domestic violence the "number one health risk for women between the ages of fifteen and forty-four. . . It's a bigger threat than cancer or car accidents."[1]

The seriousness of domestic violence is beyond question, but the extent of the problem is difficult to define, primarily because of the lack of agreement on a definition as well as the refusal of victims to report. Often domestic violence is defined as physical and sexual violence within the family, including sexual abuse of children and physical abuse of elderly parents. In this discussion domestic violence is expanded to include violence among those who are not married, engaged, or divorced from each other and have no present or former legal ties. Dating relationships are included, for personal violence in these relationships is a problem among all ages.

The difficulty of defining domestic violence and the fact that definitions vary from jurisdiction to jurisdiction create a serious problem in collecting accurate data. Other problems in data gathering are that alleged victims are reluctant to report the crimes; cases that are reported may be processed as some other crime (such as simple assault, aggravated assault, battery, sexual battery, and so on) and thus not recorded as domestic violence. Many cases are dismissed without formal processing and do not become part of the official data. This may be true particularly with domestic violence cases reported from middle- and upper-income families in contrast to lower-income and especially welfare cases.

EXHIBIT 1

Family Violence

— Annually, compared to males, females experienced over 10 times as many incidents of violence by an intimate. On average each year, women experienced 572,032 violent victimizations at the hands of an intimate, compared to 48,983 incidents committed against men.

— Women were just as likely to experience a violent victimization by an intimate or relative (33 percent) as they were to be victimized by an acquaintance (35 percent) or a stranger (31 percent). Family-related violence, however, accounted for only 5 percent of all violent victimizations against men. Men were far more likely to be victimized by an acquaintance (50 percent of all male victimizations) or a stranger (44 percent of all male victimizations) than by an intimate or family member.

— White and black women experienced equivalent rates of violence committed by intimates and other relatives. However, black women were significantly more likely than white women to experience incidents of violence by acquaintances or strangers.

— Women with lower education and family income levels were more likely to be victimized by intimates than women who had graduated from college and who had higher family incomes. Women with family incomes less than $9,999 were more than 5 times as likely to experience a violent victimization by an intimate and more than twice as likely to be victimized by an acquaintance than those with family incomes over $30,000.

— Living in suburban or rural areas did not decrease a woman's risk of experiencing an act of violence by an intimate. Women living in central cities, suburban areas and rural locations experienced similar rates of violence committed by intimates.

— Violence by strangers was more likely to occur in central cities than in the suburbs or rural area. Females living in central cities were 4 times more likely to be victimized by a stranger than rural females and almost 2 times more likely than suburban females.

— Robbery was the only crime in which women were more likely to be victimized by strangers rather than intimates, other family members, or acquaintances. Female victims of simple assault were more likely to be victimized by an intimate or an acquaintance rather than a stranger or a relative who was not an intimate.

Source: Bureau of Justice Statistics, *Violence against Women: A National Crime Victimization Survey Report* (Washington, D.C.: U.S. Department of Justice, January 1994), pp. 6–7.

A 1994 report by the BJS, based on the reports of alleged victims, noted the difficulty of measuring family violence. The report on violence by intimates includes children or other relatives as well as spouses, ex-spouses, boyfriends, or girlfriends. The crimes included rape, robbery, or assault but not murder since the data are based on victims' reports. Some of the results of the analysis are reproduced in Exhibit 1.

Domestic violence acts are not limited to the United States. Reports of domestic violence from other countries are increasing. Perhaps none are as dramatic as the Japanese wife who complained that her husband tried to feed her to the sharks.

Child abuse

In recent years considerable media attention has focused on **child abuse**, a broad term used to include neglect as well as physical and sexual abuse. Child abuse may include child stealing or parental kidnapping, in which the parent who does not have legal custody takes the child without permission and refuses to return the youngster to his or her legal guardian or parent. Child abuse may include the involvement of children in pornography. Sexual abuse includes sexual activities that are voluntary, in the sense that no force is used, but in which the child is coerced by the parent or other person to engage in sexual activities.

The 11 December 1995 issue of *Time* magazine featured a picture of six-year-old Elisa Izquierdo on the cover, along with the caption, "A shameful death: let down by the system, murdered by her mom, a little girl symbolizes America's failure to protect its children." Her story captured the hearts of foreigners as well as Americans. One month after Elisa was born to a mother who used crack cocaine, social workers discovered that her brother and sister had been abused. There were removed from the family. For a while Elisa was in the care of her loving father, who enrolled her in a Montessori Day School. When he fell behind in tuition payments, a benefactor, a Greek prince, paid Elisa's tuition and pledged to do so until she finished high school. But the child welfare system failed this little girl when workers did not associate her problems with abuse. She was beaten to death, and her mother, who was charged with murder, protested her innocence for months. In June 1996 she entered a guilty plea to second-degree murder in exchange for a reduced sentence of fifteen years to life.[2]

Within the family, child abuse may take the form of physical abuse without sexual contact. According to the health officials, child abuse is a leading cause of death for small children, claiming at least 2,000 children each year. Approximately 140,000 others are injured by child abuse. The U.S. Advisory Board on Child Abuse and Neglect, established by Congress in 1988 to study child abuse, conducted a national study for two and one-half years, releasing its report in April 1995. According to the report, many of the children die from head trauma resulting from the "shaken baby syndrome," with approximately 25 percent of children abused in that manner dying and most of the rest sustaining brain damage.[3]

Sexual abuse of children, especially within the family, is a major type of child abuse today. The increased attention given nationally to this abuse has created a greater awareness of the crime of **incest**, which refers to sexual relations between family members (other than husband and wife) who are considered by law to be related too closely to marry. Usually children cooperate with the abusing parent or siblings because they are eager to please and do not understand what is going on. Most children cooperate also in the warning not to tell anyone about the sexual behavior. Because many cases of incest are not reported, the data on this crime are not accurate.

Most cases of incest are between father and daughter; cases of incest between mother and son are rare, but they do exist. Father/son incest may occur, but less is known about this type of sexual abuse. Most of the studies of incest are about father/daughter relationships, indicating that in most cases sexual abuse does not begin with sexual intercourse; other forms of activity may take place years before sexual penetration. Usually the activity begins with exhibitionism, then masturbation, mutual masturbation, other fondling, digital penetration of the vagina and/or anus, and finally sexual intercourse. Many daughters who are involved have poor relationships with their mothers and do not feel that they can turn to them when their fathers initiate sexual activity. Many men who have sexual relations with their daughters are having problems, often sexual, with their wives, and they see their wives as threatening and rejecting.

Most fathers deny the incestuous relationship or, if it is admitted, attribute it to overindulgence in alcohol or drugs. One therapist explains father/daughter incest as "the ultimate act of hatred a man shows his wife"[4] Many incestuous relationships begin when the daughter is very young. When confronted, the father rationalizes the behavior in terms of "teaching his daughter the facts of life" or "she seduced me." Often the mother is passive and possesses other traits characteristic of battered wives: extreme dependence on her husband, poor self-image, hostility, and jealousy of her spouse. In some cases, the mother becomes an accomplice or at least a witness.[5]

Very little has been written about brother/sister incest, thought to be the least damaging of all types of incest and usually transitory. Mother/son sexual relationships are reported infrequently. "Masters and Johnson state that the most traumatic form of incest is mother/son contact. The boy's social relationships with peers of both sexes are badly damaged."[6]

Some cases of child sexual abuse do not occur within the domestic setting but in its modern-day replacements: the day care center, for example. The longest trial in U.S. history ended in January 1990 with two acquittals on fifty-two counts of child molestation at the McMartin Preschool in Los Angeles. A second trial on one charge on which the jury had deadlocked ended in a mistrial. The trials cost the city of Los Angeles over $13 million. In December 1995 Virginia McMartin, one of the major defendants, died.[7]

In 1991 the head of the Little Rascals Daycare Center in a small North Carolina town was convicted and sentenced to twelve consecutive life sentences for molesting children. His wife accepted a plea bargain in the case. Other adults were charged in the case as well, but questions were raised in a 1993 documentary after three jurors said they thought the director was not guilty. The documentary questioned the validity of the testimony form the twelve children, aged two and three when the alleged abuse occurred and five and six when they testified. In May 1995 an appellate court ordered new trials for the director, Robert Kelly, Jr., and the cook, who was sentenced to life in prison for her conviction on five counts of sexual abuse. The court ruled that some of the evidence should not have been admitted and that during closing arguments in the cook's case, the prosecutor made improper comments regarding the evidence and the witnesses. On 30 April 1996 Kelly was returned to jail to await his retrial on some charges involving the children from the day care center as well as new charges by another alleged victim of sexual assault.

Although legal evidence issues are beyond the scope of this text, it is important to understand that such matters of criminal procedure are crucial to prosecuting sexual abuse cases, especially when the alleged victim is a child. The law must balance the defendant's rights against the need for society to punish, and the law must consider also the needs of the alleged victim. Some children may suffer even greater trauma if they testify, and when they testify, they may be less than truthful.

The literature on theories of family violence and child abuse is extensive, but the approach has moved from an emphasis on the individual offender's pathology to sociological analyses, such as the social organization of the family and the culture in which family violence occurs.

Both social-process and social-structure theories are used to explain child abuse. The lack of social integration, for example, is used to explain why the mother is the most frequent child abuser in the family in those situations not involving sexual abuse. Frequently the female offender in child abuse cases is a socially isolated person who came from a background of inadequate nurturing. These are parents who are not able to sublimate or redirect their anger, yet face strains and stresses that contribute to feelings of anger. These parents have a low threshold for children's typical activities such as crying, soiling, and rejecting food periodically. One study found that battering parents "yearned for a mature response from their babies, for a show of love that would bolster their sagging egos and lack of self-esteem."[8]

Social-structural variables were the focus of a national study of family violence, including child abuse, conducted by sociologist Richard Gelles. Gelles emphasized that the causes of child abuse are complex. Clearly they are not attributed solely to mental illness or psychiatric disorder. A number of variables are involved, including "stress, unemployment and under-employment, number of children, and social isolation." Gelles examined the social characteristics of the abusing parents, the social characteristics of the abused children, and, finally, the situational or contextual properties of the child abuse itself. Gelles concluded that if we are to treat and prevent the abuse of children, we must stop thinking of the abuser as a sick person who can be cured and begin working on social-structural variables, such as unemployment and childrearing techniques.[9]

In a later publication, Gelles and a colleague reviewed the research on domestic violence, including child sexual abuse, which was conducted in the 1980s, noting that the amount was substantial, perhaps more extensive than any other area of social science research. Estimates of the extent of child sexual abuse range from victimization of 6 percent to 62 percent of girls and 3 to 31 percent of boys. The implications of this abuse are serious, too, as studies suggest that many children who are abused sexually exhibit serious problems later in life.[10]

Many child abuse victims become child abusers when they have children; some engage in violence against other children and their parents while they are children. Studies of juvenile offenders reveal that many were victims of child abuse or were witnesses to the abuse of other children. The same is true of adult offenders.[11] A psychiatrist at Columbia University's New York State Psychiatric Center notes that many of the children who commit sex crimes against other children do so after being the victims of sexual abuse. One example she cited was the case of a boy who at age nine was sodomized by his stepfather who threatened him with greater harm if he told anyone. When the victim reached twelve, he sodomized his nine-year-old brother who was afraid to report the act. Subsequently he sodomized a five-year-old neighbor who told his mother, who reported the incident.[12]

Researchers refer to the continuation of violence in families over generations as the *cycle of violence* or the *intergenerational transmission of violence*. A study of these patterns by the National Institute of Justice focused on sexual behaviors. A few of the findings reported in 1995 are reprinted in Exhibit 2.

It is important to understand, however, that sexual (or nonsexual) abuse of children does not necessarily cause them to engage in the same kind of behavior against others. "[Although] experiencing child abuse may increase the odds of subsequent antisocial behavior . . . it does not predetermine criminality." Other factors may be influential as well.[13]

EXHIBIT 2

Later Criminal Consequences of Childhood Sexual Abuse: Key Findings

— People who were sexually victimized during childhood are at higher risk of arrest for committing crimes as adults, including sex crimes, than are people who did not suffer sexual or physical abuse or neglect during childhood. However, the risk of arrest for childhood sexual abuse victims as adults is no higher than for victims of other types of childhood abuse and neglect.

— The vast majority of childhood sexual abuse victims are not arrested for sex crimes or any other crimes as adults.

— Compared to victims of childhood physical abuse and neglect, victims of childhood sexual abuse are at greater risk of being arrested for one type of sex crime: prostitution.

— For the specific sex crimes of rape and sodomy, victims of physical abuse tended to be at greater risk for committing those crimes then were sexual abuse victims and people who had not been victimized.

— What might seem to be a logical progression from childhood sexual abuse to running away to prostitution was not borne out. The adults arrested for prostitution were not the runaways identified in this study.

Source: Cathy Spatz Widom, *Victims of Childhood Sexual Abuse–Later Criminal Consequences* (Washington, D.C.: National Institute of Justice, U.S. Department of Justice, March 1995), p. 2.

Abused and neglected children may suffer physical reactions such as impairment of neurological function, retardation, or impairment of intelligence. Many of these children have personality disorders. Even when the child does not manifest immediate problems, sexual abuse may be considered a time bomb that will go off later during sexual and other experiences in the victim's adult life.

Elder abuse

In 1994 the Department of Health and Human Services (HHS) commissioned the National Center on Elder Abuse to begin a three-year investigation of the abuse, neglect, and exploitation of the elderly. Accurate data on **elder abuse** are not available, for many of the crimes are not reported. But it is estimated that 1.5 million Americans over the age of sixty suffer some type of physical or mental abuse. According to an HHS official, "Elder abuse, especially in the family, is one of the most sensitive and embarrassing problems an older person faces. . . It's the hidden shame of the American family.[14]

There are other reasons, too, for inaccurate data on elder abuse. It is difficult to prove. The fact that elderly people bruise easily and fall often accounts for three-fourths of all home accidents. Because some doctors are not trained to detect abuse, many incidents do not come to the attention of those who collect the data.

One type of elder abuse that has gained attention in recent years is the abuse of elderly parents by members of their own families. This form of violence has been referred to as the King Lear syndrome (after the aging character in Shakespeare's play who was mistreated by two of his daughters), granny bashing, and parental abuse as well as elder abuse. Abuse of the elderly includes not only violent attacks but also such acts as withholding food, stealing savings and Social Security checks, verbal abuse, and threatening to send an elderly person to a nursing home.

It has only been relatively recently that social scientists have begun to study family abuse of the elderly; our knowledge, therefore, of the problem is limited. The roots of the abuse may lie in child abuse, as suggested earlier. It may be the result of an attempt to do the right thing but an inability to cope with the problems of an aging parent or grandparent coupled with the inability, because of guilt, to place that parent in a nursing home. Transferring the responsibility for the person is difficult.

Elder abuse occurs outside the family too. Many elderly people die from neglect in nursing homes and other residences. With its large elderly population, Florida faces difficult problems in this area, and recent investigations show that the state has a long way to go toward solving them. Most of the victims are elderly women; most of the cases are reported by social services, followed closely by neighbors or friends. Some are referred by medical personnel. The *Miami Herald* reviewed hundreds of Florida cases and reported that "dozens of frail and disabled adults have died sick, starved, ridden with bedsores, bruises and broken bones—the silent casualties of abuse, neglect and a welfare system that did little to protect them."[15]

One final problem for the elderly with regard to violent crime is their fear of becoming victims. As the police commissioner in a suburb north of New York City stated the problem, "The very people who built our streets are afraid to walk them."

Female battering

Despite the seriousness of child abuse and the apparently growing incidence of parental abuse of elderly parents, the woman (wife, lover, estranged wife, former wife, girlfriend) is the one victimized most frequently by domestic violence. The problems of domestic abuse of women were dramatized for months in the trial of O.J. Simpson, who was acquitted of the brutal slaying of his ex-wife Nicole Brown Simpson and her friend Ronald Goldman. During the trial the prosecution presented dramatic evidence (for example, a 911 call from Nicole and pictures of her bruised face) of domestic violence.

Historically, by law and by social convention, husbands had the authority to control their wives, considered to be their property. Much of our law comes from English common law, which gave men the authority to chastise their wives. The *rule-of-thumb* measure referred to the specification that a husband could discipline his wife by beating her as long as he used a stick not thicker than his thumb. Medieval practices permitted beating, even killing, a wife or a serf if done for the purpose of disciplining. In the United States, wife beating was permitted by statute. This historical recognition of a husband's legal right to discipline his wife with physical brutality has changed.[16]

Data on abuse of female companions are probably less accurate than those on any other crime, including rape. Earlier publications by sociologists report that one out of every six couples in the United States engage in at least one violent act each year and that during the years of their marriages the chances are greater than one in four that a couple will engage in physical violence.

The redesigned BJS victimization studies offer some data on domestic violence. The 1995 report states that over a half million violent crimes were committed against a spouse or ex-spouse in 1993. Of those crimes 9 percent were rapes or other sexual assaults, 6 percent were robberies, 14 percent were aggravated assaults, and 71 percent were simple assaults. Women were four times more likely than men to be victimized by relatives. Recall that the victimization studies do not include murder.[17]

Domestic violence is not limited to the United States. In February 1991 the Women's Program Forum of the Ford Foundation sponsored a symposium on "Violence against Women: Addressing a Global Problem." One of the speakers emphasized that domestic violence is not limited to interactions within families. Rather, she spoke of *gender violence*, "which ranges from forced prostitution to involuntary pregnancy, infanticide, and genital mutilation. Gender violence is the most pervasive and insidious human rights abuse in the world."[18] That symposium emphasized that women all over the world are domestic violence victims.

As part of the 1994 crime control act, Congress included a section entitled, the "Violence Against Women Act of 1994." Among other provisions, such as criminalizing crossing state lines in furtherance of domestic violence, the statute enables victims to sue their offenders for damages, although this section has been declared unconstitutional by one court.[19] Within a year of the statute's signing by President Clinton, several programs for treating domestic violence were in effect in various states. According to Senator Joseph R. Biden, the chief sponsor of the legislation, "The victims of family violence and sexual assaults are finally receiving the attention, assistance, and respect they need and deserve." Over $23 million had been awarded to boost prosecution of domestic violence offenders, and steps had been taken to treat victims with greater respect and dignity. The constitutionality of the act was upheld for the first time by a federal district court judge in June 1996. The first person convicted under the statute was Christopher Bailey, of West Virginia, who kidnapped and beat his wife, Sonya. He was sentenced to life for the crimes that left his wife in a vegetative state.[20]

In October 1995 Attorney General Janet Reno announced that, due to demand for funding, the amount available for a grant program for innovative programs to prevent domestic violence would be doubled.

The male batterer

Despite the stereotype of the male batterer as a pathological male from the lower socioeconomic class, researchers have found that all races and social classes are involved. Statistically, battering may occur more often in the lower than in the upper classes, but that may be due to variations in reporting. There appear to be three major variables characteristic of men who batter their partners: frustration or stress, gender roles or learned behavior, and alcohol. Stress may occur for many reasons. Frustration and stress may result from the man's sense of inadequacy as a male, as a provider, and as a father, a husband, or a lover. Insecurities may result from his extreme dependency on his partner, coupled with his fear of losing her.

Gender roles, learned through the process of socialization, may be related to partner battering. Men learn to be aggressive and dominant and to expect women to be feminine and passive. Any show of superiority by the partner, for example, if she is employed and he is unemployed or if both are employed and she earns more money, may trigger a violent response. Many men and women adjust to changing gender roles without violence. The point is that those who continue to hold traditional gender-role differentiations may be more likely to explode when the situation gets out of hand by their definitions. This desire to maintain traditional gender-role stereotypes may explain the willingness of some women to tolerate the physical abuse.

The socialization process may trigger a violent reaction in the man. If he comes from a home in which his mother was battered, a characteristic of many batterers, he may have accepted violence as an appropriate way to handle the problems between men and women. If he were a battered child, he may have decided that it is acceptable for the one who loves you to beat you as a method of control. Another factor in abusive behavior may be alcohol. Because of the frequent association of alcohol with violence, many battered women have assumed that drinking causes the violence, but the relationship is much more complex. In some situations, both spouses are under the influence of alcohol when violence occurs.

One recent study reports that men who abuse their wives or other partners are not violent in other relationships; that is, violent men tend to specialize. Either they abuse partners and other family members or they abuse nonfamily members, but they do not abuse both groups. Only 10 percent of the sample reported engaging in violence against both family and nonfamily. Further, those who engage in violence outside the family were more likely to be blue-collar workers than those who engaged in violence against the family.[21]

Battered women: myths, stereotypes, and a research profile

There are many myths about domestic violence, especially wife battering. Research has examined the prevalent public attitudes toward the victims, who are thought to be weak, sick, guilty (she nagged him until he beat her), lower class, and willing to take physical abuse for a meal ticket.

Research on the battered woman is limited in scope and depth, but the available studies suggest that the battered woman has characteristics similar to those of the battering man. One writer has described the battered woman in these terms:

> The profile of the battered woman looks almost identical to that of her batterer: she is all ages, all ethnicities, from all socioeconomic groups, has a low self-esteem, and for the most part has very traditional notions of male and female behavior. She may feel that her husband is supposed to be in charge of the family, even if that means beating her; she must be supportive of him, even if that means allowing herself to be abused repeatedly. Her role as a woman includes marriage, even a bad marriage and to leave the home would be to admit that she is a failure as a woman.[22]

Perhaps the battered woman is understood best by analyzing why she remains in the marriage. The pioneer work on this issue was conducted by Richard Gelles, who gives three reasons battered women do not leave their husbands. First, women are less likely to leave if the violence is not frequent or severe. Second, wives who were abused by their own parents are more likely to remain with abusive husbands than those who were not abused as children. Third, the more resources and options a wife has, the more likely she is to leave an abusive spouse.[23]

Psychologist Lenore E. Walker characterizes the battered woman as a woman who is

> repeatedly subjected to any forceful or psychological behavior by a man in order to coerce her to do something he wants her to do without concern for her rights. . . Furthermore . . . the couple must go through the battering cycle at least twice. . . [And if] she remains in the situation, she is defined as a battered woman.[24]

In 1977 Walker coined the term **battered person** (or woman) **syndrome** in a case involving a battered woman who was accused of murdering her husband. The defendant was acquitted, and Walker was on her way to a career as a recognized expert on the the battered woman syndrome. The syndrome has been accepted in many courts and rejected in others. Some jurisdictions have enacted statutes declaring the admissibility of expert testimony concerning the syndrome. Walker was retained by the defense in the O.J. Simpson case, and she was criticized by many for her decision to testify for the defense. She was not called as a witness during the trial.

Similar to the battered woman syndrome is the battered child syndrome which was used by Erik and Lyle Menendez in their California trial in which they were charged with the murders of their parents. The brothers claimed that they shot their parents in self-defense after years of abuse. Although the brothers were not in imminent danger (required for self-defense), a defense of unreasonable or imperfect self-defense may be used in California and in some other jurisdictions. The defense involves a situation in which the perpetrator of a violent act believes he or she is in danger of imminent harm or death, but that belief is not a reasonable one in view of the facts as understood by an objective person. The first trial of the Menendez brothers resulted in mistrials for both defendants (who had separate juries). In the second trial the brothers were tried before one jury. Some of the evidence admitted during the first trial was excluded by the same judge in the second trial. In addition, he refused to permit the jury to consider an imperfect self-defense. In the spring of 1996 the brothers were convicted and sentenced to life in prison without possibility of parole.

Marital rape

Receiving even less attention than wife battering is **marital rape**. Historically a husband had unlimited sexual access to his wife; she was expected, and in most cases she expected, to comply with his sexual desires. He could be charged with rape only if he forced her to have sexual intercourse with a third person. No amount of force on his part would classify sexual intercourse with his wife as rape even if the couple had separated legally. This common law provision became part of most of our rape statutes. Although some jurisdictions retain the common law approach, in recent years many have changed their rules by statute or by judicial holding to permit forced sexual acts between spouses to be prosecuted as rape.

Recent research implies that marital rape is much more prevalent than previously thought and probably exceeds all other kinds of rape. Possibly as many as one of every ten wives is victimized. "The offender's goal, in many instances, appears to be to humiliate and retaliate against his wife and the abuse may often include anal intercourse."[25]

Prosecutions for marital rape are becoming more frequent. In 1977 Oregon became the first state to repeal the marital rape exemption. The state, upon complaint by Greta Rideout, filed criminal charges against her husband, John, who was tried under this statute. This was the first trial on marital rape in the country, but on 27 December 1979 John Rideout was acquitted. Shortly thereafter, the Rideouts reconciled, although the reconciliation did not last long.

In 1979 a Massachusetts defendant who was convicted of raping his estranged wife was believed to be the first person in the United States to be convicted of marital rape. On appeal, his conviction was upheld, and he was sentenced to three to five years in prison and three years on probation after release.

In a recent trial under South Carolina's new statute that permits prosecution of husbands who rape their wives, the husband was acquitted despite movies showing that he had intercourse with his wife while she was gagged and her eyes were taped. The defense claimed that the wife enjoyed rough sex and that her screams were related to her pleasure. The jury took less than one hour to reach a verdict. Two of the jurors told the press that the prosecution had not proved its case, leading many to wonder what type of proof would be sufficient in such cases.

Many states have repealed the marital rape exemption. In other jurisdictions it has been declared unconstitutional. In 1985 the Supreme Court of Georgia held that when a woman says "I do," she does not give up the right to say "I won't." In 1992 an Illinois appellate court ruled that a sexual assault committed by a person against his or her spouse is not a less serious threat than one committed by another person; the exemption was ruled unconstitutional.

The marital rape exemption has been eliminated in some other countries as well. In 1991 the highest court in England ruled that a man could be found guilty of raping his estranged wife. Declaring that a rapist is a rapist no matter what the relationship is to the victim, the House of Lords struck down a common law rule that had existed for three centuries.[26]

Male battering

Although data indicate that most domestic violence acts are committed against women by their spouses, ex-spouses, or lovers, there is evidence that some women are batterers. The redesigned BJS victimization studies permit more extensive collection of data on rape and other sexual assaults. The 1995 report discloses that in 1993 males were victims in 7 percent of all rapes and in more than 13 percent of sexual assaults, but these data do not target domestic violence in particular.[27] We do know, however, that women batter their loved ones. Some even mutilate (recall the case of Lorena Bobbitt, who severed her husband's penis after he allegedly raped her) or kill them. In 1994 a female defendant was acquitted of mayhem and assault with a deadly weapon after severing her husband's testicles with a pair of scissors. The jury deadlocked on the lesser charge of battery. Aurelia Macias testified that she feared her husband would rape her and that he abused her physically for seventeen years. The couple reconciled and did not wish for the trial to proceed. In 1995 the prosecutor announced that he would not prosecute a third time on the battery charge.

Evidence suggests that when women strike (or kill) men, many allege that they do so in self-defense. In an earlier study Richard Gelles found that women are seven times more likely than men to engage in domestic violence for self-defense, either to avoid physical attacks or physical violence in the form of rape.

It is the fear of further victimization involving serious injury or even death that is behind the legal movement toward permitting women to use the battered woman defense as a self-defense argument when they are charged with killing their husbands. Some experts argue that this fear of future violence is a factor that distinguishes male domestic violence victims from female victims. Sociologist Mildred Daley Pagelow, an expert in domestic violence, argues that a man who lives with a habitually violent woman, unlike women who live with such men, "is not tied economically or through fear. He mostly needs psychological help."[28] Many female victims of *reported* domestic abuse are tied economically to the men who abuse them. Furthermore, data suggest that once a woman is victimized by her spouse or lover, she is likely to be victimized again.

Battered men are fighting back. The Domestic Rights Coalition, located in St. Paul, Minnesota, is an example. Founded by a man for men, the organization focuses on the rights of men who are battered by their wives and lovers. Some women note that there is a big difference: Woman live in fear of men who are stronger physically and upon whom they are dependent economically. Thus, it is ridiculous to equate violence of women against men with that of men against women. Men react that violence is violence and even if men are not injured, they should not have to endure the abuse. Richard Gelles notes that women abuse men as frequently as men abuse women but that men are not as likely to be injured. He concludes that from a policy point of view the emphasis should be on protecting women from domestic violence, but that attention should be given also to domestic violence against men.

The only shelter for men who are domestic abuse victims was opened in St. Paul, Minnesota, in late 1993. A year later the director estimated that fifty-four men had utilized the shelter.

CHAPTER 6—ENDNOTES

[1]"What Penalty for a Killing Passion?" *New York Times* (21 October 1994), p. 18; "Man Released after Serving Year in Wife's Killing; Judge's Sentencing Caused Controversy," *Baltimore Sun* (31 October 1995), p.2B; "Judge Cleared over Remarks in Sentencing," *Baltimore Sun* (4 May 1996), p.1.

[2]See "She Suffered in Plain Sight but Alarms Were Ignored," *New York Times* (24 December 1995), p. 1; and *Time* (11 December 1995), front cover and pp. 33-36. See also "Mom Pleads Guilty to Elisa's Murder," *New York Daily News* (25 June 1996), p. 6.

[3]Cited in "Abuse A Leading Cause of Death for Small Children, Study Finds," *Miami Herald* (26 April 1995), p. 1.

[4]"Incest Often Hidden by Those It Tears Apart," *Miami Herald* (20 April 1995), p. 6.

[5]"The Child Victim of Incest," *New York Times* (15 June 1982), p. 22. For a discussion of the biosocial view of incest, see Joseph Shepher, *Incest: A Biosocial View* (New York: Academic Press, 1983).

[6]Geiser, *Hidden Victims*, p. 68. For more information on incest, see D. E. H. Russell, *The Secret Trauma—Incest in the Lives of Girls and Women* (New York: Basic Books, 1986).

[7]"National Digest," *Star Tribune* (3 December 1995), p. 4.

[8]Study by psychiatrists Brant Steele and Carl Pollock, cited in Ruth Inglis, *Sins of the Fathers: A Study of the Physical and Emotional Abuse of Children* (New York: St. Martin's Press, 1978), p. 69.

[9]Richard J. Gelles, *Family Violence* (Beverly Hills, Calif.: Sage Publications, 1987), pp. 32-37, 42-53.

[10]Richard J. Gelles and Jon R. Conte, "Domestic Violence and Sexual Abuse of Children: A Review of Research in the Eighties," *Journal of Marriage and the Family* 52 (November 1990): 1045-1058; data are on p. 1050. See also Ronald C. Kessler and William J. Magee, "Childhood Family Violence and Adult Recurrent Depression," *Journal of Health and Social Behavior* 35 (March 1994): 13-27.

[11]Bureau of Justice Statistics, *Report to the Nation on Crime and Deliquency*, p. 48.

[12]"Children as Sexual Prey, and Predators," *New York Times* (30 May 1989), p. 1.

[13]Candace Kruttschnitt et al., "Abuse-Resistant Youth: Some Factors that May Inhibit Violent Criminal Behavior," *Social Forces* 66 (December 1987): 501.

[14]"Abuse of Elderly Is Target of Nationwide Investigation," *Miami Herald* (17 September 1994), p.12

[15]"Abused Adults: Silent Casualties," *Miami Herald* (22 November 1992), p. 1.

[16]Bailey v. People, 130 P. 832, 835, 836 (Colo. 1913), footnotes and citations omitted.

[17]Bureau of Justice Statistics, *Criminal Victimization 1993* (Washington, D.C.: U.S. Department of Justice, May 1995), p. 6.

[18]Charlotte Bunch, Center for Women's Global Leadership, Rutgers University, New Jersey, published in *Violence against Women: Addressing a Global Problem* (New York: Ford Foundation, 1992), p. 1.

[19]Violent Crime Control and Law Enforcement Act of 1994, Public Law 103-322, Title IV, Section 40001 et seq. (13 September 1994).

[20]"Violence against Women Act Said to Spark New State Programs," *Criminal Justice Newsletter 26* (1 September 1995): 5.

[21]Elizabeth Kandel-Englander, "Wife Battering and Violence outside the Family," *Journal Interpersonal Violence 7* (December 1992): 462-470.

[22]Donna M. Moore, ed., *Battered Women* (Beverly Hills, Calif.: Sage Publications, 1979), pp. 16-20.

[23]Gelles, *Violent Home*, pp. 95-110. For information on the decision of battered wives to call the police, see I.M. Johnson, "A Loglinear Analysis of Abused Wives; Decisions to Call the Police in Domestic-Violence Disputes," *Journal of Criminal Justice* 18, no. 2 (1990): 147-160.

[24]Quoted in State v. Kelly, 478 A.2d 364, 371 (N.J. 1984). See also Lenore E. Walker, *The Battered Woman* (New York: Harper & Row, 1979)

[25]David Finkelhor and Kersti Yllo, "Forced Sex in Marriage: A Preliminary Research Report," *Crime & Delinquency* 28 (July 1982): 459.

[26]"English Law Excusing Wife Rapers Overturned," *Tampa Tribune* (15 March 1991), p. 2C. For an analysis of marital rape, see Diana E. H. Russell, *Rape in Marriage*, expanded ed. with a new introduction (Bloomington, Ind.: Indiana University Press, 1990).

[27]See Bureau of Justice Statistics, *Criminal Victimization 1993*, p. 6.

[28]"Striking Back," *Time* (21 December 1987), p. 68.

VIOLENCE, FEAR AND FIREARMS—REID

FEAR OF CRIME

According to a report of the National Research Council Committee on Law and Justice (the research arm of the National Academy of Sciences), violence has left Americans in fear of their safety and their lives, causing them to resort to locking themselves in at night and to alter their lifestyles significantly.[1] Numerous studies have been conducted on the fear of crime, what causes the fear, and how it may be alleviated.[2]

Research suggests that fear of crime varies according to where people live. People have greater fears of crime, for example, in some cities or in specific neighborhoods within cities. Fear is affected by where people live within housing projects. Also, the nature of social interaction correlates with the degree of fear. And research confirms what most people think would be obvious: fear is greater at night than during the day.[3]

Many people believe it is necessary to change their lifestyles because of their fear of crime. In recent years, after several international terroristic incidents, particularly airports, large numbers of Americans canceled their plans to travel abroad. This also occurred during the Persian Gulf War. After a series of violent crimes targeting foreign tourists in South Florida in 1992, foreign news media and travel agents warned their people about traveling to that state. Specifically, after a British tourist was killed and an American tourist wounded in Orlando, the British tabloids "painted Orlando as a war zone of gun-toting bandits."[4] By 1995 Florida had lost its position as the number one state for vacations by international travelers, having been surpassed by California.[5] This occurred despite attempts to counteract the negative publicity, extraordinary security precautions taken in some Florida cities, and a statewide system of patrolling all rest stops twenty-four hours a day. In July 1995 the security was eliminated during daylight hours.

The fear of random crime, the belief that "random mayhem has spilled out of bounds and that a sanctuary can become a killing ground almost at whim"[6] may be the greatest fear. This fear of violent crime by strangers, who pick their victims randomly, led the late Supreme Court chief justice Warren E. Burger to refer to the "reign of terror in American cities" and caused one privately funded study of crime to conclude, "The fear of crime is slowly paralyzing American society."[7]

This fear of crime has changed our lives in many other ways. We must have exact change for buses and small bills for taxi drivers, who will not change large bills. We must lock our doors, bar our windows, and install burglar alarms, paying a high price for security. Many people refuse to go out alone at night. Elderly people have suffered or even died from heat strokes in their apartments, not leaving their homes during hot weather in fear of being burglarized or attacked. We worry that on Halloween our children might be given candy or other treats that have been laced with poison or have razor blades hidden inside.

Some of these fears are realistic; others are not. [This depends on] the probability of violent crime. Americans are more likely to die from natural causes than from violent crime,[8] but people do not always respond in terms of probabilities. Research suggests that women and the elderly have the greatest fears of violent crime, but as noted in earlier discussions of victims, they are less likely than the young and males to become victims. Furthermore, frequently the most fearful are those who have not been attacked recently. But there is evidence from earlier studies that actual victimization has an *indirect* effect on creating fear of crime, resulting in even greater fear by some groups, such as women and the elderly, than had been reported previously.[9]

Both women and the elderly may perceive themselves as more vulnerable to crime and less able to protect themselves from violent predators than do men and the young. Research indicates that compared with men, women take far more precautions to protect themselves. They are more likely to avoid being on the streets at night and, when on the streets, to use what has been called "street savvy," meaning the use of "tactics intended to reduce risks when exposed to danger, such as wearing shoes that permit one to run, or choosing a seat on a bus with an eye to who is sitting nearby." They are less likely to go to a public place alone at night.[10]

The nature of crimes against women is important in understanding their fear of violent crime. Few men are raped outside of prison. Although, according to official data, rape is not a common crime, most of its victims are women. Most rapes take longer to commit than other crimes, thus increasing the victim's contact with the offender and the probability of additional personal injury. Studies of the effects of rape show that it is one of the most traumatic of all personal crimes. In addition, the victim may be blamed for the rape. Rape may be feared, too, because of the inaccurate belief that in most cases it involves violence beyond that of the rape itself.

The elderly are more vulnerable to crime and thus to fear, for they are less likely to be able to change residences to protect themselves, to be able to afford locks and other protective measures for their homes, and to be able to defend themselves should they be attacked at home or on the streets.

Scholars argue that fear of crime should be analyzed more carefully in terms of the environment and the cues that might create unrealistic fear.[11] One attempt to do so was made by two scholars who analyzed *fear spots*, defined as "those specific places or areas where individuals feel fear of being victimized but where crime may not be frequent or where the police may not have recorded any criminal incidents either during the day or at night." The results suggest that fear may be greater when people have little chance of escaping (when there are places for potential offenders to hide and wait for their prospective victims) and when there is a lack of prospect (person's ability to obtain an open view of the area by looking into or walking through the area). For example, lack of sufficient lighting affects one's ability to look through the area, perhaps even to walk through the area. If these variables are found to be widely applicable to the fear of crime, the relationship raises obvious policy issues, such as more effective lighting, fewer obstructions, and more open escape routes. The researchers conclude, "We believe that understanding the causes of fear will help to better understand the fear-generating process and to develop effective fear reduction strategies."[12]

One final variable that deserves further study is the relationship between race and the fear of crime. A study conducted by the Bureau of Justice Statistics disclosed that African Americans are three times as likely as whites to express fear of crime in their neighborhood.

In addition to altering their lifestyles because of a fear of crime, some people join neighborhood organizations such as "Crime Watch," whereas others move to what they think is a safer neighborhood. Rather than joining with others to prevent crime, some people develop a distrust of others and an unwillingness to participate in crime prevention measures. Some have alarm systems installed in their homes and/or businesses or turn to weapons to protect themselves, their families, and their property. Regulations concerning the legal use of weapons for such protection vary from state to state, but all states permit the use of weapons in situations in which it is reasonable to believe that deadly force is necessary to protect human life. Widespread ownership of guns, however, has created problems, leading to a controversy over gun control.

GUN CONTROL AND VIOLENT CRIME

The Department of Health and Human Services projects that, if current trends continue, by the year 2003 more deaths will be caused by guns than by automobiles.[14] Violent crimes committed by offenders with handguns reached a record high in 1992, accounting for approximately 13 percent of all violent crimes recorded by the BJS. The most likely victims were young African American males, who were four times as likely as white males in their age group (sixteen to nineteen) to be victimized by handgun violence.[15] According to a 1995 BJS report (on 1993 data), 1.3 million of the 4.4 million violent crime victims responded that their assailants had a firearm. The Exhibit contains more recent information regarding guns used in crime.

In a 1994 announcement of government plans to enforce the federal ban on juvenile gun possession, Attorney General Janet Reno stated, "Unless we act now, a generation of young Americans will grow up in a world where gunfire is as normal as blue jeans and school books." The 1994 ban, along with numerous other gun control measures, was part of the Violent Crime Control and Law Enforcement Act of 1994.[16]

The control of firearms has run into constitutional problems. In April 1995 the Supreme Court held that the Gun-Free School Zones Act of 1990, which provided that possession of a gun within 1,000 feet of a school was a federal crime, exceeded congressional authority. The statute violated the government's power under the commerce clause of the Constitution. In May President Clinton sent legislation to Congress that would eliminate the problem with the statute. As of May 1996 that bill remained in committee, [17] with no action taken since 21 July 1995.

Some local gun control laws have been upheld.[18] The Brady Handgun Violence Protection Act, named for James Brady, who was wounded seriously during John Hinckley's attempted assassination of President Ronald Reagan, has been challenged in courts, with initial success followed by reversal. In 1995 the Ninth Circuit upheld the statute, and at the end of its 1995-96 session, the Supreme Court agreed to hear and decide the controversy.[19] The Brady bill requires a five-day waiting period for purchasing handguns, but it has been argued that a lack of enforcement funding is rendering the statute less effective than it might otherwise be.[20] On the other hand, the Treasury Department declares that the Brady bill is effective and that about 44,000 handgun applications were denied during the bill's first year.[21]

EXHIBIT 1

Firearms, Crime, and Criminal Justice

— Although most crime is not committed with guns, most gun crime is committed with handguns.

— Although most available guns are not used in crime, information about the 223 million guns available to the general public provides a context for evaluating criminal preferences for guns.

— By definition, stolen guns are available to criminals. The FBI's National Crime Information Center (NCIC) stolen gun file contains over 2 million reports; 60 percent are reports of stolen handguns.

— In 1994, the Bureau of Alcohol, Tobacco and Firearms (ATF) received over 85,132 requests from law enforcement agencies for traces of guns used in crime. Over three-quarters of the guns traced by ATF in 1994 were handguns (mostly pistols), and almost a third were less than 3 years old.

— Surveys of inmates show that they prefer concealable, large caliber guns. Juvenile offenders appears to be more likely to possess guns than adults.

— Studies of the guns used in homicides show that large caliber revolvers are the most frequent type of gun used in homicides, but the number large caliber semiautomatic guns used in murders is increasing.

— Little information exists about the use of assault weapons in crime. The information that does exist uses varying definitions of assault weapons that were developed before the Federal assault weapons ban was enacted.

Source: Bureau of Justice Statistics, *Guns Used in Crime* (Washington, D.C.: U.S. Department of Justice, July 1995), p. 1.

Researchers differ regarding the effect of gun control statutes. Criminologist Lawrence W. Sherman found that "directed police patrols in gun crime 'hot spots' can reduce gun crimes by increasing the seizures of illegally carried guns." When gun seizures by police increased by 65 percent, gun crimes decreased by 49 percent.[22] Sherman is conducting a similar study in Indianapolis. In addition, a University of Maryland study of five urban areas reported an increase in the number of people killed by guns after the passage of laws making it easier for citizens to carry guns.[23] Others maintain that gun control may not be effective in reducing crime and that guns used for self-defense may inhibit crime.[24]

CHAPTER 7—ENDNOTES

[1]Reported in "Study Finds U.S. Most Violent of All Industrialized Nations," *Tampa Tribune* (13 November 1992), p. 2.

[2]For analyses of the problems of methodology with these studies, see Frank P. Williams III, Marilyn D. McShane, and Ronald L. Akers, "Measuring Fear of Crime: The Construction of a Reliable Scale," paper prepared for presentation at the meetings of the British Society of Criminology (York, U.K.; July 1991).

[3]For a review of the literature concerning these areas, see Bonnie Fisher and Jack L. Nasar, "Fear Spots in Relation to Microlevel Physical Cues: Exploring the Overlooked," *Journal of Research in Crime and Delinquency* 32 (May 1995): 214-239.

[4]"Tourism Industry Moves to Counteract Crime News," Orlando Sentinel (11 October 1992), p. 1. For an analysis of the effect of the fear of crime on business, see Bonnie Fisher, "A Neighborhood Business Area Is Hurting: Crime, Fear of Crime, and Disorders Take Their Toll," *Crime & Delinquency* 37 (July 1991), 363-373.

[5]"Florida Takes Tumble from Top of Tourist Mountain," *Tallahassee Democrat* (28 May 1995), p. 1B.

[6]"The Plague of Violent Crime," *Newsweek* (23 March 1981), p. 46.

[7]"The Curse of Violent Crime: A Pervasive Fear of Robbery and Mayhem Threatens the Way America Lives," *Time* (23 March 1981), p. 16. For an analysis of the fear of crime, see Steven Box et al., "Explaining Fear of Crime," *British Journal of Criminology* 28 (Summer 1988): 340-356.

[8]Bureau of Justice Statistics, *Report to the Nation on Crime and Justice*, p. 24.

[9]See Wesley G. Skogan and Michael G. Maxfield, *Coping with Crime: Individual and Neighborhood Reactions* (Beverly Hills, Calif.: Sage Publications, 1981), and Mary Holland Baker et al., "The impact of a Crime Wave: Perceptions, Fear, and Confidence in the Police," *Law and Society Review* 17 (1983): 319-335.

[10]Stephanie Riger, "On Women," in Dan A. Lewis, ed., *Reactions to Crime* (Beverly Hills, Calif.: Sage Publications, 1981), pp. 47-52.

[11]See, for example, Marcus Felson, *Crime and Everyday Life: Insight and Implications for Society* (Thousand Oaks, Calif.: Pine Forge, 1994); and Wesley G. Skogan, *Disorder and Decline: Crime and the Spiral of Decay in American Neighborhoods* (New York: Free Press, 1990).

[12]Fisher and Nasar, "Fear Spots in Relation to Microlevel Physical Cues: Exploring the Overlooked," pp. 215, 236.

[13]Bureau of Justices Statistics, *Crime and Neighborhoods* (Washington, D.C.: U.S. Department of Justice, 1994).

[14]"Guns Gaining on Cars as Bigger Killer in U.S.," *New York Times* (28 January 1994), p. 8.

[15]Bureau of Justice Statistics, *Guns and Crime* (Washington, D.C.: U.S. Department of Justice, April 1994), p. 1. For an earlier analysis of victims of handgun violence, see Bureau of Justice Statistics, *Handgun Crime Victims* (Washington, D.C.: U.S. Department of Justice, July 1990).

[16]Violent Crime Control and Law Enforcement Act of 1994, Public Law 103-322, Title XI, Firearms (13 September 1994).

[17]Gun-Free School Zones Act of 1995, 104 Bill Tracking S. 890 (December 1995), to amend Gun-Free School Zones Act of 1990, U.S. Code, Title 18, Section 922 (q)(1)(A)(1995). The case is United States v. Lopez, 115 S. Ct. 1624 (1995).

[18]See Quilici v. Village of Morton Grove, 695 F.2d 261 (7th cir. 1982), *cert. denied*, 464 U.S. 863 (1973).

[19]See Mack v. United States, 66 F.3d 1025 (9th Cir.), *cert. granted*, 116 S.Ct. 2521 (1996).

[20]"Brady Bill May Be Ineffective without Funds," *St. Petersburg Times* (29 November 1993), p. 1. The statute is codified in U.S. Code, Title 18, Section 922 *et seq.* (1995).

[21]"Administration Reports on First Year's Experience with Brady Handgun Law," *Criminal Law Reporter* 56 (8 March 1995), p. 1523.

[22]Lawrence W. Sherman et al., *The Kansas City Gun Experiment* (Washington, D.C.: National Institute of Justice, January 1995), p. 1.

[23]"Study Links Rise in Killings with Loosening of Gun Laws," *New York Times* (15 March 1995), p. 16.

[24]See Gary Kleck, *Point Blank: Guns and Violence in America* (Hawthorne, N.Y.: Aldine de Gruyter, 1991).

PART III

Groups, Violence & Conflict

GROUPS, VIOLENCE AND CONFLICT

Intergroup conflict or violence does not involve just any collectivity. It would, if the word *group* were used in the broad, generic sense. However, *group* in this book refers to aggregates of three to thirty members which are characterized by closeness, social pressure, and flexibility in meeting member's needs. (Common groups of this sort are clans, gangs, and cliques.)

Serious intergroup conflict exists in some countries. These places still have vestiges of the *vendetta*, a violent feud in which members of one group—often a kinship clan or tribe—are in constant retaliatory conflict with members of another group.[1] In the United States such feuds, like the famous one between the Hatfields and McCoys, have died out, partly because the American legal system eventually defined vendetta violence as a wrong against society rather than just a wrong against some clan. Thus society (through its courts), instead of the injured clan, was authorized to redress wrongs done by a group against another. In this way, the cycle of violence and counterviolence was finally halted. The breakdown of extended kinship systems through urbanization and migration to cities also contributed to the passing of clan vendettas in this country.

STREET GANGS

But urbanization itself created a new and different form of vendetta in many industrializing nations: intergroup warfare between street gangs. According to early observers and scholars, street gangs were a by-product of urbanization and industrialization.

Not surprisingly, then, most modern-day countries are troubled by gangs or quasi-gangs. Over the years, such groups have been called mambos in Japan, halbstarke in Germany, vitelloni in Italy, tsotsio in South Africa, and blousons noirs in France.[2] England, Sweden, Poland, Russia, Australia, and the Philippines, to name just a few countries, are afflicted with youth gangs to a significant degree. However, nowhere have gangs been as numerous or as dangerously violent as in the U.S.

Incidentally, some of the most serious gang violence today occurs between gangs in *prisons*. Prisons found years ago that street troubles were being imported. Some city gangs today reputedly have as many members inside prison as they have outside (California, Illinois, New York, and Texas have been especially plagued by prison gang violence.)

Gang troubles were also imported into American *schools*. Middle schools and high schools in urban areas have been hit particularly hard. They have experienced a great surge of violence in classrooms, hall corridors, and the like—partly because gangs have introduced street weapons into the schools. Athletic and other events have had to be redesigned and scheduled in creative ways because of the fear of gang violence.

Gangs and group-ness

In his pioneering study in the 1920s of gangs and gang activity, Frederick Thrasher emphasized the *group* aspect of street gangs. He defined gangs as "interstitial" groups with leader and follower roles and members who meet face to face with high solidarity and group awareness.[3] However, there has been some scholarly debate over what exactly this "group-ness" entails, especially since gangs have grown and changed in various ways over the ensuing decades.[*] For this reason, a closer look at the group-ness of gangs is in order. Some of the terms and system elements presented in Chapter 2 will be used here.

The group nature of gangs is important in that it is largely responsible for the frequency and intensity of gang violence. Most youths do not have the boldness, desire, or means to act violently on their own; but companionship and group pressure make the difference. (Many criminologists believe that *most* serious juvenile delinquency is a group phenomenon. Some say that three quarters of all delinquency is group-inspired and executed.)[4] While being interviewed about a gang killing they had been involved in, several different members of a New York City gang alluded to the factor of group pressure:

> I was walking uptown with a couple of friends and we rant into Magician. . . . When he asked me if I wanted to go to a fight, I couldn't say no. I mean, I could say no, but for old time's sake, I said yes.

> Everyone was pushin' and I pulled out my knife. I saw this face—I never seen it before, so I stabbed it.

> He was laying on the ground lookin' up at us. Everyone was kicking, punching, stabbing. I kicked him on the jaw or someplace; then I kicked him in the stomach. That was the least I could do was kick 'im.

> They have guys watching you and if you don't stab or hit somebody they get you later. I hit him over the head with a bat.[5]

Most present-day gangs have the four properties associated with small groups: easy interaction, informal norms, substantial cohesion, and minor division of labor. Some gangs constitute less of a group than others. They are characterized by impermanence, minimal cohesion, sociopathic leadership, meager norm consensus, and limited role definitions and expecta-

---

*There have also been other definitional problems, especially because law enforcement organizations often define "gang "and "gang-related crime" in various ways. (The Los Angeles Sheriff's Department and the L.A.P.D.—even though they work side-by-side—have had differing definitions at times.) These problems may recede as more and more police agencies start using shared computer data bases, whether they be national or local like G.R.E.A.T. (the Gang Recording, Evaluating and Tracking system).

tions.[6] Such gangs are not really genuine groups; sociologist Lewis Yablonsky calls them "near groups."

The four properties of groups have certain specific implications for gangs:

1. Face-to-face interaction among all gang members is easily attained because the average size of a gang is relatively small. When one member speaks, all can hear.

2. Since interaction is easy, most norms are informal and unwritten. Despite this informality, though, the sanctions surrounding some norms—especially those regarding "ratting" and "maintaining a rep"—are powerful and effective.

3. Cohesion is generally strong in street gangs. It poses a grave problem to authorities because of its emboldening effect on gang members. Some experts recommend that police, journalists, and others who work with gangs avoid specific gang names in public references in order to decrease gang cohesiveness.

4. Most gangs have a rudimentary division of labor, expressed in such roles as leader, strategist, and opinion leader. Each of these serves a function in the gang.

Gang violence

Drive-by shootings are probably the most well known type of gang violence. Drive-bys are known mostly because they have been featured in Hollywood movies and because of news stories about drive-by victims. There is often an outpouring of sympathy for drive-by victims, especially for those who are totally blameless: innocent bystanders or youths without gang affiliation who are mistakenly gunned down.

There is a great deal of other gang violence besides drive-bys. There are *reverse* drive-bys where people passing by in cars are shot at by gangsters standing on the sidewalk. And of course, there are endless acts of violence in the service of the various businesses gangs and gang members are involved in. Much of this violence is like the vendetta where there is an endless cycle of violence and retaliatory violence.

Many gangs also use violence to maintain the boundaries of their group social unit. Just as the "Blood in, Blood out" phrase suggests, many street gangs use violence to initiate a person into their gang and keep him or her there. (Some initiates get "beaten in" by submitting for 15 or 20 minutes to punches and blows—often with bats—from gang members. Many gangs dish out even worse violence if a member dares to leave.) Bartollas' Chapter 9 contains a chilling discussion of violence in gang initiation rites.

And some gang members also use violence in committing various conventional crimes. There seems to be a law-of-the-jungle mentality that permeates much of the gang subculture. This mentality tends to foster a fair number of rapes, robberies, and aggravated assaults on the part of gangsters.

Finally, there is gang violence which results from classic intergroup conflict.

Gang conflict and fighting

Violent gang conflict occurs in various forms with various numbers of participants. It does not necessarily involve two equal parties, and it may involve symbolic conflict where representatives of two gangs have it out in lieu of an all-out encounter.

The following is a systematic way of classifying gang conflicts:[7]

— Fights between two *unarmed members* of opposing gangs to settle a minor dispute or accidental slight.

— Fights between two *armed members* of opposing gangs to settle a serious difference (butterfly knives, nun-chuks, and guns are used.) These may or may not be symbolic conflicts.

— Fights between a *single member* of one gang *and several members* of another to settle a score or to avenge a loss incurred in a previous fight.

— Fights between *small bands* from rival gangs. Planned in advance, these are conducted so as to inflict the greatest possible damage on the enemy.

— Fights between *large bands* from rival gangs. These are all-out wars where gangs confront each other using any weapon available—up to and including automatics, and sawed-off shotguns.

There is some indication that violent conflict sustains and even strengthens gangs. In *The Gang*, Thrasher showed that gangs develop through strife and thrive on warfare.[8] This is quite in keeping with the contention of Georg Simmel and Lewis Coser that conflict usually unites and integrates each of the parties participating in it.

It should be noted that street gangs do other things besides fight; gang warring is only one of their dramatic and visible activities. One analysis of 1,259 gang incidents during a seven-year period in Philadelphia showed that only 35 percent of them could be described as gang fights.[9] A more detailed study of 217 gang incidents in the same city revealed that 22 percent could be classified as fights.[10]

There is no simple answer to the question of why gangs and gangmembers fight. They fight for many reasons, and these tend to change from decade to decade. Some of the more enduring reasons, however, include:

Status. Gang youths often fight in order to gain prestige in the eyes of their peeers and their society as a whole. They want to show that they are people worth noticing, people to be reckoned with. A homicidal youth who had "got a body"—i.e. killed—expressed this striving clearly when he said: "I'm not going to let anybody steal my 'rep'. . . . When I go to a gang fight I punch, stomp, and stab harder than anyone."[11]

Criminologists Richard Cloward and Lloyd Ohlin elaborate on the issue of fighting for a rep:

> The immediate aim of the world of fighting gangs is to acquire a reputation for toughness and destructive violence. A 'rep' assures not only respectful behavior from peers and threatened adults, but also admiration for the physical strength and masculinity which it symbolizes. It

represents a way of securing access to the scarce resources for adolescent pleasure and opportunity in underprivileged areas.[12]

Status striving in gangs is not wholly unlike status striving in corporations, where respectable people try to move ahead by virtue of dedication and hard work.

Territory. Gangs often fight over turf or territory. Since turf is scarce in urban areas, it is highly valued. Consequently gangs become possessive about sidewalks, street corners, vacant lots, and even buildings. In time they come to feel that they literally own them. A kind of urban territorial imperative causes them to attack youths—especially rival gang members—whom they catch "trespassing." Writer Barrett Seaman has noted one of the consequences of divvying up territory: "The difference between life and death can often depend on whether a boy walks on one side of a street or the other."[13]

Safety. This reason for fighting is related to the preceding one. Gangs feel they must 'protect their members' safety, although this often includes protecting intangibles such as their good name and their style of life. Gang members really need protection from time to time—mostly because they have asked for trouble—but often their fears about their safety are imaginary and paranoid. (This paranoia is not surprising, though; most people involved in on-going conflict and violence eventually begin to extend their fears from real to imagined threats.)

Girls, Guys. Serious fights often break out when gang members "want" the same girl or guy. This reason is also related to territoriality, since gang subcultures often regard the opposite sex as property.

Kicks. Gang youths frequently engage in violence merely to break the monotony of their daily existence. They thirst for challenges and new experiences. Fighting, or anything else that society forbids gives gang members the thrills they desperately seek.

Affirmation. Some violent gang youths, like a lot of other violent people, need to prove to themselves that they are alive rather than dead—emotionally and psychologically. For such people, who are utterly overwhelmed by their own alienation and hopelessness, violence provides a self-affirming existential high. They can feel and can come alive—if only for a moment.

Pride. A slur, insult, or disrespectful gesture can easily trigger a fight between gang members, expecially if the people involved are from different ethnic or racial backgrounds. Mere rumors or allegations of slights to ethnic or racial pride also precipitate violence.

Drugs. Some violence is caused by the bravado and recklessness that often result when youths use alcohol and other drugs. Drugs foster violence in other ways too. Fights occur, for instance, when gang members sell contaminated drugs, or when they sell on a rival gang's turf and thereby horn in on profits.

Discipline. Conflict sometimes erupts because one gang takes upon itself the task of disciplining another gang. Since so much gang activity is illegal or quasi-legal, gangs do not ask police and the usual authorities to maintain discipline and standards in their world. This would blow everyone's cover, so to speak. Instead, gangs enforce their own norms, punish their own wrongdoers, and generally act as social-control agents in the subculture they inhabit.

Summing up the whole issue of gang violence—and underscoring Bartollas' remarks in Chapter 9—violence often permeates relations within gangs, between gangs, and between gangs and the rest of the community in which they operate.

Past, present and future perspectives

Bartollas discusses the big picture in his chapter on gangs: the past, present and future of gang life in America. He starts with an examination of the origins of gangs in the U.S. He states that gangs have been around since the War of 1812 but that their present incarnation dates from the early 1900s and America's shift away from being an agrarian-based society.

As gangs grew and developed, Americans began to fear them, particularly their violence. In the 1950s, the movie classic *West Side Story* promulgated the image of ethnic gangs fighting over neighborhood turf and territory. Violence was often expressed using a switch-blade knife, machete, or zip-gun.

During the 1960s, street gangs seemed to be dying out in some urban areas. The prevalence of drugs is cited as one reason for this ("You can't nod and gang-bang at the same time). Another reason cited: the Civil Rights movement and the Vietnam War diverted or siphoned off the energy of many gang members. Some gangs—like the Chicago Vice Lords and Blackstone Rangers in Chicago— actually got involved for a time in constructive social and political activities.

In other urban areas, though, *super-gangs* began to emerge. In Los Angeles and Chicago, for example, certain gangs became larger and more powerful, eradicating or assimilating neighboring gangs. Saturday-night specials and automatic weapons soon replaced the less-lethal weapons of the 1950s.

As Bartollas notes, the 1970s and 1980s were a period of gang expansion, marked by more violence, more crime, and more emphasis on making money. The author describes in detail Walter B. Miller's surveys of gang growth and violent activity throughout the 1970s and 1980s.

The current gang scene

Bartollas then follows with an investigation of the current gang scene in big cities, enumerating some of the indications which denote gang involvement. This reinforces his discussion of *representing*. He then describes recent attempts by Taylor and Huff to categorize gangs into types and Jankowski's effort to dissect gang organizational structure.

Next is information about *gang migration* and drug trafficking, including a case study of how Jamaican posses can take over a town. The issue of *emerging gangs* in smaller cities and in communities is related to gang migration. Some of the spread of gangs beyond big cities is a none-too-surprising result of gangmembers' families moving from big cities to other areas.

Bartollas feels, though, that much of the development and growth of emerging gangs is due to gangmembers and others trying to cash in on the economic opportunities presented by the appearance of "crack" cocaine in America in the 1980s. Bartollas concludes this section with a description of seven possible stages that can occur when drug-trafficking emerging gangs appear in a community.

The author continues with a discussion of the four basic types of racial and ethnic gangs in the U.S.: Hispanic American, African American, Asian American and Euro-American. It is important to realize that Euro-American white gangs have begun to emerge as quite problematical in terms of violence. While there is some debate about the violence-potential of stoner gangs, there is no doubt about the potential of other white gangs. Neo-Nazi gangs, skinhead gangs and others like them have been—and will continue to be—responsible for a goodly amount of violence in the U.S., especially hate crime violence.

Subsequently, the author examines recent research on female gangs. His overview suggests that recent decades have found female gang members engaging in more and more violent behavior besides the behavior they have traditionally engaged in: sex, spying, weapons carrying, and various nonviolent crimes. This behavior should not be surprising given that gang females are often part of the urban underclass and share the same sense of hopelessness and powerlessness that young males in their neighborhoods feel.

Bartollas then briefly summarizes theoretical explanations of gang behavior. *Classic* theories delve into many broad factors, and many theories emphasize the importance of group-ness, peer pressure, and group dynamics (e.g., leadership). *Contemporary* theories include conceptualizations involving the underclass (Wilson), the loss of manufacturing jobs (Hagdorn), and the competitive struggle in poor communities (Jankowski).

Gang intervention and gang police

Chapter 9 concludes with a look at gang prevention and control, which is very important, given the great potential for further gang growth in America. Bartollas notes that some communities have denied they have a gang problem and that some have even tried to hide the fact that they do. The author quotes Spergel's findings and conclusions about the popularity and efficacy of five different strategies of gang intervention. And after looking at programs in Chicago and Paramount, California, Bartollas concludes that only an integrated, multidimensional, community-based effort is likely to have any long-term effect in preventing and controlling gangs in the U.S.

The author neglects, however, in his gang intervention discussion to deal with the important intervention role gang police play. Hence, a few words about gang police are in order.

There are several kinds of gang police as Needle and Stapleton have indicated. Depending on the organizational arrangements a police department makes, the specialized responses of gang police can be classified into three types:

— *The youth service program*: In this arrangement, traditional police-unit personnel, most commonly those in the youth bureau or section, are assigned gang control responsibility. These officers are not detailed exclusively or principally to gang control work.

— *The gang detail*: In this arrangement, one or more officers of a traditional police unit, most commonly the youth or detective unit, are assigned responsibility for the control of gang problems These officers are appointed exclusively to gang control work.

— *The gang unit*: This is the most specialized of the three arrangements. One or more officers in a unit established solely to cope with gang problems are assigned gang control responsibility. Personnel are detailed exclusively to gang control work.[14]

These specialized police programs which target gangs are common in police departments in cities with established gang problems. The tasks gang control police perform may involve:

— solving gang related crimes, using shoe leather and, say, the G.R.E.A.T. computer system.

— patrolling areas in which gangs are active

— intervening in gang violence

— collecting evidence related to gang crimes

— apprehending suspects

— testifying in court

— gathering intelligence on weapons and confiscating them.

— keeping track of the nature and symbolic meaning of gang clothing, graffiti, slogans, prayers, artwork, etc.

— role modeling nonviolent techniques for resolving conflicts

— obtaining information about gang members: their vehicles, residential addresses, aliases, etc. . .

Depending on the type of specialized program a police department has, officers may perform all or just a few of the above-noted tasks.

CHAPTER 8—ENDNOTES

[1] M.E. Wolfgang and F. Ferracuti, *The Subculture of Violence* (London: Social Science Paperbacks, 1967), 279-282.

[2] M.B. Clinard, *Sociology of Deviant Behavior* (New York: Holt, Rinehart & Winston, 1963), 195.

[3] F.M. Thrasher, *The Gang* (Chicago: University of Chicago, 1927), 57.

[4] M.W. Klein, *Street Gangs and Street Workers* (Englewood Cliffs, NJ: Prentice-Hall, 1971), 9.

[5] L. Yablonsky, "The Delinquent Gang as a Near-Group," in S. Dinitz, R.R. Dynes, and A.C. Clarke, eds., *Deviance* (New York: Oxford, 1969), 184.

[6] Yablonsky, 180.

[7] Paraphrase of New York City Youth Board, *Reaching the Fighting Gang* (New York: New York City Youth Board, 1960), 61.

[8] Thrasher, *The Gang*, 173.

[9] E. Hollingshead, *Gang Conflict: Facts and Figures* (Philadelphia: Philadelphia Youth Conservation Service, 1970), 1.

[10] B. Cohen, *Internecine Conflict* (unpublished Ph.D. dissertation, University of Pennsylvania, 1968), 18.

[11] L. Yablonsky, "The Violent Gang," in S. Endleman, ed., *Violence in the Streets* (Chicago: Quadrangle, 1968), 447.

[12] R.A. Cloward and L.E. Ohlin, *Delinquency and Opportunity* (New York: Free Press, 1960), 24.

[13] B. Seaman, *Time* (July 23, 1973), 31.

[14] Jerome Needle and Vaughan Stapleton, Police Handling of Youth Gangs (Washington, D.C.: U.S. Department of Justice, 1983), 15; quoted in Robert Regoli and John Hewitt, *Delinquency in Society* (San Francisco: McGraw-Hill, 1997), 359-361.

GANG DELINQUENCY—BARTOLLAS

> I grew up on the streets of Chicago. When I was growing up, the Lords had a big impact on me. I never saw it as a gang, but a cohesive and unified principle on which a person could organize his life. Even as a kid of nine, I was intrigued by the Lords when I first saw them outside of the Central Park Theatre. It was the first time I had ever witnessed so many black people moving so harmoniously together. They were motored by the same sense of purpose, and they all wore similar dress and insignia. There were over a hundred guys, all in black, with capes and umbrellas. To my young eyes, it was the most beautiful expression I had ever seen. They seemed so fearless, so proud, so much in control of their lives. Though I didn't know one of them at the time, I fell in love with all of them. In retrospect, I made up my mind the very first time I saw the Vice Lords to be a Vice Lord.[1]

This young man, like many others in the Lawndale community, became a member of the Vice Lords. All his friends were members; even his mother encouraged his membership. He was put in charge of the Peewees, a junior division of the Conservative Vice Lords, after his return from the Sheraton Youth Center (Illinois) in the mid-1960s. When the Peewees evolved into another youth gang, he was not selected as an officer, nor was his suggestion for a group name accepted. He, along with two friends, then decided to form a new youth gang, which they called the Unknown Conservative Vice Lords. Although the Unknown Conservative Vice Lords received considerable opposition from established Vice Lord groups, this new gang eventually was accepted as a major division of the Vice Lord nation.

That was yesterday. Today, he remains the leader of the Almighty Unknown Vice Lords, the second largest of the eleven divisions of the Vice Lord nation. Whether he is in prison, in jail, or in the community, this chief of the Almighty Unknown Vice Lords teaches his followers that it is "their obligation to extend the nation on the streets":

> We used to have three classes a week at which I taught the brothers leadership and the reconstruction of the Vice Lords here and throughout the state and eventually throughout the nation. I am the pioneer, and these guys are to be the engineers. The new concept will be called "the new movement."[2]

In the late 1980s and early 1990s, using Uzis, Soviet AK-47s, AR-15s, and other semiautomatic weapons, the Vice Lords and other street gangs evolved into small criminal empires fighting for control of thriving narcotics, auto theft, prostitution, gun-running and extortion operations. Drugs have made up the main criminal operation, particularly *crack*, or rock cocaine. The crack trade, more than anything else, transformed these street gangs into ghetto-based drug-trafficking organizations. Juveniles remained with the gangs, but the gangs are now led and controlled by adults. Estimates are that 75 to 100 gangs are involved in cocaine distribution, and some gangs have sales totaling up to $1 million a week. The most powerful drug gangs are the Bloods and Crips in Los Angeles; the Gangster Disciples, Vice Lords, Cobras, El Rukns, and Latin Kings in Chicago; the 34th Street Players and Untouchables in Miami; and the Jamaicans' Montego Bay, Reema, Riverton City, Shower, Spangler, Spanish City, Tivoli Gardens, and Waterhouse gangs.[3]

ORIGINS AND DEVELOPMENT OF GANGS

Gangs have existed in this nation since the Revolutionary War. In the War of 1812, for example, Jean Laffite led his band of pioneers and smugglers against the British in support of Andrew Jackson. The Younger and James gangs, two of the infamous gangs of the Wild West, have long been folk heroes. Youth gangs, as we know them, originated in the early decades of the twentieth century, primarily because of the shift from agrarian to industrial society. Youth gangs have been viewed somewhat differently in nearly every decade of this century: (1) the 1920s through the 1940s, (2) the 1950s, (3) the 1960s, (4) the 1970s and early 1980s, and (5) the late 1980s and 1990s.

Gangs and play activity: the 1920s through 1940s

Frederick Thrasher's *The Gang: A Study of 1,313 Gangs in Chicago* (1927) was a pioneering and as yet unsurpassed work on gangs. Thrasher viewed gangs as a normal part of growing up in ethnic neighborhoods. Adolescents who went to school together and played together in the neighborhood naturally developed a strong sense of identity that led to their forming close-knit groups. Thrasher saw these gangs, evolving from neighborhood play groups, as being bonded together without any particular purposes or goals. They were largely transitory social groupings, typically with fewer than thirty members. They were generally organized in three concentric circles: a core composed of a leader and lieutenants, the rank-and-file membership, and a few occasional members. Finally, although each gang was different, the protection of turf was universally expected gang behavior.

Thrasher was one of the first to attempt to define the juvenile gang:

> A gang is an interstitial group originally formed spontaneously and then integrated through conflict. It is characterized by the following types of behavior: meeting face to face, milling, movement through space as a unit, conflict, and planning. The result of this collective behavior is the development of tradition, unreflective internal structure, esprit de corps, solidarity, morale, group awareness, and attachment to local territory.[4]

The *West Side Story* era: the 1950s

From the late 1940s through the 1950s, teenage gangs in nearly every urban area struck terror in the hearts of citizens. These gangs spent a lot of time fighting, or "bopping," with each other. The classic movie *West Side Story* presented a somewhat accurate picture of two 1950s urban youth gangs battling over turf. The Sharks, recent immigrants from Puerto Rico, defended their neighborhood while the Jets defended theirs; territorial lines were confined to neighborhood ethnic boundaries.

The 1950s gangs did not have the lethal weapons that today's gangs have, but they were very much capable of violent behavior. I was hired to work with a white gang in Newark, New Jersey, in 1960-1961. The job became available because my predecessor, who had been on the job for two weeks, had a knife held to his chest, cutting his shirt and drawing a little blood. He was warned that bad things would happen if he did not quit. He chose to resign.

Millions of dollars in federal, state, and local money were spent on projects and programs that were designed to prevent and control the behavior of these fighting gangs. The detached workers program, one of the most widely funded efforts, sent professional workers into the community to work with gang youths. It proved to have no positive effect on reducing their rates of delinquent behavior.

Development of the modern gang: the 1960s

In the midst of a rapidly changing social and political climate in the 1960s, drugs influenced gang activity for the first time, "super-gangs" emerged in several cities, and gangs became involved in social betterment programs and political activism.

Drugs led to reduced gang activity in some urban areas. When gangs began to reduce their activities or even to disappear from some urban areas in the mid- and late 1960s, some observers thought that the problem was coming to an end. New York City is one of the urban areas in which gang activity decreased significantly in the 1960s. The major reason offered for this apparent reduction of activity was the use of hard-core drugs. Lesser reasons included the civil rights movement, urban riots, growth of militant organizations, the war in Vietnam, and an exodus from the ghettos.

A leader of a large Bronx gang in New York City reflected on the lack of gangs in the 1960s: "You can't keep a brother interested in clicking [gang activities] if he's high or nodding."[5] A college student who was a heroin addict for several years in Spanish Harlem in New York City during the 1960s also blamed drugs for the lack of gang activity:

> My brother was a big gang member. But we did not go for that kind of thing. Man, we were on drugs. That was cool. We were too busy trying to score to fool around with gang activity. It was everybody for himself.[6]

The 1960s was also the decade in which the major "super-gangs" developed. Some neighborhood gangs became larger and more powerful than other gangs in surrounding neighborhoods, and they forced these groups to become part of thier gang organization. Eventually, a few gangs would control an entire city. In the 1960s the Crips, an African American super-gang, began as a small clique in a section of south Los Angeles.[7] In Chicago the Vice Lords, Blackstone Rangers, and Gangster Disciples, all major super-gangs today, also had their beginnings during that decade.

During the late 1960s the three Chicago super-gangs became involved in social and political activism. The Vice Lords moved further than any of the other Chicago street gangs toward programs of community betterment. Their social action involvement began in the summer of 1967 when the Vice Lord leaders attended meetings at Western Electric and Sears and Roebuck. Operation Bootstrap, which resulted from these meetings, formed committees for education, recreation, and law, order, and justice. A grant from the Rockefeller Foundation in February 1967 enabled the Vice Lords to found a host of economic and social ventures. The Vice Lords also worked with Jesse Jackson on Operation Breadbasket and, in the summer of 1969, joined with the Coalition for United Community Action to protest the lack of African American employees on construction sites in African American neighborhoods.

In 1968, all three street gangs worked against the reelection of Mayor Richard Daley's Democratic machine, and this political activism brought increased strain to their relationship with the Democratic Party organization. The interrelationships between the legal and political contexts became apparent on the streets of Chicago as street gangs experienced what they perceived as harassment from the police. As soon as he began his new term, Daley announced a crackdown on gang violence, and State's Attorney Edward Hanrahan followed by appraising the gang situation as the most serious crime problem in Chicago. The courts complied with this crack-down on gangs by increasing dramatically the number of gang members sent to prison in Illinois.

Expansion, violence, and criminal operations: the 1970s and 1980s

In the 1970s and 1980s, as their leadership was assumed by adults, street gangs became responsible for an even bigger portion of muggings, robberies, extortions, and drug trafficking operations. One city after another reported serious problems with gangs in the early 1970s. It became apparent that the gangs of the 1970s and early 1980s were both more violent than the gangs of the 1950s and more intent on making money from crime. Furthermore, they were systematic in their efforts to extort local merchants, engage in robberies, shake down students for money, intimidate local residents, and sell stolen goods. The security manager of a large grocery store in Brooklyn at the time remarked:

> These gangs know exactly what they're doing. They send guys in here to watch the cash registers. They note who's getting a lot of change. Out in the parking lot, other kids try to rip them off.
>
> They'll send two guys in here. One guy deliberately acts very suspicious, to draw our attention; meanwhile, his confederate is boosting [stealing] stuff. We lose about $800 a week in meat they steal from us.
>
> You know what happens with it? They have a regular "meat route" nearby, a list of people they sell the meat to. They'll even take orders before going out to grab the stuff. [8]

Some gangs became so sophisticated that the police regarded their activities as organized crime. Those gangs kept attorneys on retainer. Some even printed up business cards to further their careers in extortion, and they sold the cards to businesses for "protection" and to warn away rivals.

Although the gang has been the major concept used to examine collective youth crime in urban areas for the past fifty years, little or no consensus exists as to what a gang actually is.

Walter B. Miller, as part of his nationwide examination of urban gangs, asked his respondents for a definition of a gang. In an analysis of 1,400 definitional elements provided by respondents, six major elements were found to be cited most frequently: being organized, having identifiable leadership, identifying with a territory, associating continuously, having a specific purpose, and engaging in illegal activity. Miller combined these elements to create the following definition:

> A youth gang is a self-formed association of peers, bound together by mutual interests, with identifiable leadership, well-developed lines of authority, and other organizational features, who act in concert to achieve a specific purpose or purposes which generally include the conduct of illegal activity and control over a particular territory, facility, or type of enterprise.[9]

Through interviews, questionnaires, and visits to major cities, Miller came to the conclusion that gang members were committing as many as one-third of all violent juvenile crimes, terrorizing whole communities and keeping many urban schools in a state of siege. In Miller's study, justice system professionals reported problems with gangs in ten of the fifteen largest metropolitan areas. Respondents in six cities (New York, Philadelphia, Los Angeles, Chicago, Detroit, and San Francisco) considered gang problems to be especially serious. Miller estimated that during the 1970s the number of gangs in these six cities ranged from 760 to 2,700 and included from 28,500 to 81,500 gang members.[10]

In a 1982 study, Miller expanded the original six-city survey to twenty-six localities in the United States, including twenty-four of the largest cities and two counties. According to Miller's estimate, 2,300-youth gangs, with 100,000 members, were found in 300 cities. In addition to Boston, Chicago, Detroit, Los Angeles, New York, Philadelphia, and San Francisco, the list of cities reporting notable gang activity included Atlanta, Buffalo, Denver, Portland, Salt Lake City, and many others. As in his earlier study, Miller concluded that law-violating youth groups accounted for a larger volume of less serious crimes, while gangs committed a smaller volume of more serious crimes. Furthermore, this study found that California's gang problems in both urban areas and smaller cities were particularly serious. In a later interview, Miller added:

> Gang problems in California were found in an unexpectedly high number of smaller cities and towns. Eighty percent of cities with gang problems were smaller than 100,000 and 20 percent were smaller than 20,000. Since gangs have been found in the traditionally large cities, their presence in so many smaller communities represents a new development.[11]

Miller found that in the mid-1970s the rate of murder by firearms or other weapons was higher than ever before; the five cities that had the most serious gang problems averaged at least 175 gang-related killings a year between 1972 and 1974. Forays by small bands, armed and often motorized, seemed to have replaced the classic "rumble."

The mid-1980s were a turning point for ghetto-based street gangs, for crack cocaine had hit the streets. With few exceptions across the nation, these urban street gangs competed with each other for the drug trade. Several Los Angeles gangs established direct connections to major Colombian smugglers, which ensured a continuous supply of top-quality cocaine. In some Chicago neighborhoods, heavily armed teams sold drugs openly on street corners, using gang "peewees" as police lookouts.

THE CONTEMPORARY SCENE: GANGS OF THE 1990S

An understanding of the 1990s gang world requires an examination of four interrelated topics: urban street gangs, emerging gangs in small communities across the nation, racial and ethnic backgrounds of gangs, and female delinquent gangs.

Urban street gangs

In urban settings, street gangs have become quasi-institutionalized as they compete for status and authority with the school and other social institutions. The violence of the school, as well as that of nearby neighborhoods, has encouraged students to seek protection in gang membership. Safety is ensured by wearing the proper color and style of clothes and flashing the correct gang sign. The exhibit on page 107 lists some of these items for the Chicago area in the early 1990s. The dysfunctional nature of many families also raises the appeal of the gang. In contrast to the chaos of their homes, the gang appears to offer security, self-esteem, and status. As one gang member said, "The gang is like a family for me. I would do anything for it."[12]

Urban gangs are sometimes able to take control of schools. This control permits them to collect fees from other students for the privilege of attending school, traversing the corridors, and avoiding gang beatings. Fear and intimidation keep both students and faculty from reporting gang activities to authorities. Many urban schools have had to adopt extreme security measures to protect themselves from gang violence and drug trafficking.

The profile of a youth gang member often includes some or all of the following indicators:

— Poor progress or achievement in school
— Truancy from school
— Lack of hobbies or something to do with leisure time
— Frequent negative contacts with the police
— Knows gang signs and insignias
— Problems at home
— Tattoos
— Residence in a neighborhood where gangs exist
— Friends are gang members or "dress down" in gang attire
— Dresses in traditional gang clothes (e.g., baggy pants, khakis, oversized T-shirts, bandannas, dark sunglasses)
— Gathers on street corners in groups where gangs are active
— Involvement in some type of illegal activity or violence[13]

EXHIBIT 1

Dress and Gang Members

Identifiers—things to remember

Please Remember: If a person has one of these items, it doesn't always mean that he/she is a gang member. The best and safest thing to do is to check for some more things, such as: tattoos, jewelry, etc.

1. **Earrings**. *Right Ear:* Disciples, Simon City. Royals, and gangs affiliated with the Disciples. *Left Ear:* Vice Lords, Latin Kings, El Rukns, and gangs that are affiliated with these gangs.

2. **Hats (generally).** *Tilted to the Right:* Disciples, Simon City Royals, etc. *Tilted to the Left:* Vice Lords, Latin Kings, etc.

3. **Hats (Civil War type).** *Blue:* Disciples, Simon City Royals, etc. *Gray:* Vice Lords, etc. (NOTE: Vice Lords have been known to cut off the bottom parts of the crossed rifles making a "V" out of the top parts.)

4. **Glove (one).** *Right Hand:* Disciples, Simon City Royals, etc. *Left Hand:* Vice Lords, Latin Kings, etc.

5. *The same "right" and "left" rule applies to other things such as; belt buckles, bandanas hanging from a pocket or tied to a leg etc.*

6. **Stars.** *Six (6) Pointed:* Disciples and affiliates. *Five (5) Pointed:* Vice Lords and El Rukns.

7. **Crowns.** *Pointed Tips:* Latin Kings. *Rounded Tips:* Imperial Gangsters.

8. **Rabbit heads.** *Straight Ears:* Vice Lords and Latin Kings. *Bent Ear(s):* Simon City Royals.

9. **Gym shoes.** The color of the shoe vs. the color of the laces or two (2) sets of laces in the shoes to represent the gang colors. Laces should be tied up the sides and not the conventional way.

10. **Graffiti.** If any graffiti is written upside-down, it shows a disrespect to that gang and was written by an opposing gang.

11. **Haircuts.** Some Vice Lords on the city's West Side have shaved the left side of their head into the shape of an arrow.

12. **Friendship beads.** Gangs have "taken over" this fad by having their gang's colors on the beads. These are worn on clothing, shoes, hair, even as an earring.

13. **Pockets.** The inside of the pocket has been colored the colors of the gang. This is used as a means of representing.

14. **Claddagh ring.** An Irish ring which means love, loyalty, and friendship. The Latin Kings have started wearing this ring because it has a crown on it.

15. **Roller skate laces.** *Tied up and down on the Right Side:* Disciples. *Tied up and down on the Left Side:* Vice Lords. *Tied up halfway on the opposite side denotes put down to rival gang.*

16. **Pant leg cuffs.** *Rolled up on the Right Side:* Disciples. *Rolled up on the Left Side:* Vice Lords.

Source: Midwest Gang Investigators' Association, *Warning Signs for Parents* (n.d.)

Ben Shapiro of the U.S. Office of Juvenile Justice and Delinquency Prevention estimates that approximately 40 percent of urban gangs are juveniles; the remainder are adult males. G. David Curry and colleagues' national survey of law enforcement agencies found that juveniles made up only 26 percent of the gang membership in established gang cities such as Chicago. Juveniles become involved in gangs as young as eight years of age, running errands and carry weapons or messages. They are recruited as lookouts and street vendors and join an age-appropriate peewee or junior division of the gang. Moreover, gangs use younger and smaller members to deal cocaine out of cramped "rock houses" that are steel-reinforced fortresses. Gangs have long known that the assistance of young people is invaluable because their age protects them against the harsher realities of the adult criminal justice system.

Types of Urban Gangs.   Richard A. Cloward and Lloyd E. Ohlin's study identified criminal, conflict, and retreatist gangs and Lewis Yablonsky's research led him to conclude that there were delinquent, violent, and social gangs. Carl S. Taylor, C. Ronald Huff, and Jeffrey Fagan found other types of gangs in the communities they studied.

Detroit urban gangs, according to Carl S. Taylor, can be classified as scavenger, territorial, and corporate. Scavenger gangs have little sense of a common bond beyond their own impulsive behavior. Without goals, purpose, and consistent leadership these urban survivors prey on people who cannot defend themselves. Their crime can be classified as petty, senseless, and spontaneous.

A territorial gang designates as a territory something that belongs exclusively to the gang. One fundamental objective of a territorial gang is to defend its territory from outsiders. In doing so, these gangs become rulers of the streets. Today, a territorial gang defends its territory to protect its narcotic business.

The organized/corporate gang has a strong leader or manager. The main focus of the organization is participation in illegal money-making ventures. Membership, as well as promotion, depends on a person's worth to the organization. Different divisions handle sales, distribution, marketing, and enforcement. Each member has a job to do, and part of that job is to work as a team member. Profit is the motivation to commit criminal acts. Though gang members have traditionally come from the lower class, some middle-class youths are attracted to these gangs. Taylor concluded that "for the very first time in modern U.S. history, African Americans have moved into the mainstream of major crime. Corporate gangs in Detroit are part of organized crime in America."[14]

C. Ronald Huff's examination of gangs in Cleveland and Columbus identified three basic groups:

— Informal hedonistic gangs, whose basic concern was to get high (usually on alcohol and/or marijuana and other drugs) and to have a good time. These gangs were more involved in minor property crime than in violent personal crime.

— Instrumental gangs, whose focal concerns were more economic and who committed a high volume of property crimes for economic reasons. Most of these gang members used drugs, and some used crack cocaine. Some individual members of these gangs also sold drugs, but doing so was not an organized gang activity.

— Predatory gangs committed robberies, street muggings, and other crimes of opportunity. Members of these gangs were more likely to use crack cocaine and to sell drugs to finance the purchase of more sophisticated weapons.[15]

Jeffrey Fagan's analysis of the crime-drug relationships in three cities identified four types of gangs. Type 1 was involved in a few delinquent activities and only alcohol and marijuana use. This type of gang, according to Fagan, had low involvement in drug sales and appeared to be a social gang. Type 2 gangs were heavily involved in several types of drug sales, primarily to support their own drug use, and in one type of delinquency: vandalism. Although this type manifested several of the subcultural and organizational features of a gang, it still seemed to be more of a party gang. Type 3 gangs, representing the most frequent gang participation, included serious delinquents who had extensive involvement with both serious and nonserious offenses. Interestingly, this type of gang had less involvement in both drug sales and the use of serious substances (cocaine, heroin, PCP, and amphetamines). Type 4 gangs had extensive involvements in both serious drug use and serious and nonserious offenses and had higher rates of drug sales. This cohesive and organized type, predicted Fagan, "is probably at the highest risk for becoming a more formal criminal organization."[16]

Organizational features of the urban gang. Martín Sánchez Jankowski, who spent over ten years studying thirty-seven gangs in Los Angeles, New York, and Boston, contended "that one of the reasons that society does not understand gangs or the gang phenomenon very well is that there have not been enough systematic studies undertaken as to how the gang works as an organization."[17] He suggested that the most important organizational features of urban gangs are structure, leadership, recruitment, initiation rites, role expectations and sanctions, and migration patterns. Jankowski observed three types of gang organizational structure:

1. The *vertical/hierarchical type* divides leadership hierarchically into several different levels. Authority and power are related to one's position in the line of command.

2. The *horizontal/commission type* is made up of several officeholders who share about equal authority over the members. The leaders share the duties as well as the power and authority.

3. The *influential* model assigns no written duties or titles to the leadership positions. This type of system usually has two to four members who are considered leaders of the group. The authority of the influentials is based on a type of charismatic authority.[18]

The most conspicious example of the vertical/hierarchical type of leadership is found in the Chicago-based gangs. The largest of these gangs—the Gangster Disciples, the Vice Lords, the Black Disciples, and the El Rukns—have leaders who have become legends. In the next Exhibit, Larry Hoover, the chief of the Gangster Disciples, and Willie Johnson, the chief of the Vice Lord Nation, answer some pressing questions about urban gangs.

The Bloods and the Crips, the two most notorious Los Angeles gangs, are representative of the horizontal/commission type. They are not gangs at all but confederations among hundreds of subgroups or sets. Sets are formed along neighborhood lines, and most sets have twenty to thirty members.

Gangs regularly go on recruiting parties, and the recruitment of younger members is easy because the life of a gang member looks very glamorous. With money from the sale of drugs, gang members are able to drive BMWs and Mercedes, flash a big roll of bills, and wear expensive jewelry. Recruitment begins early in the grade-school years; adolescent males are most vulnerable in the eighth grade. But even if a youth has enough support systems at home to resist joining a gang, it is very difficult to live in a neighborhood that is controlled by a street gang and not join. A gang leader explained: "You had two choices in the neighborhood I grew up in—you could either be a gang member or a mama's boy. A mama's boy would come straight home from school, go up to his room and study, and that was it."[19]

The methods of initiation into some gangs include some or all of the following: (1) must be "jumped in" or fight the other members, (2) must participate in illegal acts, (3) must assist in trafficking drugs and, (4) must participate in "walk-up" or "drive-by" shootings. It is the drive-by shooting that has received so much public attention.[20] One article notes:

> The drive-by killing is the sometime sport and occasional initiation rite of city gangs. From the comfort of a passing car, the itinerant killer simply shoots down a member of a rival gang or an innocent bystander. Especially common among L.A.'s Bloods and Crips, the drive-by killing is the parable around which every telling of the gang story revolves. Beyond that lies a haze of images: million-dollar drug deals, ominous graffiti, and colorfully dressed marauders armed with Uzis. The sociologists tell us that gang culture is the flower on the vine of single-parent life in the ghetto, the logical result of society's indifference. It would be hard to write a morality play more likely to strike terror into the hearts of the middle class.[21]

A street gang's clothing, colors, and hand signs are held sacred by gang members. In the world of gangs, warfare can be triggered by the way someone wears his hat, folds his arms, or moves his hands. Gang identity includes following codes for dress and behavior to make certain that the gang's name and symbol are scrawled in as many places as possible. Each gang has its own secret handshakes and hand signs, known as **representing**. Rival groups sometimes display the signs upside down as a gesture of contempt and challenge.[22]

EXHIBIT 2

Interview with Larry Hoover and Willie Johnson

Question: I have heard you talk about stopping the killing on the street. Why is this so important and how can this be done?

Hoover: We are killing each other. The mother of the murdered victim loses a child, the mother of the killer loses a child to the penal institution. When the nations come together and form a peace truce that will not be broken, then there will be a decrease in killing.

Question: Most people think of the G.D.s as "Gangster Disciples," but you have renamed the G.D.s as "Growth and Development." What is the difference between the Gangster Disciples and Growth and Development movements?

Hoover: The Growth and Development movement is a movement within the rank and file of the Gangster Disciples to advance them into becoming law-abiding citizens.

Question: I know education is important to you. What message do you give about education to those who are part of the Growth and Development movement?

Hoover: It is required for members involved in the Growth and Development movement to obtain a GED certificate or high school diploma. Members are encouraged to attend college and acquire skills to become gainfully employed.

Question: Your "Blueprint" contains the transforming vision you have. What do you consider to be its most important points?

Hoover: For a black man to have anything to say about what goes on in the world, he's got to be involved with what controls the blacks, and that's the political apparatus. To get out of the state the black man is in today, you are going to have to work within the system. You got to become part of the system. You got to make some noise. You don't make some noise, then nothing's going change. It's going to be business as usual.

Love is the most important principle for our survival. We find it easier to continue living with drugs, pimping, prostitution, gangbanging, extortion, et cetera, et cetera. But if we continue to allow our neighborhood conditions to keep our ability to love blocked by negative thoughts and attitudes, then we are standing in the way of our survival.

Knowledge is also important. Our illiteracy has been used to turn the burning hostility of poor people against one another. For a man to be illiterate and not struggle to remove his illiteracy means that he has accepted being a slave. There is no mercy for the illiterate, only exploitation, slavery, and death.

Wisdom is another of our important principles. We need a new attitude toward the world. It is our tunnel vision that has resulted in our gangbanging, shooting, robbing, and killing each other because he wore a certain color or he tilted his hat a certain way or, worse yet, he believed in a different concept or ideology than ours.

Question: You are the recognized leader of the Vice Lord Nation. What does that mean? How many divisions does your nation have?

Johnson: I am not the person the media portrays. I am a black man concerned about the plight of our youth, government, penal institutions. I want to point the nation in a positive direction in order for the membership to be looked upon as people doing positive things in their community. My nation has eleven divisions.

Question: I know you are actively involved in the Unity in Peace Movement. What is this movement and what do you and others hope to achieve?

Johnson: This movement is to stop the violence in our streets and bring harmony into our communities.

Prayers are also rituals of many gangs. They are often said before members go into battle against rivals or are chanted before wounded members die. One Chicago gang's prayer is "If I should die in battle, lay two shotguns across my chest and tell all the Kings that I did my best." The Orchestra Albany (O.A.) gang's prayer is "If I die, bury me deep with O.A.'s at my feet, with two shotguns at my side, and tell the boys I died with pride."

Loyalty is a chief value among gangs, whether prompted by blind obedience or by fear of the beatings or death that disloyalty could bring. One ex-gang member commented about the loyalty of gang members, "The gang becomes their god, and they will do anything to defend it, even die for it."

James Diego Vigil, in his study of Hispanic gangs, reported that most of the time, gang members make casual conversation and joke, drink beer or wine, play pickup games (baseball, basketball, football, and handball), and meet at the local barrio hangout. Gang youths speak a type of mixed Spanish-English slang; present a conservative appearance, with smartly combed back hair; and affect a body language that is controlled, deliberate, and methodical.

Fear is omnipresent in street life, Vigil added, particularly if one is unprotected, and must be managed. The desired state is **locura**, which denotes a type of craziness or wildness. A person demonstrates this state of mind by displaying fearlessness, daring, and other unpredictable forms of destructive behavior, such as getting loco on drugs and alcohol. Toughness also provides a sense of adventure and the emotional support that gang camaraderie provides. As one gang member expressed it:

> I was born into my barrio. It was either get your ass kicked every day or join a gang and get your ass kicked occasionally by rival gangs. Besides, it was fun and I belonged.[23]

Gang migration is another important organizational feature of urban gangs. Gang migration can take place in at least three ways: (1) the establishment of satellite gangs in another location, (2) the relocation of gang members with their families, and (3) the expansion of drug markets.

Several studies in the 1980s were unable to document the establishment of satellite gangs in other locations. In the mid-1990s, chiefs of the major Chicago gangs told the author that their gangs did not have the desire or the organizational capacity to form nationwide satellite gangs. These gang chiefs even questioned how much control they had over gangs in other locations that use their gang name.

Cheryl L. Maxson, Malcolm W. Klein, and Lea C. Cunningham, in surveying law enforcement agencies in over 1,100 cities nationwide, found that 713 reported some gang migration. The most typical pattern of gang migration was the relocation of gang members with their families (39 percent). The next most typical pattern was the expansion of drug markets (20 percent).[24] As the next section shows, some urban gangs have pursued the expansion of drug markets relentlessly.

Drug trafficking and other offenses. Beginning in the mid-1980s, street gangs with origins in the large urban centers of Los Angeles, Chicago, New York, Miami, and Detroit became criminal entrepreneurs in supplying illicit drugs. In a brief period of several years, many of these street gangs developed intrastate and interstate networks for the purpose of expanding their illegal drug market sales. High levels of violence and related criminal activity have accompanied this social phenomenon. It was the domestically manufactured crack or rock cocaine that opened the floodgates for serious gang participation in the huge profits that became available through this illicit drug trafficking.

The Crips and Bloods of Los Angeles have been the most active in drug trafficking across the nation. A study by the U.S. Congress concluded that during the latter part of the 1980s the Crips and Bloods controlled 30 percent of the crack cocaine market across the nation.[25] The Drug Enforcement Administration claimed in a 1988 report that Los Angeles street gangs were identified with drug sales in forty-six states.[26]

The Miami Boys of south Florida, the Jamacian Posses of New York and Florida, and the Vice Lords of Chicago are also among the street gangs that have entered the field on the largest scale. They followed on the heels of long-time marijuana and methamphetamine supply activities conducted by motorcycle gangs and they are being mimicked by white youths who call themselves stoner, heavy metal, neo-Nazi, and satanic cult groups. Although crack and rock cocaine are the dominant drugs that are trafficked, methamphetamine, PCP, LSD, marijuana, and brown heroin are also represented in this illicit drug market. The nationwide reach and the rapidity of the spread of this drug trafficking are astounding.

Police across the nation became alarmed by the emergence of disciplined Jamaican gangs known as *posses*. Federal sources claimed that thirty to forty posses with a total of about 5,000 members operated in the United States. Some evidence also indicated that Jamaican drug dealers had set up shop outside major urban areas. For example, Jamaicans first arrived in Martinsburg, West Virginia (population 13,000), as migrant workers, but many stayed on to peddle cocaine and crack. They transformed several blocks near the center of town into an open-air drug supermarket, where as many as 50 dealers could be found hawking dope. Martinsburg's twenty-eight-man police department was overwhelmed by the dealers, and crime soared in this small West Virginia town. In a region that was accustomed to one or two murders a year, twenty homicides, all drug-related, occurred in eighteen months as rival drug dealers fought for control.[27]

Gang participation varies by expected role behavior, rationale for affiliation, and extent of participation in antisocial activities and substance use. Gang participation may also shift over time as members move into and out of various roles. Leaders of drug-selling gangs may be significantly different from leaders of other types of gangs. Yet, despite the fluidity and diversity of gang roles and affiliation, it is commonly agreed that core members are involved in more serious delinquent acts than are situational or fringe members.

The follow-up of a sample of Cohort I to the age of thirty by Wolfgang and colleagues provided insights into the influence of gangs on delinquency in Philadelphia. They found that one-sixth of the whites belonged to gangs and were responsible for one-third of the offenses committed by whites; 44 percent of the nonwhites were gang members and were responsible for 60 percent of the offenses committed by nonwhites. Gang youths, who represented 29 percent of the total offender sample, were responsible for 50 percent of the offenses.[28]

This study also found that boys who belonged to gangs persisted in delinquent behavior nearly three years longer than did those who never joined. But when racial aspects were examined, it became clear that the persistence of delinquent behavior was traceable primarily to nonwhite gang members. Moreover, Wolfgang and colleagues found that 81 percent of the boys (90 percent of nonwhites and 60 percent of whites) became delinquent after joining a gang. Another indicator of the relationship between gang membership and delinquency is that 90 percent of the whites committed no further offenses after leaving the gang; however, for nonwhites, no clear effect of leaving the gang was evident.[29]

Furthermore, gang membership increases the likelihood of police arrest and court conviction. Catherine Ryan, the Juvenile Court's chief prosecutor in Chicago, estimated that about 80 percent of the youths handled by the juvenile justice system have some affiliation with gangs. She added that 60 percent of the juveniles in court wind up there because of street gang activity.

In sum, urban gangs are more violent, are more sophisticated, involve members for longer periods, and are more involved in drug trafficking than were the gangs of the past. Gangs have thrived because of the poverty and underclass conditions in many urban neighborhoods. The hopelessness of these environments makes drug trafficking attractive and gang membership desirable even with the high possibility of being injured, killed, or imprisoned.

Emerging gangs in smaller cities and communities

In the 1990s, nearly every city, many suburban areas, and even some rural areas across the nation have experienced the reality of youths who consider themselves gang members. Thrasher's finding that no gangs that he studied were alike appears to be true for these **emerging gangs** as well.

Curry and colleagues' 1992 national survey revealed that officials in 91 percent of the seventy-nine largest U.S. cities reported the presence of gang problems. These researchers conservatively estimated that there were 4,881 gangs with 249,324 gang members. A total of

7,205 female gang members were reported across forty cities. Twenty-seven cities reported a total of eighty-three independent female gangs. Significantly, cities with emerging gangs reported that 90 percent of the gangs were made up of juveniles.

Emerging gangs have been examined in Denver, Colorado; Kansas City, Missouri; Rochester, New York; and Seattle, Washington. Finn-Aage Esbensen and David Huizinga found that about 3 percent of the Denver sample of 1,527 youths belonged to a gang during their four-year study. But by the fourth year, the percentage of youths who claimed gang membership increased to nearly 7 percent. Esbensen and Huizinga further found that male gang members were involved in levels of delinquent activity that were two or three times greater than those of nongang members. In addition to fights with other gangs, three-quarters of the gang members reported that they were involved in assaults, thefts, robberies, and drug sales.

Mark S. Fleisher's street ethnography in Kansas City, Missouri, and Seattle among teenage gang members found gang membership to be made up of "weak social ties formed among episodically homeless, socially rejected youth reared by deviant socializers." Fleisher rejected the common assumption that gangs look upon the set as family. Instead, he found "that these kids kill each other over 'respect,' fight and kill one another in combat over girls or a gram or two of cocaine, and may severely beat or even kill a gang 'brother' in a violent ritual, known in some places as the 'SOS'—'Shoot-on-Sight' or 'Stomp-on'Sight.'"[30]

Terence Thornberry and colleagues examined the relationship between gangs and delinquent behavior in Rochester, New York, from 1988 to 1991. They found some stability among gang members; 21 percent were members in all three years. This research also revealed that gang members were much more heavily involved in street offenses while they were gang members than they were before or after their time with the gang.

The rise of emerging gangs is being reported in many cities around the nation. Salem, Oregon, reported a 97 percent increase in the number of gang members and affiliates between October 1992 and April 1993. Davenport, Iowa, has 2,000 documented gang members and a gang-related shooting nearly each week. Des Moines, Iowa, has eighteen gangs, with a total number of 1,239 members. Peoria, Illinois, decided that its gang problem was so serious that it required the intervention of Chicago-based gang consultants to negotiate a truce between two rival gangs. A statement from Rochester, Minnesota, is one to which many communities across the nation can relate:

> Gangs are a new element in the greater Rochester (Minnesota) area. In 1990, there were rumors. In 1991, there was substantiated evidence of gangs. In 1992, clear indicators emerged that there were youth gangs with a stronghold in the community. In 1993, there have been regular reports of violence, fighting, and other gang related activities in the community.[31]

This nationwide expansion began in the late 1980s, and it appeared to be fueled in four different ways. First, in some communities it took place when ghetto-based drug-trafficking gangs sent ranking gang members to the community to persuade local youths to sell crack cocaine. Second, gang-related individuals operating on their own established drug-trafficking networks among community youths. Third, urban gang members whose families had moved to these communities were instrumental in developing local chapters of urban gangs. Fourth, youths in communities with little or no intervention from outsiders developed their own versions of gangs. The latter two types were less likely to become involved in drug trafficking than were the first two types.

Behind the first wave of nationwide gang expansion was urban gang leaders' knowledge that there were a lot of new markets ripe for exploitation and that crack cocaine would command a high price in these new areas. To introduce the drug in these new markets, the representatives of most urban gangs promised the possibility of a gang satellite; that is, the emerging local gang would be connected by both name and organizational ties to the parent gang. However, urban gangs had neither the intent nor the resources to develop extentions of themselves in the emerging gang community. The promise of being a gang satellite was only a carrot to persuade local youths to sell crack cocaine for the urban gang. The development of drug-trafficking emerging gangs throughout the nation has seven possible stages, and the degree and seriousness of gang activity in a community depend on its stage of development.[32]

Stage 1: Implementation. An adult gang member, usually a high-ranking officer, comes to a city that has no gangs. On arriving, either by plane or auto, this gang member goes to a low-income, minority neighborhood, where he recruits several juveniles to sell crack and be members of the new gang. The recruited juveniles are assured of a percentage of the money they make from the sale of crack. The exact percentage seems to vary from gang to gang but is typically about 10 percent. The representative from the urban gang returns on a regular basis to supply drugs and pick up the money.

Stage 2: Expansion and conflict. The adult who came to the community tells the recruited juveniles enough about his gang that they can identify with it. They start to wear the proper clothing, to learn something about gang signs, and to experience a sense of camaraderie, yet their primary motivation is still to make money from selling drugs. One Midwestern youth claimed that he was making $40,000 a month selling crack for the Unknown Vice Lords when he was arrested and institutionalized. Conflict inevitably arises as different drug-trafficking gangs attempt to expand their markets, usually in the same neighborhoods. Fights may break out during school functions, at athletic events and shopping centers, and in parks and other common gathering places. Weapons may be used at this time, and the number of weapons increases dramatically in the community.

Stage 3: Organization and consolidation. Youths identifying with a certain gang attempt to develop a group culture during this stage. The leadership is assumed by one or more members of the core group as well as young adult males from the community. The increased visibility of the gang attracts a sizable number of "wannabes." The gang may be larger, but it is still relatively unorganized, consisting primarily of a group of males hanging around together. Recruitment is emphasized as considerable pressure is put on young minority males to join the gang. One of these males noted, "If you are black, twelve or so, they really put pressure on you to join. It's hard not to."

Stage 4: Gang intimidation and community reaction. A number of events typically take place during this stage. Some whites join the minority gangs, and other whites form gangs of their own. One youth represented the spirit of this white reaction when he said, "The blacks ain't going to push us around." Minority gangs are still more likely to wear their colors and to demonstrate gang affiliation. Drugs are also increasingly sold in the school environment, and gang control becomes a serious problem in the school. A high school teacher expressed her concern: "I've never had any trouble teaching in this school. Now, with these gang kids, I'm half afraid to come to school. It's becoming a very serious situation." Gangs are becoming more visible in shopping centers, and the older people are beginning to experience some fear of shopping when gang youths are present. Equally disturbing and much more serious in the long run, gangs are becoming popular among children in middle school, and some allegiance is being given to gangs among children as young as first and second grades.

Stage 5: Expansion of drug markets. Drugs are openly sold in junior high and senior high schools, on street corners, and in shopping centers during the fifth stage. Crack houses are present in some minority neighborhoods. Extortion of students and victimization of both teachers and students take place frequently in the public schools. The gangs are led by adults who remain in the community, the organizational structure is more highly developed, and the number of gang members shows a significant increase. Outsiders have been present all along, but during this stage they seem to be continually coming into and out of the community. In their midtwenties they roll into the community in expensive automobiles, wearing expensive clothes and jewelry, and flashing impressive rolls of money.

Stage 6: Gangs Take over. Communities that permit the gangs to develop to this stage discover that gangs are clearly in control in minority neighborhoods, in the school, at school events, and in shopping centers. The criminal operations of gangs also become more varied and now include robberies, burglaries, aggravated assaults, and rapes. Drive-by shootings begin to occur on a regular basis, and citizens' fear of gangs increases dramatically. The police, whose gang units usually number several officers, typically express an inability to control drug trafficking and violence.

Stage 7: Community deterioration. The final stage is characterized by the deterioration of social institutions and the community itself because of gang control. Citizens move out of the city, stay away from shopping centers, and find safer schools for their children. When an emerging gang community arrives at this stage of deterioration, it is fully experiencing the gang problems of urban communities.

In sum, while a community's reaction greatly affects the seriousness of the problem, non-gang and sometimes low-crime communities across the nation in the late 1980s and early 1990s began to experience the development of gangs. These emerging gangs developed from different trajectories, but the most toxic to a community was when a ghetto-based drug-trafficking gang was able to persuade minority youths to sell crack cocaine for it and these youths, in turn, developed what they thought would be a satellite to the parent gang.

Racial and ethnic gangs

Hispanic street gangs, African American street gangs, white gangs, and Asian gangs constitute the basic type of racial and ethnic gangs in the United States.

Hispanic street gangs. Hispanic, or Latino, gangs are divided into Mexican American or Chicano, Puerto Rican, Dominican, Jamaican, and Central American members, Chicano street gangs have unwritten codes of conduct and oral traditions that have evolved over generations and are referred to as *Movidas*. These street gangs usually divide themselves into groupings called *cliques*, which are generally formed by the age of the members. Some cliques may also be organized according to a specialty, such as violence. The uniform or dress readily identifies a youth or young adult as belonging to a Chicano gang. The standard dress is a white T-shirt, thin belt, khaki pants with split cuffs, a black or blue knit beanie, or a bandana tied around the forehead. Finally, one of the most distinguishing characteristics of Chicano gangs is the loyalty they receive from gang members.

African American gangs. African American gangs have received more attention in this chapter than any other racial or ethnic group because most of the ghetto-based drug-trafficking gangs that have established networks across the nation are African American. For example, the Bloods and Crips from Los Angeles, the People and Folks from Chicago, and the Detroit gangs are all African American. Furthermore, African American gangs usually identify themselves by adopting certain colors in addition to other identifiers, such as hand signals.

White gangs. A recent development on the West Coast is the solidifying of lower- and middle-class white youths into groups who refer to themselves as *stoners*. These groups frequently abuse drugs and alcohol and listen to heavy metal rock music. Some members of the group practice Satanism, including grave robbing, desecration of human remains, and sacrificing animals.[33] Stoner groups can be identified by their mode of dress: colored T-shirts with decals of their rock music heroes or bands, Levis, and tennis shoes. They may also wear metal-spiked wrist cuffs, collars, belts, and satanic jewelry. The recently emerging white gangs across the nation have used many of the symbols of the stoner gangs, especially the heavy metal rock music and the satanic rituals, but they are not as likely to call attention to themselves with their dress. They may refer to themselves as neo-Nazi Skinheads, and are involved in a variety of hate crimes and drug trafficking.

EXHIBIT 3

Gang Signs

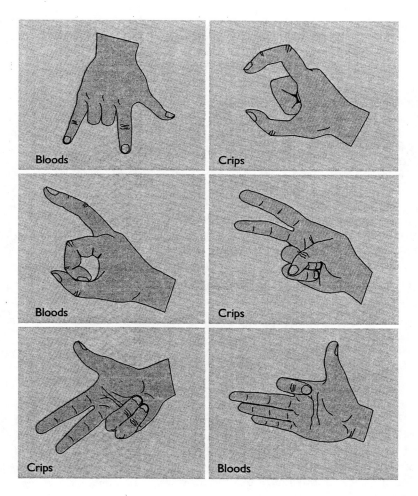

Source: Midwest Gang Investigators' Asociation, *Warning Signs for Parents* (n.d.).

Asian gangs. There is a variety of Asian gangs in California, including Chinese, Vietnamese, Filipino, Japanese, and Korean. The Chinese gangs, especially, have spread to other major cities in this nation, and some of the other gangs are also active outside of California. Asian gangs tend to be more organized and to have more of an identifiable leadership than is true of other street gangs. Ko-Lin Chin's examination of Chinese gangs found them to be involved in some of the nation's worst gang-related violence and heroin trafficking. Unlike other ethnic gangs, Chinese gangs are closely tied to the social and economic life of their rapidly developing and economically robust communities. A study of Vietnamese youth gangs in Southern California found that these youths experience multiple marginality but that they attained the American dream by robbing Vietnamese families of large amounts of cash that such families keep at home.[34]

Female delinquent gangs

More attention has recently been given to adolescent girls who join gangs. Traditional sociologists considered the female gang almost a contradiction in terms. Albert K. Cohen argued:

> Again the group or the gang, the vehicle of the delinquent subculture and one of its statistically most manageable earmarks, is a boy's gang. . . . If, however, female delinquents also have their subculture, it is a different one from that which we have described. The latter [gang] belongs to the male role."[35]

Thrasher's account of Chicago gangs also found them to be primarily male. He described the gangs that did include adolescent females as immoral rather than conflict gangs. Their chief activities included petting, illicit sex, necking, and mugging. They had names like the Lone Star Club, the Under the L gang, the Tulips, and the Night Riders. Using clandestine signals in the classroom, they arranged secret meetings in vacant lots.

In 1984, Anne Campbell estimated that in New York City, 10 percent of the membership of the 400 gangs was female. Female gang members ranged in age from 14 to 30. Some were married, and many had children.[36] A CBS News report in 1986 estimated that about 1,000 girls were involved in more than 100 female gangs in Chicago alone. These gangs, according to the report, were not sister organizations or auxiliaries to male gangs but were independent female gangs. Like their male counterparts, these female gangs staked out their own turf, adopted distinctive colors and insignia, and had physical confrontations with rival gangs.

In *Sisters in Crime*, Freda Adler discussed female gangs in Philadelphia and New York. Walter B. Miller and E. Ackley investigated two female gangs, the Molls and the Queens, in the inner-city district of an eastern seaport in the early 1970s. The gangs' illegal offenses included truancy, theft, drinking, property damage, sex offenses, and assault. Truancy took place about three times as frequently as the next most common offense, theft (largely shoplifting). Peggy C. Giordano's 1978 examination of institutionalized adolescent females in Ohio revealed that 53.7 percent of the 108 institutionalized females had been part of a group that they called a gang, and 51.9 percent said that their gang had a name. She noted that the names of these gangs (e.g., the Outlaws, the Cobras, Mojos, Loveless, Red Blood, White Knights, East Side Birds, and Power) conveyed neither a particularly feminine image, nor suggested a subordinate position to a male gang.[37]

Waln K. Brown, an ex-gang member himself, carried out a more comprehensive study of female participation in youth gangs in Philadelphia in 1970. He suggested that female gang participation was usually limited to sexually integrated gangs. Their functions within these integrated gangs in Philadelphia included serving as participants in gang wars or individual and small group combat fights and acting as spies to gain information about activities being planned by other gangs. Brown noted that most females joined Philadelphia gangs to be popular and to be "where the action is." But he did find one all-female African American gang. The Holy Whores were heavily involved in the subculture of violence, being accused of knifing and kicking pregnant females and of badly scarring and mutilating "cute" girls. "Getting a body" (knifing) was said to be an important part of their "rep."[38]

Lee Bowker and Malcolm W. Klein studied a group of African American gang females in Los Angeles in 1980 and reported that they never planned a gang activity; the planning was done by the males, who usually excluded the females. But the female gang members would participate in violent crimes and drug-related gang activities. J. C. Quicker studied Mexican American adolescent female gangs in East Los Angeles in 1983 and drew four conclusions about these gangs. First, he found that the gangs always had a connection to a male gang; indeed, they derived their names from those of their male counterparts. Second, adolescent females were not coerced into the gang but had to prove their loyalty and undergo an initiation procedure. Third, these females usually operated in a democratic manner. Finally, loyalty to the gang rivaled loyalty to the family, and most friends came from within the gang. The gang, according to Quicker offered "warmth, friends, loyalty, and socialization" as it insulated its members from the harsh environment of the barrio.

A. Harris's 1988 study of the Cholas, a Latino gang in California's San Fernando Valley, revealed that these adolescent females were becoming more independent of male gangs. In rejecting the traditional image of the Latina as wife and mother, the gang supported a more "macho" homegirl role. Gang affiliation also supported members in their estrangement from organized religion, as it substituted a form of familism that "provides a strong substitute for weak family and conventional school ties."[39]

Campbell's 1984 examination of the relationships among adolescent females in three New York female gangs also revealed that there was intense camaraderie and strong dependency among these gang members. But she still concluded that female gangs continued to exist as an adjunct to male gangs and that males dictated and controlled the females' activities. Campbell observed, "Girls are told how to dress, are allowed to fight, and are encouraged to be good mothers and faithful wives. Their principal source of suffering and joy is their men."[40]

Taylor found in Detroit in 1993 that women were involved in many disparate gang types, ranging from compatriots to corporate. They were frequently represented in drag-trafficking gangs. Fifteen-year-old Tracie responded, "Girls is in crews, gangs, money, shooting . . . they in it all! What makes you ask that question, is you from somewhere where the girls don't count." DeLores added, "Girls got guns for the same reason guys got 'em . . . It's wild out here, you need to protect yourself. . . . It doesn't matter if it's selling crack, weed, or any kinda dope, business is business. Guns protect you and your business, right."[41]

David Lauderback, Joy Hansen, and Daniel Waldorf studied the Portrero Hill Posse, an African American girl group in San Francisco in 1992. After sharing the common experiences of being abandoned by the fathers of their children and being abused and controlled by other men, this group of girls began hanging around together. They found that selling crack and organized "boosting" (shoplifting) were among the few resources available for supporting themselves and their children.

In 1993, Beth Bjerregaard and Carolyn Smith, using data from the Rochester Youth Development Study, found that involvement in gangs for both females and males was associated with increased levels of delinquency and substance abuse. For example, female gang members reported a serious delinquency rate of 66.8 percent, compared to 6.6 percent for non-gang members. Although there was some similarity in the factors associated with gang membership for males and females, lack of school success was a particularly important factor for female gang members.

In sum, most studies have found that girl gangs still serve as adjuncts to boy gangs. Yet an increasing number of important studies show that female gangs provide girls with the necessary survival skills to survive in their harsh communities while allowing them a temporary escape from the dismal future awaiting them. What these studies reveal is that girls join gangs for the same basic reasons that boys do and share with boys in their neighborhood the hopelessness and powerlessness of the urban underclass.

THEORIES OF GANG DELINQUENCY

The classical theories about the origins of juvenile gangs and gang delinquency have come from Herbert A. Bloch and Arthur Niederhoffer; Richard A. Cloward and Lloyd E. Ohlin, and Albert K. Cohen, Walter B. Miller, and Lewis Yablonsky.

Bloch and Niederhoffer's theory was based on the idea that joining a gang is part of the experience male adolescents need to grow up to adulthood. The basic function of the gang thus is to provide a substitute for the formalized puberty rites that are found in other societies. Cloward and Ohlin's theory was based on the notion that lower-class boys interact with and gain support from other alienated individuals. These youngsters pursue illegitimate means to achieve the success they cannot gain through legitimate means. Cohen's theory was that gang delinquency represents a subcultural and collective solution to the problem of acquiring status that faces lower-class boys when they find themselves evaluated according to middle-class values in the schools. Miller held that there is a definite lower-class culture and that gang behavior is an expression of that culture. Miller saw gang leadership as being based mainly on smartness and toughness. He viewed the gang as very cohesive and with high conformity to gang norms. Finally, Yablonsky suggested that violent delinquent gangs arise out of certain conditions that are found in urban slums. These conditions encourage the development of the sociopathic personality in adolescents, and such sociopathic individuals become the core leadership of these gangs.

These classical theories of gangs focused on sociological variables such as strain (Cloward and Ohlin), subcultural affiliation (Miller, Cohen), and social disorganization (Yablonsky). Cohen, Cloward and Ohlin, and Miller also stressed the importance of the peer group for gang membership. Each of the five theories of gang formation has received both support and criticism, but research is needed into current expressions of gang activity because the existing theories were based primarily on 1950s gangs.

Other theories of gangs are associated with social disorganization theory. This theory is based on the assumption that poor economic conditions cause social disorganization to the extent that there is a deficiency of social control. This lack of social control leads to gang formation and involvement because youths in low-income neighborhoods seek the social order and security that gangs offer.

More recently, underclass theory has been widely used to explain the origins of gangs. In the midst of big-city ghettos and barrios filled with poverty and deprivation, it is argued, gangs are a normal response to an abnormal social setting. John M. Hagedorn documented the loss of manufacturing jobs in Milwaukee during the 1980s that resulted in an increasingly segmented labor force in which minorities were consigned to low-wage or even part-time work, welfare, and the illegal economy. Gangs provided a means for the unemployed underclass, especially adults, to take refuge in illegal markets, such as trafficking crack cocaine, prostitution, muggings, and extortions. J. D. Vigil added that people who join gangs are pushed into these groups by their condition of poverty and their status as minorities. Marginal to the wider society, to their communities, and to their families, they are subject to difficulties in all areas. This multiple marginality makes them the most likely candidates for gang membership, for in a real sense they have little else going for them. Vigil added that this "dialectic of multiple marginality [also] applies to why females now are more active in gangs."

Jankowski contended that gang violence and the defiant attitude of young men are connected with the competitive struggle in poor communities. Being a product of their environment, they adopt a "Hobbesian view of life in which violence is an integral part of the state of nature."[42] The operations and survival rate of gangs vary greatly but, according to Jankowski's theory, can be accounted for by the interaction of four elements:

> (1) inequality, and individual responses to reduce inequality; (2) the ability of the gang (both leadership and rank and file) to manage the desires and behavior of people with defiant individualist characters; (3) the degree to which a collective of individuals has been capable of developing a sophisticated organization to carry out its economic activities; and (4) the extent to which it has been able to establish ties to institutions belonging to the larger society.[43]

Michael F. de Vries proposes that an integrated approach is needed to understand why juveniles become involved with gangs. For African American youths, strain theory is "the heart of why African Americans find gang associations worthwhile." Gangs offer deprived African American youths opportunities to obtain status and financial gain that is denied them in the larger culture. Asian immigrants, he argues, are also experiencing such strain. Although African Americans are more "likely to engage in illicit drug distribution to counteract their inherited inferior position in society, Asians are more apt to engage in home invasions, theft, and intimidation as their way of coping with a similar strain." According to de Vries, subcultural theory appears to be helpful in explaining Hispanic gangs. Largely spared from Anglo-American culture by their own traditions, "this subcultural group places a high degree of value on an individual's prowess (machismo), territorial identity, pride, and loyalty to their own group identity." Control theory, especially for middle-class whites, helps explain why these youths become involved in gang activity. Social bonds are coming under attack as the family unit is becoming weaker.[44]

GANG PREVENTION AND CONTROL

There is every indication that the gang problem is getting worse. If the analogy to Prohibition is accurate, as some analysts believe, the gangs have only begun to consolidate their hold on drug trafficking. Given their growth throughout the 1980s and early 1990s, it seems reasonable to anticipate that gangs, like the Mafia before them, will become even more skillful in evading apprehension and conviction.

Communities across the nation have had a tendency to deny that they have gangs even when gang youths are causing considerable problems at school and in the neighborhoods. Then a dramatic incident takes place, such as the killing of an innocent victim or a shoot-out in which one or more gang youths are killed, and what began as a process of denial eventually becomes one of attempting to repress, or make gangs invisible. In 1984 and 1985, for example, Columbus, Ohio, abandoned the stage of denial when gang assaults took place on the governor's daughter at a local fast-food restaurant and the mayor's son at a high school football game. But in spite of such efforts as establishing gang units in police departments, increasing the size of these units, and harassing gang members at every opportunity, gangs begin a process of intimidation and terror that touches all aspects of community life.

Another reason that successful interventions must be found is that gangs are destructive to their members. Gangs that originated as play groups frequently become involved in dangerous, even deadly, games. Joining a gang may be a normal rite of passage for a youth, yet gangs minister poorly to such basic adolescent needs as preparation for marriage, employment, and learning to adapt to the adult world. Adolescent males who join gangs for protection are often exposed to dangers that most nongang youth are able to avoid. Adolescent females may join because they are attracted to male members but then are exploited sexually. Gang members are more likely both to commit delinquent acts and to become victims of crime than are youths who do not join gangs. Finally, joining a gang may provide status and esteem in the present, but gang membership also ensures incarceration in juvenile and adult facilities.

Irving Spergel and colleagues' 1989 survey of forty-five cities with gang problems identified five strategies of intervention. These were (1) community organization, including community mobilization and networking; (2) social intervention, focusing on individual behavioral and value change; (3) opportunities provision, emphasizing the improvement of basic education, training, and job opportunities for youths; (4) suppression, focusing on arrest, incarceration, monitoring, and supervision of gang members; and (5) organizational development and change, or the creation of special organizational units as well as procedures.

In examining the implementation of these strategies, Spergel and colleagues found that suppression (44 percent) was most frequently used, followed by social intervention (31.5 percent), organizational development (10.9 percent), community organization (8.9 percent), and opportunities provision (4.8 percent). Community organization was more likely to be used in programs in emerging gang cities, whereas social intervention and opportunity provision tended to be primary strategies of programs in cities with chronic gang problems. But in only seventeen of the forty-five cities was there any evidence of improvement in the gang situation.

Spergel and colleagues, in developing a model for predicting general effectiveness in dealing with gang problems, stated:

> A final set of analyses across all cities indicate that the primary strategies of community organization and provision of opportunity along with maximum participation by key community actors is predictive of successful efforts at reducing the gang problem.[45]

Some promising initial efforts to prevent and control gangs are taking place that incorporate elements of a community organization model. One Chicago suburb, newly plagued by gangs, established block patrols, watched neighbors' homes, telephoned neighbors to keep them abreast of crimes, appeared in court to support victims, and pressured the police to enforce curfews for youths. Letty Cooper, a mother of ten children and a leader of an inner-city Chicago community group, contended that community organizations can work. She said, "The simple fact is that there are more honest and caring people in this city than there are thugs, and if the good ones work together, I don't think the bad ones can win."

Paramount, California, developed a very successful Alternative to Gang Membership Program. In six years, only fifteen of the 3,000 youths who participated in the antigang curriculum in school joined gangs. In addition, more than 250 neighborhood meetings on gang awareness attracted 2,500 parents. The city is proud of the fact that the $75,000 cost of the program is much cheaper than putting one patrol car on the streets. Twelve other California communities have also adopted the Paramount plan.

Although the above approaches are promising, only an integrated, multidimensional, community-organized effort is likely to have any long-term effect in preventing and controlling gangs in the United States. This gang prevention and control model must have several components: (1) the community must take responsibility for developing and implementing the model; (2) it must be a structural model that takes very seriously the hopelessness arising from the unmet needs of underclass children; (3) prevention programs, especially in the first six years of school, must be emphasized; (4) supporters of this model must coordinate all the gang intervention efforts taking place in a community; and (5) sufficient financial resources must be available to implement the model.

CHAPTER 9—ENDNOTES

[1]Interviewed in 1982 at the Iowa State Penitentiary at Fort Madison.

[2]*Ibid.*

[3]"The Drug Gangs," *Newsweek*, 28 March 1988, p. 27.

[4]Frederick Thrasher, 1927. *The Gang*. Chicago: University of Chicago Press, p. 57.

[5]Craig Collins, "Youth Gangs of the 70s," *Police Chief* 42 (September 1975), p. 50.

[6]Interviewed in March 1974.

[7]John C. Quicker and Akil S. Batani-Khalfani, "Clique Succession among South Los Angeles Street Gangs, the Case of the Crips." Paper presented at the Annual Meeting of the American Society of Criminology, Reno, Nevada (November 1989).

[8]Collins, "Youth Gangs of the 70s," p. 52.

[9]Walter B. Miller, "Gangs, Groups, and Serious Youth Crime," in *Critical Issues in Juvenile Delinquency*, edited by David Shicor and Delos H. Kelly. Lexington, Mass.: Heath 1980, p. 121.

[10]Walter B. Miller, *Violence by Youth Gangs and Youth Groups as a Crime Problem in Major American Cities* (Washington, D.C.: U.S. Government Printing Office, 1975). Much of the following material is derived from Chapter 15 of Miller's study.

[11]Interviewed in 1988.

[12]Interviewed in 1991.

[13]"Warning Signs for Parents." Mimeographed handout by the Los Angeles Police Department (1989), p. 1.

[14]Carl S. Taylor, "Gang Imperialism," in *Gangs in America*, edited by C. Ronald Huff (Newbury Park, Calif.: Sage, 1990), p. 113.

[15]Huff, "Youth Gangs and Public Policy," *Crime and Delinquency* 35 (October 1989), pp. 528-529.

[16]Fagan, "The Social Organization of Drug Use and Drug Dealing among Gangs," pp. 649-651.

[17]Martín Sánchez Jankowski, *Islands in the Street: Gangs and American Urban Society* (Berkeley: University of California Press, 1991), p. 5.

[18]Jankowski, pp. 64-66.

[19]Interview conducted in 1985.

[20]For more information about the drive-by shooting, see William B. Sanders, *Gangbangs and Drive-Bys: Grounded Culture and Juvenile Gang Violence* (New York: Aldine De Gruyter, 1994).

[21]"When You're a Crip (or a Blood)," *Harper's Magazine*, (March 1989), p. 51.

[22]William Recktenwald, "Street Gangs Live—and Often Kill—by Their Sacred Symbols," *Chicago Tribune*, 9 January 1984. Source of prayer and loyalty quotes, too.

[23]Quoted in Vigil, "The Gang Subculture and Locura," p. 6.

[24]Cheryl Maxson, Malcolm W. Klein, and Lea C. Cunningham, "Street Gangs and Drug Sales." Report to the National Institute of Justice, 1993.

[25]General Accounting Office, *Nontraditional Organized Crime* (Washington, D.C.: Government Printing Office, 1989).

[26]Drug Enforcement Administration, *Crack Cocaine Availability and Trafficking in the United States* (Washington, D.C.: U.S. Department of Justice, 1988).

[27]"The Drug Gangs," *Newsweek*, 28 March 1988, p. 24.

[28]Marvin E. Wolfgang, Terence P. Thornberry, and Robert M. Figlio, *From Boy to Man: From Delinquency to Crime* (Chicago: University of Chicago Press, 1987), pp. 155-156.

[29]*Ibid.*, pp. 156-158.

[30]Mark S. Fleisher, "Youth Gangs and Social Networks: Observations from a Long-Term Ethnographic Study." Paper presented at the Annual Meeting of the American Society of Criminology, Miami, Florida (November 1994), p. 1, 4.

[31]"Youth Violence: Gangs on Main Street, USA," *Issues in Brief* (Winter 1993), p. 3.

[32]This seven-stage development scheme was developed from conversations with a variety of individuals across the nation, ranging from gang leaders and gang members to police administrators, school officials, and newspaper reporters.

[33]For an examination of the seriousness of the problem of Satanism among U.S. youths, see Philip Jenkins and Daniel Maier-Katkin, "Satanism: Myth and Reality in a Contemporary Moral Panic." Revised paper presented at the American Society of Criminology, Baltimore, Maryland (November 1990).

[34]See Ko-Lin Chin, "Chinese Gangs and Extortion," in *Gangs in America*, pp. 129-145 and James Diego Vigil and Steve Chong Yun, "Vietnamese Youth Gangs in Southern California," in *Gangs in America*, edited by C. Ronald Huff (Newbury Park, Calif.: Sage, 1990), pp. 146-162.

[35]Cohen, Albert K., 1955 *Delinquent Boys: The Culture of the Gang*, Glencoe, Ill.: Free Press, pp. 46-48.

[36]Anne Campbell, *The Girls in the Gang: A Report from New York City* (New York: Basil Blackwell, 1984), p. 5.

[37]Peggy C. Giordan, "Girls, Guys and Gangs: The Changing Social Context of Female Delinquency." *Journal of Criminal Law and Criminology* 69 (1978), p. 130.

[38]Waln K. Brown, "Black Female Gangs in Philadelphia," *International Journal of Offender Therapy and Comparative Criminology* 21 (1970), pp. 221-229, pp. 223-227.

[39]M. G. Harris, *Cholas: Latino Girls and Gangs* (New York: AMS Press, 1988), p. 172.

[40]Campbell, *The Girls in the Gangs.*

[41]Carl S. Taylor, *Girls, Gangs, Women and Drugs* (East Lansing: Michigan State University Press, 1993), p. 48, 95, 102-103.

[42]Jankowski, *Islands in the Street*, p. 139.

[43]*Ibid.*

[44]Personal correspondence from Michael F. de Vries, October 1995. For another integrated theory of gangs, see J. F. Short, "Exploring Integration of Theoretical Levels of Explanation: Notes on Gang Delinquency," in *Theoretical Integration in the Study of Deviance and Crime: Problems and Prospects*, edited by S. F. Messner, M. D. Krohn, and A. E. Liska (Albany: University of New York Press, 1989), pp. 243-259.

[45]I. A. Spergel, G. D. Curry, R. A. Ross, and R. Chance, *Survey of Youth Gang Problems and Programs in 45 Cities and 6 Sites*. Tech. Report No. 2, National Youth Gang Suppression and Intervention Project (Chicago: University of Chicago, School of Social Service Administration, 1989), p. 218.

PART IV

Organizations, Violence & Conflict

10

ORGANIZATIONS, VIOLENCE AND CONFLICT

Larger than groups but smaller than communities, organizations usually have a number of rules and goals that are formally written down. Some of the rules have to do with communication channels because it is impossible for all organization members to deal with everyone else in the social unit at once, face to face. Organizations—or associations as they are sometimes called—have a moderate amount of division of labor, and this results in a variety of organizational roles.

Of late in America, violent conflict between organizations has taken place between law enforcement organizations and *religious* (e.g., cult) organizations as happened at Waco, Texas a few years back. And to a lesser degree, violent conflict has occurred between law enforcement organizations and *political* (e.g., militia) organizations.

A few decades ago, the main kinds of interorganizational clashes were between law enforcement organizations and campus, anti-war, and civil rights organizations. And prior to that, the main conflicts were between labor and management organizations, farmer and banker organizations, and cattlemen and railroader organizations. (These were often termed *industrial* organizations.) Law enforcement agencies were involved in many of these clashes, either acting on their own or on behalf of one of the conflicting parties.[*]

Before turning attention to cult, militia, and police organizations, a few words about violence between industrial organizations are in order.

INDUSTRIAL ORGANIZATIONS, UNIONS, AND VIOLENCE

While conflicts between workers and managers have occurred in most nations, they have rarely been as severe—or as helpful in the long run—as they have been in the United States.

---

[*]Throughout much of this century in America, *criminal* organizations have likewise been involved in violent conflicts. Some kinds of organized crime violence go way back in American history (battles among mafia "families") and some kinds are more recent (struggles among drug cartel organizations). As with other interorganizational violence, law enforcement organizations have been involved in some but not all of these conflicts.

One social scientiest summarized the industrial violence that took place in America during the peak years this way:

```
┌─────────────────────── EXHIBIT 1 ───────────────────────────────────┐
│                                                                      │
│  Industrial Conflict & Peacekeeping Since New Deal[1]                │
```

Year	Interventions (5 yr. periods)		Fatalities (1 yr. periods)	
	Natl. Guard	Military	Number	Location
1945			*	
1946			*	
1947			0	
1948	5	1	1	Maryland
			3	Illinois, Iowa
1949			1	Kentucky
1950			1	Tennessee
			1	Alabama
1951			1	Georgia
			1	Arkansas
	1	2	1	Tennessee
1952			0	
1953			1	West Virginia
			1	Pennsylvania
1954			0	
1955			1	Louisiana
1956			0	
1957			2	Tennessee
1958	6	1	1	New York
			2	Florida
1959			4	Kentucky
			1	Louisiana
1960			1	Wisconsin
1961			1	New York
1962	1	0	3	Tennessee
1963			*	
1964			*	

*Exact number unknown or uncertain.

There were the bloody railroad strikes in 1877 that killed 150; the Rocky Mountain mining wars that took the lives of 198, including a governor, at the turn of the century; the brutal Molly Maguires, a secret band of Irish miners in Pennsylvania, the Wobblies, or Industrial Workers of the World; the industrial and railroad police who brutally beat laborers from

Pennslyvania to California; the garment workers' strike in Chicago in 1910 that resulted in 7 deaths, an unknown number of seriously injured, and 874 arrests; the 20 lives lost in the Illinois Central Railroad strikes in 1911; the 1919 steel strike in which 20 persons perished; the national cotton textile labor dispute of 1934 that spread from Georgia and South Carolina to Alabama, even to Rhode Island and Connecticut, with 21 deaths and 10,000 soldiers on strike duty.[2]

Not surprisingly, some experts claim that "The United States has had the bloodiest and most violent labor history of any industrial nation in the world."[3] The period of major strife was 1870 to 1930, and during this period violence occurred *primarily* in coal and railroad industries from 1870 to 1890; in coal, textile, and streetcar industries from 1890 to 1910; and in coal, steel and transportation industries from 1910 to 1930.

Labor-management conflict was significantly reduced with the passage of New Deal legislation, which routinized and institutionalized it by means of protocols and collective bargaining. (Simply defined, collective bargaining involves negotiation between unionized workers and their employers for the purpose of reaching agreements on wages, hours, and working conditions.)

But some sporadic violence has occurred between workers and managers since the New Deal. As noted in the exhibit, many people have been killed or wounded in post World War II clashes, and the U. S. military and National Guard have been called up several times to keep the peace, as they had to long ago in the famous 1894 Pullman strike, the 1913 Colorado coal strike, and the 1919 West Virginia mine strike.[4] In recent decades there has been occasional violence between Caesar Chavez's United Farm Workers Organizing Committee (UFWOC) and various other union and management organizations in California's lush agricultural valleys. There also has been occasional violence in disputes involving management organizations (and their scab workers) and organizations of say, teamsters, transit workers, or coal miners.

RELIGIOUS ORGANIZATIONS, CULTS, AND VIOLENCE

In America these days, religious organizations—whether they be formal organizations like Louis Farrakhan's Nation of Islam or informal ones like David Koresh's Branch Davidian cult—have demonstrated that they can be involved in conflict and violence as much as any other kind of organization. Religious conflicts, of course, bedevil many other areas of the world: Northern Ireland, the Middle East, and India to name just a few. And as any student of history knows, there have been times when most of the violence in the world was caused by churches and other such organizations waging war in the name of religion.

Because of the violence and tragedy in Waco, Texas a few years back, cult-type religious organizations like the Branch Davidians will be examined in some detail in this book. There are all manner of cults as the following partial list of past and present ones indicates:

— Kip McKean's Church of Christ, in Boston, Los Angeles, etc.

- Reverend Moon's Unification Church (& CARP which one may encounter on a college campus)

- Jim Jones' Peoples Temple in San Francisco and Guyana

- Heaven's Gate in Rancho Sante Fe, California

- Bhagwan Rajneesh's cult in Antelope Valley, Oregon

- Christ Miracle Healing Center in Arizona

- Elizabeth Clare Prophet's Church Universal and Triumphant in Montana

- First Church of Satan in San Francisco

- MOVE in Philadelphia

- White Brotherhood in the Ukraine

- Covenant, the Sword and Arm of the Lord in the Ozarks

- Synanon in the San Francisco Bay Area

- Family of God in California and Argentina

Interestingly, the approach of the year 2000 may bring forth more encounters between cults and other organizations because of the symbolic meaning of the millennium, especially for the subtype known as "doomsday" cults. This is going to require fairly sophisticated conflict management and resolution techniques on the part of government officials and law enforcement organizations.

Cult experts believe that *destructive* cults are more likely to be involved in violence than *constructive* ones. Destructive cults are those that manipulate and exploit their followers. They tend to *mis*represent themselves both to their followers and to the outside world. Destructive cults are also more likely than constructive ones to use so-called "brainwashing" techniques to "program" their followers to believe certain things.

"Religion "must be defined broadly in any study of contemporary cults because seemingly secular cults (from Marc "Yo" Tizer's ultramarathoner cult to L. Ron Hubbard's Scientology organization) also manifest a religious devotion to some person, object, idea or movement. *Religion*, here, is defined as sociologist Durkheim defined it: namely, the beliefs and practices that hold some person or thing as sacred and unite its adherents.

In his chapter, Henslin explains that *cults* exist at one end of a continuum, with *sects* and *churches* in the middle and *ecclesia* at the other end. He notes that all religions begin as cults, and that Christianity and Islam are good examples. (Early believers in Christ constituted a cult and were persecuted as a result. So, too, were early believers in Mohammed.)

Successful cults often become sects, that is, aggregates larger than cults that still feel substantial hostility from and toward society. The reverse can happen as well: David Koresh took over a former Seventh-day Adventist sect and turned it into his own personal cult. Sects tend to put their emphasis on saving *society* rather than on saving *individuals* as cults often do.

A sect may *then* grow into a church which is a highly developed organization—with elaborate rules, regulations and structures—which emphasizes more sedate worship in contrast to a cult or sect.

And finally, a church may slowly, inexorably become an ecclesia over time. As Henslin explains, an ecclesia is a religious aggregate so integrated into the dominant culture that it is difficult to tell where the one begins and the other leaves off. Sometimes an ecclesia is also called a *state religion*.

In his chapter, Henslin presents four major patterns of adaptation which occur when cults and other religious organizations find themselves in conflict with the culture of which they partake.

Interestingly, Henslin concludes Chapter 11 with a discussion of the secularization of religion, that is, the replacement of a religious organization's "otherworldly" concerns with concerns about "this world." Henslin discusses how the secularization of a sect can be the result of changes in the economic well-being of sect members.

David Koresh and Waco

A brief examination of Koresh's Branch Davidian cult is appropriate here because it was involved in some of the most controversial government violent action in recent history. To some, the two government assaults on the cult are classic examples of legitimate violence that is really illegitimate.

The cult that David Koresh led had had a chaotic history in Texas dating back to the the 1930s and 1940s. The cult was an offshoot of the Davidian Seventh-day Adventists who felt regular Adventists had become spiritually lax. Koresh was a dyslexic school drop-out who happened to have an impressive memory for biblical scripture and a lesser facility for playing rock music on his guitar. He joined the cult around age 18, looking for meaning and wanting a God who was a father figure. (He grew up as an out-of-wedlock child in Houston, Texas.)

Koresh had many power struggles with other would-be leaders of the cult, and some struggles even involved gun battles. Koresh finally emerged as the undisputed leader around 1990.

Koresh had always had a fondness for women—from young innocent girls to worldly older women—and eventually rationalized his promiscuity with cult members as an effort to populate a new House of David. He fathered many of the 20 or so children who perished in the fire during the final showdown with the government. (The mothers of several of these children were underage girls. Koresh told them they were chosen by God to bear his children.) At one point, Koresh annulled the marriages of many of the older couples in the cult and declared that God wanted only him to have sex at Ranch Apocalypse. He had males and females sleep in different parts of the Ranch compound.

Koresh controlled his followers in two major ways. He brainwashed them—as a self-styled messiah—with his fervent readings and quotings of the Bible during sermons that went on for hours. He also used his familiarity and obsession with guns and weapons to intimidate cult members. He had an armed guard stationed outside the cult compound around the clock.

Law enforcement organizations eventually became concerned with Koresh's stockpiling of assault weapons and large amounts of ammunition. Koresh claimed the weapons and ammo were needed to deal with the coming apocalypse as well as with external threats to the cult. This stockpiling set the stage for the ATF's effort to serve Koresh with an arrest warrant which resulted in one of the deadliest days in U.S. law enforcement history. (The deaths of four ATF agents during the serving of this warrant were soon eclipsed in numbers by the deaths of many agents in the Federal Building during the Oklahoma City bombing.)

The FBI, ATF and Waco

In their attempt to serve the arrest warrant for gun law violations, more than 100 ATF agents in jumpsuits and flak jackets surrounded the sprawling cult compound that included a "gun" tower that dominated the windswept, desolate plains outside Waco. ATF had hoped to surprise Koresh and arrest him, but a furious gun battle ensued because the cult had been tipped off that the ATF was coming. Outgunned by the 100 or so cultmembers inside the compound (who had countless assault rifles and untold ammunition), the ATF frantically negotiated a cease-fire. ATF agents gathered up their dead and wounded and retreated.

Immediately after the fiasco, the FBI took over control of the situation from the ATF. The FBI encircled the sprawling, well-maintained compound with 400 federal agents, reinforced by state and local police as well as SWAT teams. Eventually, the FBI's elite Hostage Rescue Team, armored personnel carriers, Bradley fighting vehicles, and M-60 tanks were brought in.

In Chapter 12, Reid details a variety of failed promises made by Koresh. The FBI tried almost every tactic imaginable to break the cult's will—including deal-making, inching troops closer each day, cutting off the cult's electricity, and directing bright light and annoying music and sound at the compound. Finally after 51 days, authorities decided to inject the buildings with CS gas, a chemical agent more debilitating than normal tear gas.

The gas attack began early in the morning of April 19th and continued off and on until 12 noon when smoke appeared in different parts of the compound. Allegedly, four separate fires had been intentionally set by cult-members, but there is still debate as to whether the final debacle was a mass murder or a mass suicide. Eighty-six people died in the conflagration. (Five cult members had already died in the first ATF raid.)

Only a few cult members escaped from the raging inferno alive. One such cultist carried with her a computer disk with a 13-page manuscript about the Book of Revelation's Seven Seals which Koresh said he was working on. (He regularly claimed to be the "lamb" of God who alone could open the mysterious book sealed with Seven Seals.) Koresh had promised to come out of the compound when his manuscript was done, and some scholars say the manuscript was a carefully reasoned exegesis, not the rantings of a psychotic mind.

In her exposition, Reid summarizes the allegations against the ATF, the Congressional hearings into the tragedy, and the sanctions levied against certain government decision-makers. Many felt that the ATF had succumbed to a "paramilitary mentality" during the first raid—

what with their ninja-type outfits and helicopters—when a simple arrest of Koresh while he was outside his compound might have sufficed. Reid neglects to mention it, but one of the strongest allegations against the ATF was that the presence of 38 young children inside the compound made frontal assault the wrong tactic. In fact, the policy in most law enforcement organizations is to always negotiate when there are women or children involved in hostage or barricade situations.

The FBI, other organizations, and Janet Reno (Attorney General at the time) came in for much criticism, too, for many different issues: their faulty intelligence about the cult, their dismissal of experts' advice to "go slow," their decision to inject nerve gas into the compound on a windy day, and their failure to have firefighting equipment ready at hand. Despite shakeups at ATF and various other political fallout, there still seem to be many unanswered questions about the government's handling of the Waco situation. While a "go slow" approach was used a while later during the government's standoff with the Freeman militia in Montana, it is not clear whether law enforcement organizations have learned important lessons from the Waco tragedy.

POLITICAL ORGANIZATIONS, MILITIAS, AND VIOLENCE

Violence and conflict involving *political* organizations in days gone by was noted earlier: to wit, clashes involving campus, anti-war, and civil rights organizations as parties to violent conflict. Currently, there is occasional violent conflict involving other political organizations such as pro and con gay-rights associations, pro and con abortion-rights organizations, and pro and con hate organizations. These conflicts often involve police organizations acting as third parties in the middle of the two parties.

Militias are a type of political organization, and they take their name from the Second Amendment reference to a "well regulated militia." Experts claim militias are growing especially fast in California, Arizona, New Mexico, Colorado, Idaho, New Hampshire, Virginia, North Carolina, and Florida. Militias are forming in urban as well as rural areas.

In "A Call to Arms," author Bill Wallace notes that throughout California, angry citizens are forming combat-ready militias to protect themselves against a federal government they believe wants to take their guns and tell them how to live. These militia members fear the weakening of individual rights and the strengthening of government rights. They feel federal government power has grown too large.

Wallace observes that the organizational structure of each militia is somewhat different. Militias differ organizationally in terms of security, activities, goals, and beliefs:

Security:

Some militias are obsessed with security and secrecy. Others have open and public meetings with published minutes.

Activities:

Some militias engage in everything from simulated combat and counterinsurgency tactics to firearms practice at ranges. Some are content, however, to engage in the mundane work of registering voters with an eye toward rolling back gun-control laws and search and seizure statutes.

Goals:

Some militias are very ambitious and proselytize for new members. For example, one militia in El Dorado Country, California has the ambitious goal of creating a 7,000-person army, ready for combat. Other militias seem content to meet occasionally, dress up in battle-fatigues, and essentially function as a forum for discussion.

Beliefs:

Some militias believe in elaborate conspiracy theories ("The United Nations and U.N. troops will take over America;" "FEMA is poised to impose martial law across the U.S.," etc.). Other militias believe in the racist, anti-Semitic rhetoric of right-wing extremist organizations. Some even claim common-cause with neo-Nazis, skinheads and other hate-groups. However, many California militias go to great lengths to distance themselves from white supremacists.

In sum, as Wallace notes, most militia members in California seem united in their general dissatisfaction with current American politics. They fear crime, social disorder, and increasing federal power. In terms of federal power, they worry most about law enforcement organizations like the ATF and the FBI. Militia members generally despise the ATF and FBI actions at Waco, and see such actions as proof that the U.S. government will do almost anything to disarm its citizens.

Randy Weaver and Ruby Ridge

So, how do government and law enforcement organizations deal with militia members and others of their ilk? In her article, "Is deadly force justifiable," Michele Ingrassia reviews how federal marshals confronted Randy Weaver and his rag-tag band in northern Idaho in 1992. She describes the events at Ruby Ridge and the court debate over the violence that occurred there.

Ingrassia explains that the bloody events at Weaver's ramshackle compound foreshadowed in an uncanny way the Waco siege which took place six months after Ruby Ridge. The events also may have triggered a number of similar situations with other militias in recent years. Among them:

— An impasse between authorities and a militia which announced it had seceded and formed a government called the Republic of Texas. The incident finally ended with the laying down of arms by the secessionists. However, a gunbattle several days later with police resulted in the killing of one of two militia members who had fled just before the laying down of arms.

— A standoff with the Freeman militia at "Justus township" in eastern Montana. The militia finally gave in after an 80-day standoff. Local law enforcement organizations apparently learned some lessons from Waco because they showed considerable patience in this standoff.

— A surveillance of twelve suburban militia members resulted in arrests for an alleged plot to blow up government buildings in Phoenix, Arizona. The middle-class militia members called themselves the "Viper Militia."

— A similar situation, involving a small militia calling itself "The Republic of Georgia," resulted in arrests just before the Atlanta Olympics were to begin in 1996. Militia members were charged with conspiracy and possession of unregistered explosives.

As Ingrassia explains, the Ruby Ridge standoff started with militia members holed up in their compound, armed to the teeth. The members had been the targets of 16 months of surveillance by federal law enforcement agents. Their leader, Randy Weaver, was a former Green Beret just like the well-known, ubiquitous militiaman, Bo Gritz. Weaver was something of a political and religious zealot, espousing a variety of anti-government and anti-Semitic ideologies.

At one point during the 11-day standoff, there was gunfire which each party claimed the other initiated. In the resulting shootout, a deputy U.S. Marshal was killed as was Weaver's 14-year-old son. The next day, Weaver's wife was killed by an FBI sharpshooter as she held her baby daughter in her arms. Despite being injured, Weaver and his sidekick, Kevin Harris still resisted capture. Law enforcers then brought in helicopters, armored personnel carriers, and 200 more agents. This ultimately caused Weaver and Harris to surrender a week later. In the end, three people had died and $1 million in government funds had been spent on manpower and equipment.

After the Ruby Ridge court case which Ingrassia discusses, there were investigations of the possibility of evidence tampering by the government. There was a Congressional hearing in 1995 during which allegations were made that unnecessary "shoot-to-kill" orders were given at Ruby Ridge. As a result of all of this, six senior FBI officials were suspended. A blistering report in 1997 called for "aggressive disciplinary action" against former FBI deputy director Larry Potts and three other senior bureau officials who were all suspended without pay in 1995 for their conduct.

LAW ENFORCEMENT ORGANIZATIONS, POLICE, AND VIOLENCE

Engaged in *social* control as they are, police and other law enforcers often fail to engage in *self* control during their efforts to deal with violence. As a consequence, police brutality often results. This brutality sometimes involves more than just individuals losing control over themselves; it involves entire *law enforcement* organizations losing control over their officers because of improper training, supervision, or command structure. This kind of violence can be termed *illegitimate* violence as noted in Chapter 2.

Many experts have pointed out that brutality often provokes violence from the victim(s) of it:

> "The most fundamental human response to force is counterforce. Force threatens and angers men, especially if they believe it to be illicit or unjust. Threatened, they try to defend themselves. Angered, they want to retaliate."[5]

The Rodney King beating case illustrates a variety of problems regarding brutality. First, of course, the notorious case was an instance where several individual officers lost control of themselves. Second, and perhaps as troubling, the case involved a situation where many other officers stood around, watching the brutality and doing nothing. None of these officers even minded that a citizen drove by in a car and observed the scene. Somehow, the police felt they could cover up what was happening. Their word would be believed in court over a citizen's word. (They had not reckoned with "videotape.") Third, the King case highlighted an organizational issue: namely, the role of leadership in preventing brutality. Essentially what was on trial in the second King case was the leadership of Chief Daryl Gates. The allegation was that the L.A.P.D., under Chief Gates' leadership, sanctioned the use of excessive force. Thus, the organizational norms, socialization, and culture of the L.A.P.D. were on trial since they all seemed to tolerate, even excuse, brutality. Incidentally, this same issue may be replayed in court regarding the New York Police Department where officers are accused of savagely sodomizing an arrested Haitian immigrant male with a wooden stick handle in 1997.

Before turning attention to Reid's chapter on violence and the police, it is worth looking at some of the findings regarding police brutality and the use of deadly force. The following list is Roberg and Kuykendall's summary of the most important research findings in this area .

1. While police use of force is a rare event, there is considerable variation in how often it occurs in different neighborhoods and cities.

2. The number of times police shoot and hit their targets also tends to vary among departments, based on restrictiveness of shooting policies, training, and skill levels of the officers.

3. Minorities are shot disproportionately to whites when compared to their numbers in the population, but not when compared with the minority arrest rate or number of police contacts.

4. Historically, a substantial number of citizens have been shot who posed no threat to officers, but this is changing.

5. Those situations that have the greatest probability of officer injury or death involve crimes in progress and any arrest situation.

6. Black officers are more likely to use deadly force and to be shot than white officers because black officers are assigned more frequently to high-crime-rate, black neighborhoods.

7. Police officers who utilize deadly force may experience a decline in productivity and performance afterward.

8. The decision to shoot or not to shoot largely appears to be the result of the officer's perception of a threat.

9. Women may utilize deadly force less frequently than men because they have no ego involvement with suspects.[6]

These nine findings are worth keeping in mind as one reads Chapter 15, especially as they relate to some of the police organizational factors examined by Reid: namely, *rules* (e.g., have restrictive shooting regulations), *policies* (e.g., keep good police-citizen relations), and *division of labor* (e.g., have gang squads, SWAT units, domestic dispute teams).

Violence and the police

Early on in her chapter, Reid cites sociologist Albert Reiss' discovery that many citizens see police brutality—"blue-collar" crime, if you will—as more than just excessive violent force. Citizens see it as ranging from the use of abusive language (which results in status degradation of citizens) through commands to "move on" or "get home" to the unwarranted use of deadly force. This is quite a range.

In her treatment of police brutality, Reid focuses on the use and misuse of deadly force. Historically such force was allowed against fleeing felons. This was because apprehension was quite difficult in times past. As police weapons and communications improved, apprehension became easier. As a result, the U.S. Supreme Court changed the fleeing felon rule in 1985 (*Tennessee v. Garner*) into a more restrictive rule. The new guideline is: the use of deadly force must be reasonable to be lawful. Reid goes on to itemize the circumstances required for force to be "reasonable."

As Reid points out, violence against police is a significant factor in the issue of police violence. This is because "violence begets violence." Police violence in some cases is a reaction to citizen brutality against them. Some police officers work in a "hostile work environment," to say the very least—with profanity, abusive epithets, and threats being standard fare.

Violence against the police is significant, too, because of the impact it has on the emotional health of officers and their families and friends.

Controlling police organizations and violence

In Chapter 16, Reid discusses police violence by examining the control mechanisms both inside and outside police organizations. In her discussion of *inside*-the-organization controls, she deals with the typical "internal affairs" solutions. Her discussion, however, needs to be augmented by an examination of other issues such as officer personality and background, officer training, and officer professionalism. Hence the following:

Personality, background. Since the eye-opening police brutality publicity of the 1960s, police organizations have made great progress in screening out police applicants who, for example, are sadistic, authoritarian, or overly fascinated with guns, nightsticks and the power bestowed by a badge.

Training. Training is a critical police brutality factor, too, because unprepared officers often panic and brutality results. Police "overreaction" can result from inadequate training as can police "underreaction" which can also have dire consequences. (Chapter 18 includes discussions of underreaction and indecision in police riot control activities. Classic examples of underreaction were the Watts riot, the Detroit and Washington DC riots of 1967, and the Los Angeles "Rodney King" riot of 1992.)

Professionalism. The police professionalism movement encourages law enforcement organizations to put top value on efficient, non-political, legalistic enforcement of the law. The use of science, technology, continuing education, and organizational self-assessment is encouraged as are specialized units for substance abuse, juvenile crime, and family crisis intervention.

In Reid's discussion of *outside*-the-organization controls, she begins with the effort to control police misconduct by means of the exclusionary rule. The exclusionary rule prohibits the introduction at a trial of evidence obtained illegally by the police. As the Fuhrman-over-the-wall debate in the O. J. murder trial illustrated, the exclusionary rule and its exceptions—good faith and inevitable discovery—can get very complicated.

The use of criminal and civil liability suits are also outside-the-organization methods to control police brutality and violence. They are being used more and more often, as evidenced by the Rodney King criminal and civil trials.

A control measure not touched on by Reid is the proliferation of video recorders which played such a crucial role in the Rodney King case. Ubiquitous camcorders in the hands of citizens—and also video cameras installed in police vehicles—provide a deterrent against police violence. And, incidentally, these cameras reveal that citizens frequently start violent encounters and that citizen vigilantes are sometimes as brutal as cops are.

Finally, Reid talks about controlling the police by means of community relations, including community-oriented policing. (In the latter, both the police and the community work together, and often they improve their relationship as well as their perceptions of each other.) Relatedly, civilian review boards have proven to be of some value in controlling police misconduct. However, they often lack the financial resources to investigate and try cases in a timely manner. Ultimately, their effectiveness depends on the legal teeth they have in carrying through disciplinary recommendations.

CHAPTER 10—ENDNOTES

[1] Adapted from tables in H. Graham and T. Gurr, eds., *Violence in America* (New York: Signet, 1969), 349; and J.F. Coates, *Nonlethal Weapons for Use by U.S. Law Enforcement Officers* (Springfield: National Information Service, 1967), 31.

[2] M.E. Wolfgang, "Violence and Human Behavior," in M. Wertheimer, ed., *Confrontation* (Glenby: Scott Foresman, 1970), 175.

[3] P. Taft and P. Ross, "American Labor Violence: Its Causes, Character, and Outcome," in H. Graham and T. Gurr, eds., *Violence in America* (New York: Signet, 1969), 270.

[4] E.E. Wittee, *The Government in Labor Disputes* (New York: McGraw-Hill, 1932), 201.

[5] Ted Gurr, *Why Men Rebel* (Princeton, NJ: Princeton University Press, 1970), 232.

[6] R. Roberg and J. Kuykendall, *Police Organization and Management* (Brooks Cole, 1990), 356-357. The nine statements are based on:

M. Blumberg, "Research on the Police Use of Deadly Force," in A.S. Blumberg and E. Niederhoffer, eds., *The Ambivalent Force* (New York: Holt, Rinehart & Winston, 1985), 340-350;

J.J. Fyfe, *Shots Fired: An Examination of New York City Police Firearms Discharges* (Ph.D. dissertation, University of New York at Albany, 1978);

J.J. Fyfe, "Administrative Interventions on Police Shooting Discretion," *Journal of Criminal Justice 7*, no. 4 (1980): 309-323;

J.J. Fyfe, "Blind Justice," *Journal of Criminal Law and Criminology 73*, no. 2 (1982): 707-722;

J.J. Fyfe, Interview, *Law Enforcement News* (June 24, 1985), 9-12;

W.A. Geller, "Deadly Force: What We Know," in C. Klockars, ed., *Thinking About Police* (New York: McGraw-Hill, 1983), 313-331; and

P. Scharf and A. Binder, *The Badge and the Bullet* (New York: Praeger, 1983).

11

TYPES OF RELIGIOUS ORGANIZATIONS—
HENSLIN

Just as different religions have distinct teachings and practices, so *within* a religion different groups contrast sharply with one another. Let's look at the types of religious organizations sociologists have identified: cult, sect, church, and ecclesia. The typology presented here is a modification of analyses by sociologists Ernst Troeltsch (1931), Liston Pope (1942), and Benton Johnson (1963). The Exhibit illustrates the relationship between each of these four types of religious organizations.[1,2,3]

Cult

The word cult conjures up many bizarre images—shaven heads, weird music, unusual clothing, brainwashing, children estranged from their parents. Secret activities under cover of darkness, even images of ritual murder, may come to mind.

Cults, however, are not necessarily weird, and few practice "brainwashing" or bizarre rituals. In fact, *all religions began as cults* (Stark 1989).[4] A **cult** is simply a new or different religion, whose teachings and practices put it at odds with the dominant culture and religion. Cults often begin with the appearance of a **charismatic leader**, an individual who inspires people because he or she seems to have extraordinary qualities. **Charisma** refers to an outstanding gift. Finding something highly appealing about such an individual, people feel drawn to both the person and the message.

The most popular religion in the world today began as a cult. Its handful of adherents believed that an unschooled carpenter who preached in remote villages in a backward country was the Son of God, that he was killed and came back to life. Those beliefs made the early Christians a cult, set them apart from the rest of their society, and created intense antagonisms. Persecuted by both religious and political authorities, these early believers clung to one another for support, many cutting off associations with their unbelieving families and friends. To others, the early Christians must have seemed deluded and brainwashed.

EXHIBIT 1

A Cult-Sect-Church-Ecclesia Continuum

Less

More

Characteristics of the unit
1. Number of members
2. Wealth or organization
3. Wealth of members ("worldly success")
4. Formal training of clergy

CULT SECT CHURCH ECCLESIA

More

Less

The unit emphasizes:
1. The need to reject society
   (hostility should be directed toward the culture)
2. That it is rejected by society
   (the group feels hostility directed toward itself)
3. Hostility toward other religions
4. Hostility from other religions
5. Personal salvation
6. Emotional expression of religious beliefs
7. Revelation
   (God directly speaking to people)
8. God's direct intervention in people's lives
   (such as providing guidance or healing)
9. A duty to spread the message
   (evangelism)
10. A literal interpretation of Scripture
11. A literal heaven and hell
12. Becoming a member by conversion

Note: Any religious organization can be placed somewhere on this continuum, based on its having "more" or "less" of these characteristics.

Based on Troeltsch (1931), Pope (1942), and Johnson (1963).

So it was with Islam. When Muhammad revealed his visions and said that God's name was really Allah, he was alone. Only a few people believed him at first. To others, he must have seemed crazy, deranged.

Each cult (or new religion) meets with rejection from society. Its message is considered bizarre, its approach to life strange. Its members antagonize the majority, who are convinced that they have a monopoly on the truth. The new message may claim revelation, visions, visits from God and angels, some form of enlightenment, or seeing the true way to God. The cult demands intense commitment, and its followers, confronting a hostile world, pull into a tight circle, separating themselves from nonbelievers.

Most cults fail. Not many people believe the new message, and the cult fades into obscurity. Others, however, succeed and make history. Over time, large numbers of people may accept the message, and become followers of the religion. If this happens, the new religion changes from a cult to a sect.

Sect

A **sect** is a group larger than a cult, whose members still feel a fair amount of tension with the prevailing beliefs and values of the broader society. The sect may even be hostile to the society in which it lives. At the very least, its members remain uncomfortable with many of the emphases of the dominant culture, while nonmembers, in turn, tend to be uncomfortable with members of the sect.

Ordinarily, sects are loosely organized. They are still fairly small and have no national organization that directs their activities. Even if they belong to local or regional associations, individual congregations retain much control. Sects emphasize personal salvation and an emotional expression of one's relationship with God. Clapping, shouting, dancing, and extemporaneous prayers are hallmarks of sects. Like cults, sects also stress active recruitment of new members, an activity that some call evangelism.

If a sect grows, over time its members tend to make peace with the rest of society. They become more respectable in the eyes of the majority and feel much less hostility and little, if any, isolation. To appeal to the new, broader base, the sect shifts some of its doctrines, redefining matters to remove some of the rough edges that created tension between it and the rest of society. If a sect follows this course and becomes larger and more integrated into society, it has changed into a church.

Church

At this point, the religious group is highly bureaucratized—probably with national and international headquarters that give directions to the local congregations, enforce rules about who can be ordained, and control finances. The group's worship service is likely to have grown more sedate, with much less emphasis on personal salvation and emotional expression. Written prayers, for example, are now likely to be read before the congregation, sermons to be much more formal, and the relationship with God to be less intense. Rather than being recruited from the outside by fervent, personal evangelism, most new members now come from within, from children born to existing members. Rather than joining through conversion—seeing the new truth—children may be baptized, circumcised, or dedicated in some other way. When older, children may be asked to affirm the group's beliefs in a confirmation or bar mitzvah ceremony.

Ecclesia

Finally, some groups become so well integrated into a culture, and so strongly allied with their government, that it is difficult to tell where one leaves off and the other takes over. In these state religions, also called **ecclesia**, the government and religion work together to try to shape the society. There is no recruitment of members, for citizenship makes everyone a member. The majority of the society, however, may belong to the religion in name only. The religion is part of a cultural identification, not an eye-opening experience. In Sweden, for example, where Lutheranism is the state religion, most Swedes come to church only for baptisms, marriages, and funerals.

Where cults and sects see God as personally involved and concerned with an individual's life, requiring an intense and direct response, an ecclesia's vision of God is more impersonal and remote. Church services reflect this view of the supernatural, for they tend to be highly formal, directed by ministers or priests who have undergone rigorous training in approved schools or seminaries and follow set routines.

Examples of ecclesia include the Church of England (whose very name expresses alignment between church and state), the Lutheran church in Sweden and Denmark, Islam in Iran and Iraq, Confucianism in China until this century, and, during the time of the Holy Roman Empire, the Roman Catholic church, which was the official religion for what is today Europe.

VARIATIONS IN PATTERNS

Obviously, not all religious groups go through all of these stages. Some die out because they fail to attract enough members. Others, such as the Amish, remain sects. And since only a limited number of countries have state religions, very few religions ever become ecclesias.

In addition, such neat classifications as those in this typology are not perfectly matched in the real world. For example, some groups become churches but retain a few characteristics of sects, such as an emphasis on evangelism or a personal relationship with God. Some sects, such as the early Quakers, stressed a personal relationship with God, but shied away from emotional expressions of their beliefs. (They would quietly meditate in church, with no one speaking, until God gave someone a message to share with others.) Some sects, like the Amish, place little or no emphasis on recruiting others.

Finally, although all religions began as cults, not all varieties of a particular religion did so. For example, a **denomination**—a "brand name" within a major religion, for example, Methodism or Reform Judaism—may begin as a splinter group. Although splintering, or schism, usually gives birth to sects, on occasion a large group within a church may disagree with *some aspects* of the church's teachings (not its major message) and break away to form its own organization. An example is the Southern Baptist Convention, formed in 1845 to defend the right to own slaves (Ernst 1988).[5]

A closer look at cults and sects

As we have seen, because of their break with the past, cults and sects present an inherent challenge to the social order. Four major patterns of adaptation occur when religion and the culture in which it is embedded find themselves in conflict.

First, the society may reject the religious group entirely, or even try to destroy it. The early Christians are an example. The Roman emperor declared them enemies of Rome and determined that all Christians were to be hunted down and destroyed until not one was left alive. Even the memory of their heresy was to be removed from history.

In the second pattern, the religious group rejects the dominant culture and withdraws from it geographically. Believing that the survival of their religion is at stake, its members migrate. In some cases, they cannot tolerate the surrounding society and feel too uncomfortable to remain. In other cases, they face persecution and decide that they had better leave.

The Mormons provide an example of the latter type of migration. Their rejection of Roman Catholicism and Protestantism as corrupt, accompanied by their belief in polygamy, led to their persecution. In 1831, they left Palmyra, New York, and moved first to Kirtland, Ohio, and subsequently to Independence, Missouri. When the persecution continued, they moved to Nauvoo, Illinois. There a mob murdered the founder of the religion, Joseph Smith, and his brother Hyrum. The Mormons then decided to escape the dominant culture altogether by founding a community in the wilderness. Consequently, in 1847 they settled in the Great Salt Lake valley of what is today the state of Utah (Bridgwater 1953).[6]

A third pattern is the members of a religion to reject the dominant culture and withdraw socially. Although they continue to live in the same geographical area as others, they try to have as little as possible to do with nonmembers of their religion. They may withdraw into closed communities, like the Essenes, a Jewish sect that existed in the second century A.D.

Such is the case of the Amish, who broke away from Swiss-German Mennonites in 1693. The Amish try to preserve the culture of their ancestors, a simpler time when life was uncontaminated by television, movies, automobiles, or electricity. To do so, they emphasize family life, traditional male and female roles, and live on farms, which they work with horses. They continue to wear the same style of clothing as their ancestors did three hundred years ago, to light their homes with oil lamps, and to speak German at home and in church. They also continue to reject electricity and motorized vehicles. They do mingle with non-Amish to the extent of shopping in town—where they are readily distinguishable by their form of transportation (horse-drawn carriages), clothing, and speech.

In the fourth, a cult or sect rejects only specified elements of the prevailing culture; and neither the religion nor the culture is seriously threatened by the other. For example, religious teachings may dictate that immodest clothing—short skirts, swimsuits, low-cut dresses, and so on—is immoral, or that wearing makeup or going to the movies is wrong. Most elements of the main culture, however are accepted. Although specified activities are forbidden, members of the religion are able to participate in most aspects of the broader society. They are likely to resolve this mild tension by either adhering to the religion or by "sneaking," doing the forbidden acts on the sly.

The secularization of religion

Sociologists use the term **secularization of religion** to refer to the replacement of spiritual or "otherworldly" concerns with concerns about "this world." Secularization occurs when religious influence over life is lessened, both on a society's institutions and on individuals. (The term **secular** means "belonging to the world and its affairs.") Cultures, too, become secularized when other social forces replace the functions traditionally fulfilled by religion. Secularization is thus an important type of social change.

The splintering of American churches. The secularization of religion can explain a question that has perplexed many: Why have Christian churches splintered into so many groups? Why don't Christians have just one church, or at least several, instead of the hundreds of sects and denominations that dot the American landscape?

The simplest answer, of course, is that Christians have disagreed about doctrine (church teaching). As theologian and sociologist Richard Niebuhr pointed out, however, there are many ways of resolving doctrinal disputes besides splintering off and forming another religious organization. Niebuhr (1929) found that the answer lies more in *social* change than in *religious* conflict.[7]

The explanation goes like this. As noted earlier, when a religion becomes more churchlike, tension between it and the main culture lessens. Quite likely, its founders and first members were poor, or at least not too successful in worldly pursuits. Feeling estranged from their general culture, they received a good part of their identity from the cult or sect. Their services and practices stressed differences between their values and cosmology and those of the dominant culture. They also probably stressed the joys of the coming afterlife, when they would be able to escape from their present pain.

As time passes, however, the group's values—such as respect for authority, frugality, the avoidance of gambling, alcohol, and drugs—may actually help the members to experience worldly success. As they become more middle-class and respectable in the eyes of society, they no longer experience the isolation or the hostility felt by the founders of their group.

As this change occurs, the group's teachings—in the official literature as well as in sermons—begin to center more on this world. Life's burdens don't seem as heavy, and the need for relief through an imminent afterlife doesn't seem as pressing. Similarly, the pleasures of the world no longer appear as threatening to salvation or to "true" belief. There follows an attempt to harmonize religious beliefs with the changing orientation to the culture.

Protestant sects such as the Church of the Nazarene and the Church of God provide examples. In their early years, they stressed that jewelry, makeup, and movies were worldly and that true believers had to separate themselves from such things. Over time, the groups became less vocal about movies, and then fell silent about them. Similarly, after initial protests, they gradually objected less and less to their younger members wearing makeup, which at first was "light," and barely discernible, and later became a "normal" amount.

Finally came accommodation with the secular culture to such an extent that ministers' wives now dye their hair and wear makeup and jewelry. A sociological cycle has been completed, and what was formerly called the "Jezebel" has become a role model for young women. The teaching changes also, and one hears, "Outward appearances aren't really important. It's what's in your heart that counts."

This is just an example. The particulars vary from one group to another, for not many chose movies, makeup, and jewelry as central identifiers. But the process is the same. As a group becomes more middle-class, the worldly success of its members leads it to change its teachings.

While the secularization of a sect is occurring, however, one segment of the group remains dissatisfied: those members who have had less worldly success. They continue to feel estranged from the broader culture. For them, the tension and hostility remain real, making their group's gradual accommodation to the culture uncomfortable. They view the change as a "sellout" to the secular world.

In short, changes in social class create different needs. As a religious organization changes to meet the changing social status of some of its members, it thereby fails to meet the needs of those whose life situation has not changed.

This, says Niebuhr, creates irreconcilable tension. The group whose needs are not being met then splinters off, forming a sect in which its members feel more comfortable. This newly formed group again stresses its differences with the world, the need for more personal, emotional religious experience, and salvation from the pain of living in this world. The cycle then repeats itself.

The secularization of religion also occurs on a much broader scale. As a result of modernization—the industrialization of society, urbanization, mass education, wide adoption of technology, and the transformation of *Gemeinschaft* to *Gesellschaft* societies—people depend much less on traditional explanations of life (Berger 1967). Thus, religious explanations become less significant as people turn to answers provided by science, technology, modern medicine, and so on. Although the members of a religion, including its priests, ministers, and rabbis, depend on religion less for answers to everyday questions and problems of living, many hold onto its rituals. This, of course, is one of the reasons that sects come into existence in the first place.

CHAPTER 11—ENDNOTES

[1]Ernst Troeltsch, *The Social Teachings of the Christian Churches* (New York: Macmillan, 1931).

[2]Liston Pope, *Millhands and Preachers: A Study of Gastonia* (New Haven, CT: Yale University Press, 1942).

[3]Benton Johnson, "On Church and Sect," *American Sociological Review* 28 (1963): pp. 539-549.

[4]Rodney Stark, *Sociology,* 3rd ed. (Belmont, CA: Wadsworth, 1989).

[5]Eldon G. Ernst, "The Baptists," in Charles H. Lippy and Peter W. Williams, eds., *Encyclopedia of the American Religious Experience: Studies of Traditions and Movements,* Vol. 1 (New York: Scribners, 1988), pp. 555-577.

[6]William Bridgwater, ed., *The Columbia Viking Desk Encyclopedia* (New York: Viking, 1953).

[7]H. Richard Niebuhr, *The Social Sources of Denominationalism* (New York: Holt, 1929).

12

THE FBI, ATF AND WACO—REID

In the summer of 1995 two House subcommittees of Congress investigated the government's handling of the Waco Davidian compound, and in November 1995 the Senate Judiciary Committee held a two-day hearing to determine what the FBI had done to prevent similar situations. Federal agents from the Bureau of Alcohol, Tobacco and Firearms (ATF) had stormed a seventy-seven-acre, heavily fortified cult compound in Waco, Texas, on 28 February 1993. The agents intended to arrest the cult leader, Vernon Howell, also known as David Koresh, who claimed to be Jesus Christ. They had arrived in livestock trailers, dressed in black, prepared for a surprise attack. The gunfire from agents and those inside the compound lasted about forty-five minutes. Four ATF agents were killed, and many were wounded. Several members of the religious sect within the compound were killed or injured.[1]

FBI agents were called in to assist federal ATF and local law to lay siege to the compound. On 2 March 1993 Koresh indicated the he and his followers would leave the compound when they received a message from God. Several members, mostly women and children, had been permitted to leave earlier. The week before Easter, Koresh delivered to federal agents a four-page letter he claimed was from God. FBI agents responded that they did not have verification that the message was from God and were trying to get that confirmation. "But if it is the message from God, then we have to know what the heck the message is." The FBI would not disclose the contents of the communication.[2]

Various other promises were made by Koresh, and in early April he told the FBI that he and his followers would come out after he finished a religious manuscript. Later he asked for word processing equipment to facilitate his writing. On 19 April 1993 the fifty-one-day standoff was ended. Federal agents used armored tanks to punch holes in the walls of the compound. Tear gas was injected. According to the FBI, the cult members were told that they should surrender, but they responded instead by firing rounds of gunfire. The compound was set on fire, allegedly at the instruction of Koresh. Only nine members of the cult survived; it was estimated that more than eighty were killed including seventeen children.

Attorney General Janet Reno, in taking responsibility for the attack, stated that the information received by the FBI suggested that the children were in increasing danger from disease and abuse. There was no indication that the cult would commit mass suicide; thus the decision to move. "Obviously, if I had thought that the chances were great of a mass suicide, I would never have approved the plan."[3]

Not everyone agreed with the government action, however, as the congressional investigations revealed. ATF agents blamed each other, with ATF agent Robert Rodriguez, who had worked undercover at the compound, testifying that he told his bosses that the element of surprise in the February attack was lost and that they lied to the American people about that. Phillip Chojnacki and Chuck Sarabyn, Rodriguez's supervisors, said he had not made himself clear and they were not aware that the Davidians knew of their plans. Chojnacki and Sarabyn were fired and then rehired with full benefits and back pay. Director Stephen F. Higgins resigned but was not punished; nor did he lose his benefits or pension. He had been with ATF for thirty-one years and served as its director since 1983.[4]

At the November 1995 Senate hearings, retired FBI negotiator Clint Van Zandt testified concerning some mistakes admitted by FBI officials. He concluded, "The American people have the right to expect better." The former negotiator told senators that the 1993 Waco siege was "almost beyond repair" when the FBI became involved. He blamed his former colleagues and the ATF for the disaster, stating that the ATF agents "should never have been ordered into such a confrontation."[5]

Also in 1995 Congress held hearings into the bloody siege at Ruby Ridge, Idaho, in August 1992, in which government agents shot and killed the fourteen-year-old son of white separatist Randy Weaver after a fight erupted between the son and officials. An FBI agent, Lon Horiuchi, shot and killed Weaver's wife, who was holding their ten-month-old baby. Another member of the Weaver household was shot and seriously wounded. Horiuchi refused to testify at the Senate hearings, invoking his Fifth Amendment rights. At Weaver's trial in Idaho, however, he did testify that he fired a shot at Randy Weaver, who he thought was preparing to shoot at an FBI helicopter (Weaver denied that claim) and that he shot Weaver's wife accidentally. FBI Director Louis J. Freeh supported that version of the shooting in his testimony before the congressional hearing. The shooting has resulted in the most intensive investigations of the FBI in recent history. Six senior bureau officials have been suspended.[6]

In the Ruby Ridge hearings, Senator Dianne Feinstein, Democrat from California, asked FBI Director whether the FBI had succumbed to a "paramilitary mentality." He said no, but others disagree. One legal journalist described the Waco and the Ruby Ridge fiascoes in these words: "In both . . . the FBI and the ATF dressed up in camouflage and ski-masks and deployed armored vehicles and helicopters to solve problems that, reflection suggests, might well have been solved by making an ordinary arrest."[7]

CHAPTER 12—ENDNOTES

[1] "U.S. Agent Say Fatal Flaws Doomed Raid on Waco Cult," *New York Times* (28 March 1993), p. 1.

[2] "Cult Leader Presents F.B.I. with 'Letter from God'*, *New York Times* (11 April 1993), p. 13.

[3] "Reno Says Suicides Seemed Unlikely," *New York Times* (20 April 1993), p. 1 See also "Scores Die as Cult Compound Is Set Afire after F.B.I. Sends in Tanks with Tear Gas," New York Times (20 April 1993), p. 1.

[4] "Hearings Show Why Waco Became a Rallying Cry," *Denver Post* (30 July 1995), p. 6D.

[5] "Ex-FBI Negotiator Says Agency Faced Hopeless Situation at Waco," *Los Angeles Times* (2 November 1995), p. 14.

[6] "Ruby Ridge Probe Now Looking into Possible Cover-Up," *The Recorder* (7 November 1995), p. 1.

[7] "Shared Fantasies: We have Met the Enemy, and He Is Us," *New Jersey Law Journal* (6 November 1995), p. 26.

13

A CALL TO ARMS—WALLACE

With his close-cropped gray hair and a pair of clip-on black suspenders stretched tightly over his barrel chest, Harry Infalt looks more like a kindly grandfather than the leader of a band of citizens arming to resist a hostile government. Despite his gentle mien, Infalt, a 67-year-old retired building inspector, is the interim commander of the Unorganized Militia of El Dorado County. His mission: to create a 7,000-member citizens' army—armed and prepared for combat—among the residents of this small Gold Country community nestled in the foothills of the Sierra Nevada.

At his small office on Main Street, Infalt gestured toward a large map showing El Dorado County broken down into electoral precincts. The map was studded with scores of multicolored push pins representing individual militia members.

"There are 77,000 registered voters in this county," he said, "We hope to sign up about 10 percent . . . We are going to have people in every precinct in this county." Like members of other militias that have sprouted up around the state, those in Infalt's group are worried about growing federal power, erosion of individual rights and possible government confiscation of privately owned firearms.

They believe that their voluntary army may be the only protection they have against a government they see as dangerously out of touch with its citizens.

"We are losing our freedom by degrees, and I think it's time for a big no-no," said Allen Westerson, a medical electrical engineer and former reserve Los Angeles police officer who serves as captain of El Dorado County's Georgetown militia district.

Citizen militias—which take their name from the "well-regulated militia" mentioned in the Second Amendment to the U.S. Constitution—are scattered widely and lack formal affiliation and a centralized method of communications.

Nevertheless, the movement is growing rapidly, and boasts branches in Arizona, Colorado, Florida, Idaho, Indiana, Michigan, Missouri, Montana, New Hampshire, New Mexico, North Carolina, Ohio and Virginia.

Although militias began forming several years ago, the movement seemed to reach critical mass last summer when promoters held organizational meetings in Arizona, Colorado, Florida and Indiana. Nationwide, promoters estimate the militia's membership already stands more than 10,000 strong.

The movement has touched a nerve in California. Currently there are 27 different militia units operating in 22 counties. Their locations range from urban centers such as Los Angeles and San Bernardino to rural redoubts like West Point in Calaveras County and Jamestown in Tuolumne. When two residents of Freedom, a tiny town in Santa Cruz County, recently convened a public meeting to discuss forming a local militia, more than 150 people turned up.

Each militia is different in its organizational structure, leadership and rules of operation. Some meet in private and use military-style security measures to keep their plans secret. Others—like Infalt's group in Placerville—have open public meetings, with a formal agenda and published minutes.

At several recent meetings most members appeared to be white males. The vast majority were middle-aged with a few in their 20s and 30s. They lined the parking lots outside their meeting places with elderly Volkswagons, late-model sedans, station wagons with ski racks, camper vans with "Good Sam Club" bumper stickers and dusty Chevy pick-ups with Marine Corps decals in the windows.

Although each militia has a unique philosophical perspective and world view, all agree on one fundamental principal: The U.S. government can no longer be trusted to defend and protect the Constitution.

"Our whole political system is perverse," said Mike Howse, commander of a militia unit in Fort Bragg. "It's changed to where an honest man can't get elected unless he has millions of dollars to run with . . . I don't think this is what the founding fathers had in mind."

The militias are involved in a wide variety of activities. Some members don camouflage uniforms to practice counter-insurgency techniques in isolated area. Others wear warm-up suits and jeans while they plink at targets in local rifle ranges. Still others engage in voter registration drives, or assist local law enforcement agencies in flood-relief efforts, search and rescue operations or other types of emergency response.

Although leaders hope it will never be necessary, the militias are also getting ready to meet any threat to the U.S. Constitution that might arise.

"This is a preparedness group," Placer County militia commander Doug Fales grimly told 30 supporters during a recent meeting in Roseville. "We prepare for the worst and hope for the best."

With the Cold War over, the customary threats to the United States have vanished.

However, some supporters of the movement worry that the United Nations is preparing to take this country over. Others fear that the government—operating under a secret scheme drawn up by the Federal Emergency Management Agency—is poised to implement martial law.

EXHIBIT 1

CITIZEN MILITIAS IN CALIFORNIA

- *Citizens' militia groups are being organized in these 27 California communities:*

Whenever militia members get together, their conversation runs to rumors of mysterious "black helicopters" that have been sighted swooping down over communities and spying on the populace. They exchange stories about government preparations for martial law and reports of U.N. troops massing in isolated parts of the country in preparation for military action.

During a recent militia meeting in Shingle Springs (El Dorado County), Vernon Weckner, a columnist for a militia-oriented newspaper called "Of, By and For the People," told a reporter he had heard about hundreds of men in camo uniforms recently practicing military maneuvers in the rugged bluffs of Butte County.

"Nobody knows who they were," he said. "One thing's for sure—they weren't up there hunting deer."

In Roseville, militia supporters who met on the second floor of a bank last month expressed concern over steps to re-name the old Flag Day holiday "U.N. Flag Day," and about U.N. efforts to draft a world charter guaranteeing certain human rights to all children.

As more than two dozen neatly dressed supporters listened intently, Commander Fales exhorted them to lobby against a pending federal statute that would allow evidence to be seized during questionable searches, so long as the investigating officers acted in good faith.

"This bill literally guts the Fourth Amendment," Fales warned.

Despite all the talk about U.N. takeovers, government crackdowns, "black helicopters" and hidden troops, most militia members seem to have joined the movement because of dissatisfaction with U.S. policies and politics. The militia gives members an opportunity to take direct action to stop what they see as the country's slow slide into chaos.

The world view of militia members seems to be based on natural fears of crime and social disorder. It is nourished by a distrust of the federal government that has grown stronger in the wake of a series of White House scandals, including Watergate, the Iran-Contra affair and the current "White Water" imbroglio.

As proof of federal perfidy, militia members point to the Alcohol, Tobacco and Firearms Bureau's February 1993 armed siege at the headquarters of the Branch Davidian sect in Waco, Texas. The fiery shootout—which led to the deaths of 85 people, including more then a dozen children—convinced many militia members that the federal government will do almost anything to disarm U.S. citizens.

"In every country where the government has succeeded in taking firearms away from the citizenry, they have been reduced to slavery or chattel," said Fort Bragg militia leader Howse.

Although watchdog groups that track extremist organizations suggest the militia movement is linked to dangerous right-wing ideologues, the offer little supporting evidence. Though most California militia supporters are white, militia leaders deny that they discriminate on the basis of race or ethnic origin.

Militia organizers deny links to neo-Nazis. They note that news stories characterizing militias as extremist organizations make it more difficult to recruit members.

As an indication of how far militia leaders will go to avoid being tarred, Howse notes that a benefactor in Monterey County offered the Fort Bragg unit a 1,500-acre parcel of land to use in organizing and training, but a check into the man's background revealed that he was a white supremacist.

"We turned him down," Howse said. "If we took land from somebody who was known as a white supremacist, even if the intentions were good, we would end up being labeled as white supremacists. That's not what we're about."

Local law enforcement officials have shown little interest in the activities of the militias, and the FBI says it is precluded by law from scrutinizing them.

"That's what we call free speech," said Rick Smith, a spokesman for the FBI's San Francisco field office.

So far, occasional news stories alleging right-wing ties do not seem to have impeded the militia movement's growth. In its first open meeting January 14, the El Dorado County group drew 200 interested citizens, many of whom paid a $20 fee to join on the spot. In a second meeting February 18, 100 people turned out to see five district captains sworn in.

A youth auxiliary might even be possible, said Infalt, the El Dorado unit's acting commander. Two young men recently walked into the malitia's offices in a former fruit packing warehouse that has been converted into a mini-mall and asked Infalt for permission to speak to local high school students on the group's behalf.

"I'm thinking about sending them to Toastmasters for training in pubic speaking," he said with a smile. "I think they would make excellent representatives."

14

IS DEADLY FORCE JUSTIFIABLE?—
INGRASSIA, SHAFFER, AND MURR

The similarities are eerie. Well-armed religious zealots barricade themselves in their rural compounds surrounded by their families and convinced by their faith that the end of the world is near. Federal agents launch paramilitary operations to take them by force, but the deadly crackle of gunfire dissolves into a long, uneasy stalemate. Attempts to negotiate sputter. The federal force grows. As the fugitives vow not to be taken alive, the specter of destruction looms.

One version of this scenario played out for 51 days this spring in Waco, Texas. The other unwound last August in the remote mountains of northern Idaho, in a bloody 11-day stand-off between federal marshals and white separatists Randy Weaver, 45, and Kevin Harris, 25. Its cost: the lives of Weaver's wife, Vicki, son, Sam, 14, and Deputy U.S. Marshal William Degan—and $1 million in manpower and equipment.

Weaver's case might have been overlooked if not for David Koresh. But in the wake of the Texas inferno, brutal questions are being pressed as the murder-and-conspiracy trial of Weaver and Harris enters its ninth week in U.S. district court in Boise. How much government force is necessary? How should it be applied? And, in trying to get its man, how scrupulous must the government be? More ethical than it has been, argues Weaver's attorney, Gerry Spence. "The relationship between this and Waco is the ungodly power of the federal government against individuals," he said last week after announcing the defense would not put on a case because the prosecution "didn't prove" its own. Federal attorneys refused to comment on the case.

What unfolded before U.S. district court Judge Edward Lodge could chill the fur off a grizzly: grim photos of Weaver's slain son; tales of government evidence tampering; wrenching details of how Vicki Weaver was shot while holding her infant daughter. Everything about the case is rough-edged—including Weaver, a former Green Beret who, though he had never even had a traffic ticket, was no boy scout. Linked to extremists who label the Unites States part of an international Jewish conspiracy, he was a renegade who lived a spartan existence with Vicki and four children: their house on Ruby Ridge was a plywood cabin with no electricity or running water; they ate what they grew or shot.

But even in a spot where guns were as common as fir trees, Weaver's love of firearms seemed unusual: in an October 1989 sting, federal officials said, he sold two sawed-off shotguns to a Bureau of Alcohol, Tobacco and Firearms operative. He was indicted but says he was given

163

an incorrect trial date. When he didn't show in March 1991, he was declared a fugitive. Convinced he was the object of "trickery," Weaver barricaded the clan inside the ramshackle compound. In an ominous letter, Vicki told prosecutors Weaver would not obey a government he deemed his enemy. The U.S. attorney took it as a threat and summoned marshals to bring Weaver in. They set up surveillance and waited—for 16 months.

Mother's Blood. Everything changed on August 21, 1992. Degan and two other agents were scouting for a new lookout when the family dog chased them down the mountain. They were followed by Weaver, Sam and family friend Harris, all armed. What happened next is the crux of the case: who fired first, igniting the bloody standoff? Whatever the spark, Degan was dead, a bullet piercing his lung; Sam was killed by a shot in the back. The next day, Weaver and Harris were wounded and Vicki slain by an FBI sniper; she was found clutching baby Elisheba, showered in her mother's blood. Though only Harris, Weaver and his three daughters remained, the government brought in an arsenal—helicopters, armored personnel carriers, 200 agents. A week later, Weaver surrendered.

But the furor endured, in part because of the FBI's handling of evidence. Bullets recovered from the shoot-out were lost. Transcripts from FBI interviews, including the sniper's account of Vicki's death, were received by the defense after the agent testified, prompting Lodge to sanction the prosecution for "inexcusable and extremely poor judgement" and force it to apologize.

Weaver's is one of four cases in the past decade in which extremists and Feds clashed to disastrous end; Waco is the most recent. As it inches toward trial, the painful questions of Ruby Ridge will resonate. Again and again, the question is whether maximum force is being used with minimum judgement.

Law Enforcement Organizations, Police, and Violence

15

VIOLENCE AND THE POLICE—REID

Historically, police have been viewed as necessary in establishing law and order, often by applying justice on the spot. Although violence between police and citizens was reported earlier, the violence and unrest that occurred in the 1960s led to demands for larger and better trained police forces. During that decade predominantly white police and minority citizens clashed in hot, crowded cities. Many student protesters found themselves in conflict with the police, and the police experienced disillusionment with a system that they did not believe protected their interests. They, too, became more active. Police unions were established. They were viewed by many as representing hostility by the police.

In short, the decade of the 1960s brought open violence between police and citizens, and the 1970s brought more cases of police violence and corruption. Meanwhile, crime rates began to rise and citizens demanded greater police protection. Demands for a more professionalized police force were heard, but the allegations of police misconduct were predominant. The 1991 incident of alleged police brutality in Los Angeles, described in Exhibit 1, focused national attention once again on the use of excessive violence by police.

POLICE VIOLENCE

In a classic and frequently cited article on police brutality published in 1968, Albert J. Reiss, Jr., began his discussion with a 1903 quotation by a former police commissioner of New York City:

> For 3 years, there has been through the courts and the streets a dreary procession of citizens with broken heads and bruised bodies against few of whom was violence needed to affect an arrest. Many of them had done nothing to deserve an arrest. In a majority of such cases, no complaint was made. If the victim complains, his charge is generally dismissed. The police are practically above the law.[1]

Police Actions in the 1990s: Focus on Los Angeles

The alleged brutality of white police officers against a black suspect might have gone unnoticed, but an eyewitness taped the actions of 3 March 1991. National television brought the details of a police beating into our homes as we saw Rodney King, a twenty-five-year-old black suspect, fired on by a white police officer carrying a 50,000-volt Taser stun gun. Three other officers kicked and beat the suspect on his head, neck, legs, and kidneys with their nightsticks. King suffered multiple skull fractures, a broken ankle, crushed cheekbone, internal injuries, severe bruises, and some brain damage.

The incident prompted investigations by the FBI, the Los Angeles County District Attorney's office, and the Internal Affairs Division of the Los Angeles Police Department. Mayor Tom Bradley, a former police officer, after calling for a thorough investigation, said "This is something we cannot and will not tolerate. I am as shocked and outraged as anyone."[2] President Bush said he was "sickened" by the beating, referred to those "shocking videotapes and transcripts," and ordered then-Attorney General Dick Thornburgh to begin a nationwide review of police brutality. A few days later, Thornburgh announced that a review would be made of every police brutality case over the past six years. Bush ordered that any violations of federal law involved in this case be prosecuted.[3]

Allegations of racial bias discrimination within the Los Angeles Police Department and against minority citizens surfaced after the King incident occurred. Throughout the nation police reexamined their departmental policies while citizens called for improved police-minority relations. Despite pressure to resign immediately, Police Chief Daryl F. Gates retained his office until his retirement in the early summer of 1992, resulting in severe criticism from inside and outside the police department.

All four officers in the King incident were charged with assault with a deadly weapon and excessive force by an officer under cover of authority; two were charged with filing a false police report, and one was charged with being an accessory after the fact. In the spring of 1992, the officers were tried by a jury in Simi Valley, California, a predominantly white community to which the trial had been moved when defense attorneys argued successfully that their clients could not get a fair trial in Los Angeles. All of the officers were acquitted of the assault and secondary charges, but the jury could not reach a verdict on the excessive force charge against one officer. The judge declared a mistrial on that charge. The prosecutor announced plans to retry the officer, and the judge ruled that the trial would be held in Los Angeles.

The reaction in Los Angeles was violent. The resulting rioting and looting led to the deaths of sixty persons, although later reports indicated that approximately fifteen of those deaths were not related to the rioting. Still, it was the "most deadly U.S. disturbance in the twentieth century." In the weeks following the rioting, authorities reduced their estimates of fires from more than 5,000 to 623 and their estimates of arrests from over 19,000 to about one-half of that number.[4] Approximately $1 billion in property damage occurred in the Los Angeles area, while less severe riots caused property damage in other cities, too.

Local and national leaders called for peaceful resolution of the problems, with President Bush addressing the nation on prime-time television with his concerns. While the media featured experts who discussed the causes and the solutions to this most deadly of all riots to occur in a single U.S. city in decades, volunteers began assisting residents in rebuilding their homes and businesses.

Until recently little research had been conducted on police brutality. During the summer of 1966, Reiss conducted a study of the interactions of police with citizens in Boston, Chicago, and Washington, D.C. In discussing the results of that study, Reiss pointed out the difficulty of defining police brutality, but he listed six of the most common complaints of citizens:

1. The use of profane and abusive language

2. Commands to move on or get home

3. Stopping and questioning people on the street or searching them and their cars

4. Threats to use force if not obeyed.

5. Prodding with a nightstick or approaching with a pistol

6. The actual use of physical force or violence itself[5]

This list covers a wide range of behavior, not all of which would be considered brutality by everyone. Reiss emphasizes the importance to the citizen of the status degradation aspect of police behavior, "the judgement that they have not been treated with the full rights and dignity among citizens in a democratic society."[6] Police brutality may cause serious injury or even death, and the use of deadly force by the police is the root of most controversy surrounding police behavior.

POLICE USE OF DEADLY FORCE: THE FLEEING FELON RULE

The use of **deadly force** by police has been defined as "such force as under normal circumstances poses a high risk of death or serious injury to its human target, regardless of whether or not death, serious injury or any harm may actually result."[7] Police officers may use deadly force under some circumstances. If they use deadly force improperly, the officers may be criminally liable and both the officers and the police department may be liable to the injured person (or, in the event of death, to the family of the deceased) in a civil suit. Most rules for the use of deadly force come from federal statutes. Most of the suits are concerned with police use of deadly force to arrest fleeing suspects who apparently were engaging in nonviolent felonies. Violent felonies are felonies, such as armed robbery, that create a risk of bodily harm or death. Most unarmed burglars, however, do not represent a substantial risk of serious bodily harm or death to a police officer if they are not apprehended immediately.

Shooting any fleeing felon was permitted historically. Because all felonies were punishable by death, it was assumed that any felon would resist arrest by all possible means. The rule permitting officers to shoot *fleeing felons* developed during a time when apprehending criminals was more difficult. Police did not have weapons that could be used for shooting at a long distance, nor did they have communication techniques that would enable them to notify other jurisdictions quickly that a suspect had escaped arrest. Therefore, it was possible for fleeing felons to escape if not immediately apprehended and begin a new life in another community without fear of detection by the local police.[8]

As more efficient weapons were developed, it became easier for police to apprehend felons, and many did so by use of deadly force, even though the fleeing felons were not dangerous. Such actions were not necessary to protect the officer and others, nor were they necessary to apprehend felons. Despite these developments, however, many states codified the common-law rule that permitted police officers to use deadly force in apprehending fleeing felons. This practice was condemned by many commentators and scholars, but the practice was not prohibited by most courts before 1985.

On 27 March 1985, the U.S. Supreme Court ruled that Tennessee's fleeing felon statute was unconstitutional under the facts of the case. *Tennessee v. Garner* involved an unarmed boy who was killed by a police officer as the youth fled from an unoccupied house. The officer could see that the fleeing felon was a youth and apparently unarmed. But the officer argued that he knew that if the youth got over the fence, he could escape; so he fired at him. The Tennessee statute allowed the officer to shoot a suspect if it appeared to be necessary to prevent the escape of a felon.[9]

In *Garner*, the Court emphasized that the use of deadly force by police officers must be reasonable to be lawful. It is reasonable in the following circumstances:

1. To prevent an escape when the suspect has threatened the officer with a weapon.

2. When there is a threat of death or serious physical injury to the officer or others.

3. If there is probable cause to believe that the person has committed a crime involving the infliction or threatened infliction of serious physical harm and, where practical, some warning has been given by the officer.

The Tennessee statute that permitted an officer to shoot a fleeing felon may be constitutional in some instances. But used against a young, slight, and unarmed youth who apparently had been involved in a burglary, deadly force was unreasonable and therefore unlawful...

Police use of deadly force is necessary, but when used improperly, it violates he rights of others and may lead to serious injuries or death as well as a loss of confidence in the police. In addition, it may escalate into violence against police. How much abuse occurs is unknown, although some recent research indicates that abuse is relatively rare.[10] That is not the perception of many people, especially minorities, as illustrated by the reaction to the acquittal of the police officers who beat Rodney King. (see Exhibit 1). One problem is that guidance in the use of deadly force is difficult, although there is slowly-accumulating knowledge on what works and what is appropriate. Many police officers and others stated that the beating of Rodney King involved excessive force. The first jury found otherwise.

VIOLENCE AGAINST THE POLICE

In 1990, sixty-five law enforcement officers were killed feloniously in the line of duty. This was the lowest number for one year since the FBI began collecting such data in the 1960s.[11] Research indicates that the killing of police officers in New York City, in most cases, is a functional act done to avoid arrest.[12] Not all police officers are convinced, and some place the cause in the structure of society. "It's a more violent society, and police are its victims as much as everyone else."[13]

The tension between a predominantly white police force and a large minority population in high-crime areas may be a factor in violence against police as well as police violence against others. In January 1988, John Glenn Chase, a Dallas police officer, was killed in a downtown parking lot while some bystanders urged a black, mentally ill, homeless man to kill the officer who was pleading for his life. Hundreds of Dallas police officers flew to Des Moines, Iowa, for the slain officer's funeral, also attended by numerous police and citizens in that city.

Chase's death and the circumstances under which it occurred became a "major issue in this city—one of race." White police chief Billy Prince accused black city council members of spreading malicious rumors about the police department and referred to these critics as "little more than freeze-dried experts." Blacks called for Prince's resignation, which was tendered, although Prince and others claimed he was not forced to resign.[14]

The reactions of Dallas citizens, many of whom demonstrated strong support for the police department, are not unusual. Killings of police officers in the line of duty elicit strong public reaction. It is common after each of these crimes to hear demands for more police, banning of hand guns, reinstituting capital punishment (where it does not exist, for example, in New

York State), incarcerating violent offenders in special prisons, imposing stiffer sentences, and abolishing parole for violent offenders.

The number of police officers killed by citizens does not tell the complete story. Police encounter growing hostility from a public that, in many cases, results in verbal abuse and physical attacks short of murder. Although it is debatable which comes first and which causes which, there are indications that violence against police officers is accompanied by violence by police officers. The Police Foundation, in a 1977 study, focused on police use of deadly force, but the authors indicated that they were "acutely aware of the interrelationship between acts committed *by* the police and acts committed *against* them."[15]

EFFECTS OF UNREASONABLE FORCE BY POLICE AND CITIZENS

The effects of unreasonable force, especially force that causes death, go beyond the immediate victims and their families. One reaction to police use of excessive force is the feeling by minorities that the police are out to get them. Approximately 50 percent of the persons killed by police officers are black. Studies indicate, however, that this high percentage for blacks might not necessarily represent a policy of discrimination against minorities, although some investigators believe there is evidence that "police have one trigger finger for blacks and another for whites."[16]

Presidential commissions studying urban riots have noted the effect of police brutality on such incidents. When the public perceives an act by a police officer to be unfair, unreasonable, unnecessary, or harassing, especially when minorities are the victims, that perception may provide the impetus for urban riots.[17] This is not to suggest that police actions *cause* the riots. Police have no control over the root causes of civil disturbances, such as unemployment, lack of educational opportunities, poor housing, and inadequate health care facilities; but police may escalate or reduce violent confrontations by the policies they adopt.

The U.S. Commission on Civil Rights, in its report issued after field investigations and public hearings in Philadelphia and Houston, along with the results of a national conference of police experts and community officials, emphasized the importance of hiring more racial minorities and upgrading their positions on police forces. The commission cited the study of the National Minority Advisory Council on Criminal Justice:

> Central to the problem of brutality is the under representation of minorities as police officers...
> It has been shown that the presence of minority police officers has a positive effect on police-
> community relations.[18]

This report of the Commission on Civil Rights emphasized the far-reaching effect of police brutality. In Miami, for example, after a white police officer was acquitted in the killing of a black citizen he had pursued in a high-speed chase for a traffic violation, rioting began in the black community, resulting in destruction, violence and the death of eighteen people. Earlier commissions underscored police violence as a catalyst in urban rioting in the 1960s.[19]

Violence against police has serious repercussions too. Officers who survive may have physical injuries or psychological problems that preclude further work as police officers. Families and friends of those who are killed are victims of such violence as well. One study indicated the following reactions of survivors of police who are killed in the line of duty:

— Having difficulty concentrating and making decisions, feeling confused, having one's mind go blank

— Feeling hostile

— Feeling different from others, feeling alone, being uncomfortable in social situations

— Fearing people, places, and things, and being anxious of one's ability to survive

— Reexperiencing the traumatic incident through flashbacks, dreams, or thoughts

— Feeling emotionally numb, having less interest in previously enjoyed activities, or being unable to return to prior employment

— Having less ability to express positive and negative emotions

— Having difficulty falling asleep or remaining asleep

— Feeling guilty about the way one acted toward the deceased or as if one could have prevented the death.[20]

[1]Albert J. Reiss, Jr., "Police Brutality," *Transaction Magazine* 5 (1968), reprinted in *Police Behavior: A Sociological Perspective*, ed. Richard J. Lundman (New York: Oxford University Press, 1980), pp. 274-75.

[2]"Tape of Beating by Police Revives Charges of Racism," *New York Times* (7 March 1991), p. 10.

[3]"President Assails Beating by Police," *New York Times* (22 March 1991), p. 13.

[4]"One-Fourth of L.A. Riot Deaths Found Unrelated to Violence," *St. Petersburg Times* (2 June 1992), p. 4.

[5]*Ibid.* p. 276. See also Albert J. Reiss, Jr. , *The Police and the Public* (New York: Ballantine, 1973).

[6]Reiss, "Police Brutality," p. 276.

[7]Catherine H. Milton et al., *Police Use of Deadly Force* (Washington, D.C.; Police Foundation, 1977), p. 41.

[8]Lawrence W. Sherman, "Execution Without Trial: Police Homicide and the Constitution," *Vanderbilt Law Review* 33 (January 1980); pp. 74-75.

[9]Tennessee v. Garner, 471 U.S. 1 (1985).

[10]See, for example, David H. Bayle and James Garofalo, "The Management of Violence by Police Patrol Officers," *Criminology* 27 (February 1989); pp. 1-25.

[11]*Uniform Crime Reports*, 1990, p. 237. For an analysis of the killing of police, see S.G. Chapman, *Cops, Killers and Staying Alive—The Murder of Police Officers in America* (Springfield, Ill; Charles C. Thomas, 1986).

[12]Mona Margarita, "Killing the Police: Myths and Motives," *The Annals of the American Academy of Political and Social Science* 452 (November 1980); p. 63.

[13]"When Police Officers Use Deadly Force," *U.S. News & World Report* (10 January 1983), p. 58.

[14]"Police Death Divides Dallas," *Tulsa World* (28 January 1988), p. 9.

[15]Milton et al., *Police Use of Deadly Force*, p. 3.

[16]Arnold Binder and Peter Scharf, "Deadly Force in Law Enforcement," *Crime & Delinquency* 28 (January 1982) 1, 23. See also Frank Horvath, "The Police Use of Deadly Force: A Description of Selected Characteristics of Intrastate Incidents," *Journal of Police Science and Administration* 15 (September 1987): 226-38. For an analysis of police shootings in Philadelphia and New York, see James J. Fyfe, "Police Shooting: Environment and License," in *Con-*

troversial Issues in Crime and Justice, ed. Joseph E. Scott and Travis Hirschi (Beverly Hills, Calif.; Sage Publications, 1988), pp. 79-94.

[17]See Milton et al., *Police Use of Deadly Force,* pp. 3-4, for a discussion of such findings.

[18]National Minority Advisory Council on Criminal Justice, *The Inequality of Justice: A Report on Crime and the Administration of Justice in the Minority Community* (October 1980), pp. 15-16, as quoted in Commission on Civil Rights, *Who Is Guarding the Guardians?* p. 2.

[19]Commission on Civil Rights, *Who Is Guarding the Guardians?* p. vi.

[20]Frances A. Stillman, *Line-of-Duty Deaths: Survivor and Departmental Responses,* National Institute of Justice (Washington, D.C.; U.S. Department of Justice, January 1987), pp. 2, 3.

16

THE CONTROL OF POLICING—REID

Although only a minority of police officers may be guilty of misconduct, any misconduct should be subject to discipline; more important, policies and programs should be developed to avoid as much misconduct as possible. Police misconduct may be controlled from within the department or by outside agencies.

REGULATION BY POLICE DEPARTMENTS

The efficient operation of any department requires internal discipline of employees; in the case of police departments, it is important that the public's image of internal operations be positive. It is essential, said the Commission on Civil Rights, that police departments have an effective system of internal discipline that will "include clear definition of proper conduct, a reliable mechanism for detecting misconduct, and appropriate sanctions, consistently imposed, when misconduct has been proven." Policies must be articulated clearly.[1]

Police departments should enforce their written policies actively and fairly. If police believe that they will not be reprimanded for violating the policy, the policy may be ineffective in curbing abuse of discretion. The Commission on Civil Rights recommended that "every police department should have a clearly defined system for the receipt, processing, and investigation of civilian complaints." Once a violation of policy is found, "discipline imposed should be fair, swift, and consistent with departmental practices and procedures."[2] Police departments should take measures to identify violence-prone officers in an attempt to avert problems.

REGULATION BY COURTS: THE EXCLUSIONARY RULE

Courts have attempted to regulate police behavior, too. If police seize evidence illegally or secure confessions improperly, the evidence may be excluded from trial. This procedure is the result of the U.S. Supreme Court's **exclusionary rule**. In 1914 the Supreme Court held that the Fourth Amendment (which prohibits unreasonable searches and seizures) would have no meaning unless the courts prohibited the use of illegally seized evidence. Consequently, when the police violate that provision, the evidence they seize may not be used in *federal* cases. In 1961 the Court held that the exclusionary rule applies also to the states.

The exclusionary rule is controversial, mainly because it applies after the fact. When the illegally seized evidence is excluded from the trial, we know who the suspect is and, in many cases, believe the guilt is obvious. Thus, when the judge rules that the gun allegedly used in a murder cannot be used against a suspect because the evidence was obtained illegally by the police, and the suspect goes free because we do not have enough legal evidence for a conviction, there is a strong pubic reaction of disbelief and outrage.

Arguments in favor of the exclusionary rule

The exclusionary rule serves a symbolic purpose. If police violate individual rights to obtain evidence to convict alleged criminals, the government, in a sense, is supporting crime. When this occurs, the government becomes a lawbreaker, and "it breeds contempt for law, it invites. . . anarchy."[3]

The symbolic purpose is important, but the second reason for the exclusionary rule is a practical one: it is assumed that the rule prevents police from engaging in illegal searches and seizures. According to the Supreme Court, the exclusionary rule "compels respect for the constitution guarantee in the only effectively available way—by removing the incentive to disregard it."[4]

It is difficult to know whether that statement is true because most illegal searches that may be conducted to harass or punish take place in secret and may not be reported. Research on the issue reports inconclusive evidence. There is evidence, however, that the rule has lead some police departments to increase the quantity and quality of police training, thus educating officers in what they may and may not do regarding search and seizure.[5]

Arguments for abolishing the exclusionary rule

In recent years the exclusionary rule has come under severe attack, with many people calling for its abolition or at least its modification. Most of their arguments are the reverse of the arguments in favor. First is the argument of the symbolism of abolition, based on the view that, when people see guilty persons going free as a result of a technicality, they lose respect for law and order, and the entire criminal justice system is weakened. The public's perception of letting guilty people go free is crucial.

Second, the abolitionists contend that the exclusionary rule should be eliminated because it results in the release of guilty people. It makes no difference how many: one is too many, argue the abolitionists. Third, the possibility of having evidence excluded from a trial because it was not seized properly leads defendants to file numerous motions to suppress evidence, which consumes a lot of court time and contributes to the courts' congestion. In criminal cases, objections to search and seizure are the issues raised most frequently.

Exceptions to the exclusionary rule

Several exceptions to the exclusionary rule have been suggested; some have been adopted. Under the good faith exception, illegally obtained evidence is not excluded from trial if it can be shown that police secured the evidence in good faith; that is, they reasonably believed that they were acting in accordance with the law. The good faith exception has been rejected by some state legislatures and adopted by others. It is opposed by the American Bar Association and the American Civil Liberties Union. In *Massachusetts* v. *Sheppard*, the Supreme Court adopted the good faith exception, holding that when police conduct a search in good faith, even though the technical search warrant is defective, the seized evidence should not be excluded from the trial.

The Court has interpreted the Constitution to permit the use of evidence seized by officers who had a warrant to search one apartment but searched the wrong apartment and found illegal drugs. In *Maryland* v. *Garrison*, the Court reasoned that because the search was in good faith and excluding its use in such cases would not deter police, who thought they were searching an apartment included in the warrant, nothing positive would be gained by applying the exclusionary rule.

The Supreme Court has ruled that evidence secured by police who conducted a warrantless search through garbage left for collection outside an individual's home need not be suppressed under the exclusionary rule. According to the Court, the individuals who left the garbage outside their dwelling did not have a reasonable expectation that such garbage would not be viewed by others.

> It is common knowledge that plastic garbage bags left on or at the side of a public street are readily accessible to animals, children, scavengers, snoops, and other members of the public.[6]

A variation of the good faith exception to the exclusionary rule occurred in November 1988, when the Court ruled that a defendant's constitutional rights are not violated when police officers lose or destroy evidence that might have been used to establish the defendant's innocence, provided the officers' actions were made in good faith. The case, *Arizona* v. *Youngblood*, involved an Arizona case in which Larry Youngblood was convicted of the kidnapping, molestation, and sexual assault of a ten-year-old boy.

The police in *Youngblood* had failed to refrigerate the victim's semen-stained clothing or to make tests capable of showing whether the semen came from Youngblood. Results of such tests might have shown that Youngblood was not the offender. Justice Rehnquist, writing for the majority, argued that omission can "at worst be described as negligent."[7]

Since the Supreme Court adopted the good faith exception to the exclusionary rule, some state courts have held that it does not apply under their state constitutions, and thus all illegally seized evidence must be excluded at trial, regardless of the motivation of the officer who seized the evidence. Because this involves enlarging, not reducing, a Supreme Court interpretation of the federal constitution, as it decreases the amount of evidence that can be used against a defendant, such interpretations are permissible.

The Supreme Court has approved the inevitable discovery rule exception to the exclusionary rule. According to this rule, evidence that police seize illegally will be admitted at trial if it can be shown that eventually the evidence would have been discovered by legal methods. Writing for the Court in *Nix* v. *Williams*, Chief Justice Warren E. Burger said, "Exclusion of physical evidence that would inevitably have been discovered adds nothing to either the integrity or fairness of a criminal trial."[8]

The Court has continued to relax the exclusionary rule, holding in 1990 that a state may use as evidence a statement made by the defendant outside of his home even though that statement was taken after an arrest made in the home in violation of a previous case, which was decided to protect the "physical integrity of the home, not to grant criminal suspects protection for statements made outside their premises where the police have probable cause to make an arrest."

In March 1991 a sharply divided Supreme Court demonstrated the impact of its recently appointed associate justice, David Souter, who joined the majority 5-4 decision that permits the use of coerced confessions in some circumstances. In 1967 the court had articulated the *harmless error rule*, which holds that if a confession is coerced, it must be excluded at trial. In *Arizona* v. *Fulminante* the Court held that the constitution does not require the automatic exclusion of the coerced confession. Rather, it is to be considered like any other trial error; it is to be analyzed under the circumstances and the trial court is to make a decision regarding whether it was a harmless error beyond a reasonable doubt. If so, it must be excluded; if not, it may be used against the suspect.

This decision confirmed what many Supreme Court watchers had expected: Justice Souter's elevation to the high court would tip the balance toward the conservatives and away from defendant's rights. As a University of Chicago law professor said, "They've finally got enough votes." With the retirement of liberal Justice Thurgood Marshall at the end of the 1990-1991 term and the appointment of Clarence Thomas, this prediction could be even more accurate.

COMMUNITY RELATIONS

Another method of controlling police activities is through community involvement and improved police-community relationships. It is vital that relationships between police and the community be improved. Already we have seen that police are not in a position to apprehend most criminals without the support of citizens. The U.S. Commission on Civil Rights emphasized that the men and women who are authorized to make arrests in this country depend to a great extent on the cooperation of the public. "Perhaps the most valuable asset these officers can possess is credibility with the communities they serve."[9]

Good police-community relationships take on an even greater importance as budgetary restraints force reductions in police forces, making police even more dependent on citizen assistance in crime control. The importance of these contacts is emphasized by studies indicating that citizens who have positive images of the police are more likely to report crimes than those who have negative images. Those most likely to have negative images of the police are members of the lower class, blacks, and other nonwhites—persons who feel a general alienation from the political process and those who perceive an increase in crime in their neighborhoods.

One problem with these studies, however, is that they tend to be descriptive and based on socioeconomic, racial, or ethnic factors. It has been argued that, in studying police-community relationships, attention should be given to such factors as "the frequency and nature of past contacts with police officers, residential history, and arrest records." After conducting that type of study, investigators found evidence to refute the argument that certain segments of the population will have negative images of police, not matter how the police behave.

> Socioeconomic factors such as race, age, and income appear to have little direct effect on attitudes toward police. The primary factor determining general satisfaction with police and police service seems to be actual personal contact with specific police officers in a positive context.[10]

The findings of this study minimized the effect of efforts by the police to educate the community, finding instead that what really counts is contact with the police in an *official* capacity.

One the whole, police do not receive extremely high marks for their work, but contrary to what might be expected, negative reactions to the police are not necessarily related to police performance of the job. For example, *not* giving a ticket when one should have been given may be seen as a negative, not positive. In one study, negative reactions to the police resulted mainly from the way police behaved when they took action. Regulatory actions of police were seen as positive when they

> resulted from a prompt response, being informative about the reasons for the police actions, and for being nice, polite, and helpful (e.g., calling an ambulance or aiding the citizen to cope with consequences of the situation). . . In no case did the policeman have to engage in dangerous or extraordinary feats to be positively evaluated; he simply had to respond in a sincere and personal way to the individual.[11]

A study of community-oriented policing (COP) by several investigators who observed police work in Newark, Detroit, Denver, Houston, Oakland, and Santa Ana, indicates that COP has been effective in reducing crime as illustrated by the 25 percent reduction in Newark, New Jersey.[12] Similar results were found by Albert J. Reiss, Jr., in his study of policing in Oakland, California.[13]

COP may take many forms, such as foot, motorcycle, or horse patrol, in which the officers have a chance to learn firsthand the problems of the community and community citizens have an opportunity to know their police. Crime prevention programs are important, too. Police educate the community about various approaches to crime prevention. Community organization activities in which police and the community work together to identify community problems are helpful as well. Herman Goldstein, who has written extensively on numerous criminal justice issues, concludes that full development of the overall concept of community policing, including a "concern with the substance of policing as well as its form," could "provide the integrated strategy for improving the quality of policing."[14]

CIVILIAN REVIEW BOARDS

Members of the community may be involved in improving police-community relationships by means of civilian review boards that review citizen complaints against police officers. These boards became popular after the civil disturbances of the 1960s and 1970s, primarily in areas in which minorities believed that police were discriminating against them. They were opposed bitterly by some police, and most lasted only a short time or were not very powerful.

The Civil Rights Commission emphasized that the civilian review boards created to hear complaints against police have not always been successful. "Their basic flaws were that they were advisory only, having no power to decide cases or impose punishment, and that they lacked sufficient staffs and resources." The commission recommended that, although the primary responsibility for disciplining police rests with police departments, it is imperative that the disciplinary process "be subject to some outside review to ensure . . . that a citizen not agreeing with the department's disposition of a complaint has an avenue of redress to pursue."[15]

Some civilian groups are not merely advisory, however, and have proven quite effective. For example, an out-of-court settlement was reached in Los Angeles, giving the Los Angeles Police Commission (composed of civilians) full authority to authorize future undercover investigations by the police (an authority that previously was held by the chief of police). Under the terms of the settlement, the city was required to pay $900,000 to 143 plaintiffs who claimed that their civil rights were violated by the police, who spied on legal, political, and civil activities. The city had to pay the fees of the American Civil Liberties Union attorneys who represented the plaintiffs. Guidelines were created and accepted; the attorneys reported that they had numerous requests from other police departments and civil liberties groups for copies of those guidelines.

TORT ACTIONS

Torts are the area of law referring to civil wrongs as opposed to criminal wrongs. A tort action is a wrongful act—other than a mere violation of contract—which entitles the victim to compensation, usually determined in a civil suit. Civil suits may be brought in some cases that involve crimes as well as torts. The use of civil suits to bring actions against police (or other authorities) who violate civil rights of citizens is thought to be an effective deterrent for such illegal actions. Even if they do not deter other violations, tort actions, if successful, permit victims of abuse (or their families when the victims die) to recover monetary damages for physical injuries (or death) and also for emotional and psychological damages.

Tort actions are brought under the Civil Rights Act and commonly called *1983 actions*, after the section of the U.S. Code in which the provision for such action is codified. Section 1983 actions may be brought by persons injured as a result of police negligence, as, for example, in high-speed chases that result in injuries (or death) to bystanders. In 1992, Los Angeles Police Chief Daryl F. Gates and nine officers were ordered to pay $44,000 to the families of three robbers slain by the officers and a surviving suspect shot in a fast-food restaurant two years previously. The suit alleged that the officers constituted a "death squad" that shot rather than arrested the suspects. Gates said he would ask the city to appeal the award.

CHAPTER 16—ENDNOTES

[1]Commission on Civil Rights, *Who Is Guarding the Guardians?* p. 35.

[2]*Ibid.*, pp. 157, 159; see also pp. 58-79.

[3]Olmstead v. United States, 277 U.S. 438, 485 (1928), Justice Brandeis, dissenting.

[4]Elkins v. United States, 364 U.S. 206, 217 (1960).

[5]See Stephen H. Sachs, "The Exclusionary Rule: A Prosecutor's Defense," *Criminal Justice Ethics* 1 (Summer-Fall 1982). This journal contains a symposium on the pros and cons of the exclusionary rule and is an excellent source on the topic.

[6]California v. Greenwood, 486 U.S. 35 (1988).

[7]Arizona v. Youngblood, 488 U.S. 51 (1988), *reh'g. denied*, 488 U.S. 1051 (1989), *remanded*, 790 P. 2d 759 (Ariz. App. 1989).

[8]Nix v. Williams, 467 U.S. 431 (1984), *remanded*, 751 F.2d 956 (1985), *cert. denied*, 471 U.S. 1138 (1985).

[9]Commission on Civil Rights, *Who is Guarding the Guardians?* p. 2.

[10]Richard Scaglion and Richard G. Condon, "Determinants of Attitudes Toward City Police," *Criminology* 17 (February 1980): p. 493

[11]Theodore Groves et al., "An Approach to Problems in Police-Community Relations," *Journal of Community Psychology* (October 1980): pp. 359, 360.

[12]See Jerome H. Skolnick and David H. Bayley, *The New Blue Line: Police Innovation in Six American Cities* (New York; Free Press, 1986).

[13]Albert J. Reiss, Jr., *Policing a City's Central District: The Oakland Story* (Washington, D. C.; National Institute of Justice, 1985).

[14]Herman Goldstein, "Toward Community-Oriented Policing: Potential, Basic Requirements, and Threshold Questions," *Crime & Delinquency* 33 (January 1987); p. 28.

[15]Commission on Civil Rights, *Who is Guarding the Guardians?* p. 163.

PART V

Communities, Violence & Conflict

17

COMMUNITIES, VIOLENCE AND CONFLICT—
REID

Part V of this book deals with the violence and conflict that stem from racial and ethnic issues as well as from various macrosocial political issues. Included here are important chapters on *collective violence* (riots and civil disorders) and *terrorist violence* (incidents which try to influence how a community or society should govern itself).

COMMUNITIES

Before getting into the substance of the chapters, it is important to understand the social units or aggregates known as communities. Communities are more than just large numbers of people connected by sewer lines. Communities are generally comprised of countless individuals, groups and organizations; and they share many of the characteristics of organizations: for example, written rules, formal roles and extensive division of labor. Communities are quite different from other social units such as groups and organizations, though, in that they are localized populations, rooted in territory.

Communities provide for most of their member's daily needs. These needs range from simple food and shelter to government, education, and protection from deviants, especially criminals. Slogans and bumper stickers have proclaimed—even to this day—the importance of meeting local people's needs: "Keep your local police/schools local!" There is a strong feeling in many communities that no one should interfere with how the community chooses to police itself or how it educates and socializes its young.

Historically, members of communities tend to be alike or homogeneous in terms of race, ethnicity, language, and culture. In the United States, there are African-American communities, Polish-American communities and Chinese-American communities, to name but a few.

In the early days, communities were relatively isolated from one another in America and rarely interacted with other communities. When they did interact, it was usually economically, i.e., for needed goods and services (furs and black-smithing, say). To get these, they traded or sold what they specialized in (canoes, weaving) that other communities did not have.

Thus, despite some economic dependence on one other, communities started out being fairly autonomous—culturally and politically. This meant that communities often had goals, values, and practices different from other communities. The threat of conflict with one another, then, was always present. This conflict was expressed in all kinds of nonviolent and violent ways. Among the violent manifestations were lynchings, pogroms, riots and other disturbances.

However, despite innumerable nonviolent and violent conflicts, population growth, intermarriage, assimilation, and a host of other factors caused communities to lose their distinctness and homogeneity. In addition, economic commerce among communities increased; and governments of all sorts (county, state and federal) started to expand their influence. In a blur of cause and effect, communities experienced continuing conflict and assimilation, but finally became less and less autonomous and self-determining.

Two of the most important community distinctions—from the point of view of violent conflict—are race and ethnicity. What exactly is meant by the terms race and ethnicity? Acknowledging that there is much current debate about these terms and especially their academic origins, the following working definitions are suggested:

An *ethnic community* is one whose members are part of a coherent culture or subculture; that is, members "share an accent, style of dress, food habits, family arrangement, or any other cultural cluster that distinguishes them.[1] (Culture is usually thought of as all the ideas, customs, traditions, and artifacts generated by a people that can be historically transmitted from person to person.)[2]

A *racial community* is one whose members through biological descent share distinctive common hereditary characteristics: that is to say, on the average, they differ in some genetic pattern that produces observable differences vis-a-vis other communities.[3*]

Let us turn our attention now to the two chapters in this part of the book.They describe how violent conflict among communities has continued over recent decades in the U.S. and how terroristic violence has been used to influence communities.

Communal violence

After noting the spectacularly destructive nature of racial and ethnic violence, the communal violence chapter sets forth definitions for such phenomena as riots, civil disorders, and mob behavior. The chapter continues with a reminder that America is not alone in its worrisome ethnic and racial conflict. Though America ranks very high among societies with respect to chronic communal violence, this is partly because America has been a pioneer from the start regarding diversity and multiculturalism. Many recently-diversified nations which were rel-

---

*It is not always clear whether a given collectivity is an ethnic or racial community. For example, the Hispanic collectivity in America generally includes Mexican Americans, Cuban Americans, Mainland-Puerto Ricans, Central and South Americans, and a residual subcategory of Other Hispanics.[4] "Hispanic" thus may include racial as well as ethnic aggregates, and so the category includes such diverse people as: Mexican immigrants, Cuba immigrants, Spanish-speaking Native Americans, South Americans who are mulatto or black, and people who trace their origins to Spain. Because of the complexity that arises from these issues of racial ancestry and national origin, some people want the U.S. Census to have a category called "Mixed."

atively untroubled by communal violence in the past are finding it is one of the growing pains of becoming more multiracial and multiethnic.

The author of the chapter presents the current demographic percentage breakdown of racial and ethnic communities in America. (See Chapter 18 of the Study Guide for a fascinating exercise using the projected breakdown for the year 2050.) The author says it is not surprising that a good deal of America's current racial and ethnic angst relates to black-white conflict because the black and white communities constitute the two largest communities in the percent breakdown presented.[†] However, it is worth adding that America experiences a lot of other communal conflict besides violent black-white, majority-minority conflict. Here are just a few examples of several of the different generic types of communal conflict in the U.S.:

— *majority-minority conflict*
There is a long history in the U.S. of *non*violent as well as *violent* conflict between blacks and whites.

— *majority-majority conflict*
There has been substantial *violent* as well as *non*violent conflict within the white majority, e.g., recently established Italian-American, Irish-American, etc. communities often clashed with longer-established Euro-American communities.

— *minority-minority conflict*
There has been *violent* minority-minority conflict, where the white community has not really been a party to the trouble (e.g., the recent Black-Latino conflict in the city of Compton, California and the Black-Korean violence during the post Rodney King verdict riots).
There has been a lot of *non*violent minority-minority conflict likewise, as the, following sampling of cases indicates:

— ethnic conflict among Southeast Asians (e.g., Vietnamese vs. Laotians)

— Japanese-Korean tensions in Culver City and Monterey Park in L.A. county

— Salvadoran-Guatemalan problems in Los Angeles

— Latino-Black troubles and violence in America's prisons

— chronic conflict and tension between Hispanics identifying as northerners (Nortenos) and southerners (Surrenos)

— Asian-Black problems in San Francisco and Orange County California schools

---

†Probably the most accurate and *formal* terms for racial and ethnic communities in the U.S. are Native-American, African-American, Asian-American, Hispanic-American and European-American.[5] However, using these terms repeatedly in a discussion of communal conflict can get wordy and unwieldy. As an example, consider this sentence: "*Eventually, European-American versus Native-American conflict gave way symbolically to European-American versus Asian-American trouble and European-American versus African-American conflict.*" Therefore, the terms black, white, etc.—which are the *informal*, everyday terms—will be generally used here. No disrespect is intended, and reader indulgence and forbearance are appreciated.

Survey of consequences

The author of Chapter 18 moves on to a general survey of violence among ethnic and racial communities in recent times in U.S. history. His survey makes it clear that many different ethnic and racial communities have engaged in collective violence for a variety of reasons. However, the particularly chronic and troublesome history of back-white communal conflict gets special attention in the survey. There is a decade-by-decade accounting of black-white racial violence and its consequences over the last 40 years.

The author goes into great detail in his account of the deadliest urban disorder of this century: namely, the conflagration that broke out in South Central Los Angeles after the first Rodney King verdict was announced. The author notes that more was going on in this disorder than just black anger at a criminal justice system that seemed biased in favor of white police officers. Other communal hostilities were expressed, too: for instance, animosity between blacks and recent Asian immigrants. And underclass resentment was expressed, too. The rioting often pitted, say, chronically unemployed Latinos against seemingly successful Latino shopowners. In short, a complex of factors was involved in the South Central riot as is often the case in modern-day communal violence.

Riots and civil disorders

In the course of his survey of riots and disorders, Schonborn points out the different configurations racial and ethnic rioting has taken over recent decades:

communal rioting, featuring attacks on opponents

commodity rioting, featuring attacks on property or symbols of the opponent

terroristic rioting, featuring firebombings, shootouts, sniper attacks

composite rioting, featuring a combination of all of the above

There has been a progression of sorts through these configurations, but any given riot may have elements of all four types. By the end of the survey, it is evident that the form and nature of communal rioting has evolved over the decades.

Next, the author discusses the financial consequences of communal violence in recent American history. It is interesting to note that the Rodney King South Central violence was the fourth most expensive riot besides being the deadliest riot (50 people died) in U.S. history.

Chapter 18 continues with a discussion of several theories about why and how riots occur. Among the explanations discussed are theories of underclass desperation, frustrated expectations, and absolute and relative deprivation. The notion of media instigation and contagion is examined also as are theories of institutional racism and riots as "protests" or chances to express grievances.

Schonborn suggests that the burning cities of the 1960s can best be understood by the theories of institutional racism and frustrated expectations. Regarding frustrated expectations, James C. Davies points out that violence is most likely to occur when there is a sharp reversal of fortune in the middle of a long-awaited period of economic prosperity.

Schonborn concludes his chapter by calling for more research and inquiry—as well as social action to address the underlying causes of collective communal violence.

TERRORISTIC VIOLENCE

The next chapter in Part V is devoted to a discussion of terrorism. At the heart of terrorism is the effort to influence those with power and authority by means of shocking and random uses of violence.

Reid starts her discussion of terrorism by distinguishing it from other political crimes such as treason and sedition. She then emphasizes the role played by fear in terrorism and the need for an audience which is what differentiates *communal* from *individual* terror. The author lists *civil disorders* as a form of terror. As Schonborn points out in his chapter, terroristic riots and civil disorders are a relatively new development. They may have elements of a "protest" riot which uses violence as a way to coerce policymakers rather than to persuade them.

In Chapter 19, Reid mentions two forms of terrorism that are important enough to highlight and worthy of elaboration. The following is a reiteration of Reid's description as well as an elaboration on how political and state terrorism operate:

Political terrorism

Political terrorism is an effort to pressure a government into over-reacting to the terror so that citizens then rise up and overthrow the government because of the extreme infringements the government makes upon citizens lifestyles. (Terrorists hope governments will over-react with intrusive curfews, omnipresent checkpoints, and endless security measures).[6] Or—as noted in the chapter—political terrorism tries to get citizens to lose confidence in their present government and favor a new government which promises to end the terror and return the community or country to stability. (Usually the new government is run by the people behind the terrorism.) In short, terror can be a means to seize control of a government. And it is an attractive technique for factions that lack traditional power—that is, arms, money, and connections.

State terrorism

State terrorism, by contrast, is an effort by a government (say, the former Nazi Germany) to keep a governed or oppressed people so frightened and disoriented that they become paralyzed and do nothing. (At one stage, the Nazis seized and incarcerated randomly selected people in the middle of the night. No one could figure out a pattern or rhyme or reason, and so a kind of paralysis set in.) This paralysis often allows the state to do almost anything it wants. And in addition to this, the citizenry may develop a kind of hypnotic "suggestibility"—due to feelings of helplessness—which makes it swallow almost any propaganda the state puts out to rationalize its brutal actions.[7]

Reid continues her chapter on terror by discriminating between xenofighters and homofighters which is essentially a distinction between international terrorists and domestic terrorists.[8] The author also argues that the ultimate goal of terrorists is the establishment of a bargaining position. She states that victims are often just a bargaining chip for publicity, money, escape, the release of prisoners, etc.

Case studies of terrorism

In a presentation of case studies of some of the major terrorist attacks of late, Reid attempts to define and categorize various types of terrorism. Included among these are the World Trade Center bombing in New York City and the unusual, but long-lived string of bombings by the so-called Unabomber.

Chapter 18 concludes with an examination of the specific as well as general efforts to control terrorist violence. Attention is given to the details of the Antiterrorism and Effective Death Penalty Act, a bill passed by the U.S. Congress partly in response to the devastating and horrific Oklahoma City bombing.

CHAPTER 17—ENDNOTES

[1] G.R. Leslie, R.F. Larson, and B.L. Gorman, *Order and Change* (New York: Oxford University, 1973), p. 471.

[2] J. Brislin, "Definitions of Culture," in R.J. Corsini, ed., *Encyclopedia of Psychology*, 2nd ed. (New York: John Wiley, 1994).

[3] Kenneth Monteiro, *Ethnicity and Psychology* (Dubuque, IA: Kendall/Hunt, 1996), p. 12; and Robin Williams, *The Reduction of Intergroup Tensions* (New York: Social Science Research Council Bulletin No. 57, 1947), p. 42.

[4] Juan Gonzales, *Racial and Ethnic Groups in America* (Dubuque, IA: Kendall/Hunt, 1990), p. 200.

[5] Monteiro p. 13; Gonzales p. 200.

[6] Anthony Burton, *Urban Terrorism: Theory, Practice, and Response* (New York: Free Press, 1975).

[7] Peter Bruckner et al., "Terrorism and the Violence of the State," *Working Papers in European Criminology* 1: 1979 pp. 1-86.

[8] Ariel Merari, "A Classification of Terrorist Groups," *Terrorism* 1, no. 2 (1978): pp. 332-347.

18

COMMUNAL VIOLENCE: RIOTS AND CIVIL DISORDERS

Racial and ethnic communal violence that involves rioting, looting, and burning catches our attention, riveting us to our TV sets. The violence may be triggered by anger over a court decision, a rumor about police brutality, or a demonstration that gets out of hand. These triggers or *precipitating incidents* are generally not the root cause of the trouble, as will be seen later in the section on theories of causation.

Collective violence need not be racial or ethnic in character.* It can emanate from almost any community (e.g., a campus community, a gay community) and can concern almost any issue or set of issues (e.g., anti-war concerns, abortion rights, student rights, the environment). There have been some extremely serious disorders in America that have not been racial or ethnic such as those during the 1968 Democratic National Convention in Chicago.

However, conflicts between racial and ethnic communities—along with their accompanying social and political issues—have triggered some of the most destructive collective violence in America. Although a relatively rare occurrence, this kind of intercommunal violence is fairly common in American history, especially between black and white communities.

America is not alone in suffering violent communal conflict with serious consequences. Such conflict occurs in many other industrial and post-industrial countries—Europe is a prime example—and will probably increase as racial and ethnic issues continue to trouble the post

---

*A few relevant definitions:

Communal violence is violence whose source can be traced back to intercommunal conflict. As such it may entail a single act by an individual committing, say, a hate crime. Or it may entail rioting and mob behavior by thousands of people. The latter is often considered a civil disorder.

Civil disorders are public disturbances by citizens of a community. (They are sometimes called urban disorders because the rioting and looting which are typical of civil disorders frequently happen in cities, especially inner cities.)

Riots are a form of civil disorder marked by violent mob action, characterized by hostility, resentment and rebellion. While a riot or civil commotion may have an objective and be selective in its targets, it is usually marked by undisciplined behavior.

Mob behavior is activity of an active crowd bent on an aggressive, destructive act.[1]

Protest. An unconventional activity in opposition to a policy or condition.[2]

Cold War world. Rather than choosing sides, as happened for so long, in superpower conflicts between the U.S. and the USSR or in other global conflicts, more and more people these days seem to be putting their energies into fighting their ethnic neighbors. This phenomenon may have been part of the reason—as well as the death of longtime Yugoslavian leader Tito—that ethnic communal conflicts recently tore Bosnia apart. Similar communal conflicts have kept the former Union of Soviet Socialist Republics Union busy—what with 10 or more major ethnic communities represented in the vast geographical area known as the USSR.

Exhibit 1 shows the current demographic percentage breakdown of racial and ethnic communities in America. (See Student Guide for projections for the year 2050.)

EXHIBIT 1

Racial and Ethnic Percentages in U.S. Population[3]

European-American	74%
African-American	12
Hispanic-American	10
Asian-American	3
Native-American	1
	100%

From the Exhibit figures, it is not surprising that a good deal of this country's racial and ethnic angst relates to black-white conflict because the black and white communities constitute the two largest communities in the percent breakdown presented.[†] However, there is a long history in the U.S. of a lot of other communal conflict besides majority-minority, black-white conflict. Recently there has been minority-minority conflict in the city of Compton, California. Many Hispanics there in the 1990s feel the black-dominated police department and city government "oppresses" their community. There was also a good deal of Black-Korean violence during the Rodney King verdict riots.

---

†Probably the most accurate and *formal* terms for racial and ethnic communities in the U.S. are Native-American, African-American, Asian-American, Hispanic-American and European-American.[4] However, using these terms repeatedly in a discussion of communal conflict can get wordy and unwieldy. As an example, consider this sentence: *"Eventually, European-American versus Native-American conflict gave way symbolically to European-American versus Asian-American trouble and European-American versus African-American conflict."* Therefore, the terms black, white, etc.—which are the *informal*, everyday terms—will be generally used here. No disrespect is intended, and reader indulgence and forbearance are appreciated.

What follows is a review of some major categories of communal conflict in the U.S. which have almost invariably involved the majority community, the European Americans (whites). The listings within each category do not purport to be comprehensive. Since conflict involving African Americans and European Americans has been the predominant form of inter-communal conflict in recent times, more emphasis will be placed on this kind of violence in this survey.

Native Americans

Red-white conflict began when European whites arrived in North America and started to compete with Native Americans for land and resources. Warfare, massacre, expulsion, and forced assimilation followed. This tragic chapter in American history reached its nadir in 1890 when three hundred Sioux (two-thirds of whom were women and children) were slaughtered by five hundred Seventh Calvarymen at Wounded Knee Creek, South Dakota. The modern-day occupations of Wounded Knee and Alcatraz island in the San Francisco Bay, together with many other protests, are reminders that ages-old red-white conflicts have yet to be fully resolved.

European Americans

White-white conflicts were quite common in nineteenth century America. Anti-Italian and anti-Irish riots were often instigated by white communities further up the socio-economic ladder who felt threatened by rapidly growing communities of new European immigrants. Long-established white communities worried that newly arrived ethnic communities (especially those professing Catholicism) would get "too big or too close." An ethnic riot involving the Irish cost over three-hundred lives in 1863. Irish immigrants were treated and regarded by native-born whites in much the same way blacks have been over the years in America. Not surpisingly, Irish immigrants reacted to discrimination in much the same way blacks have. As black author Bayard Rustin notes:

> In the year 1863, in New York, the Irish were called "shanties," which means "nigger." In the year 1863, amongst the Irish in New York there was 44 per cent unemployment. In the year 1863 Irish could not buy property in certain parts of New York. In the year 1863, policemen used to come into the Irish district five and six together.[5]

Hispanic Americans

Brown-white communal conflicts have also been frequent in America, but mainly in the West and Southwest. During World War II in California, there was a tendency for the press to stir up public opinion against Mexican American residents. Also, much police brutality resulted during this period, which basically bore witness to an extended harassment campaign against Mexican Americans. In many situations, police stopped and searched anyone who looked Mexican at various road blocks. At one point, police arrested 600 Mexican Americans and booked and incarcerated almost 200 of them.

The famous " zoot-suit" riots did much to stigmatize Mexican Americans as violence-prone in the eyes of whites.[‡] This stigmatization, in turn, caused inhabitants of the "barrio" to substantially increase their feelings of resentment against Anglos (whites).

A variety of tensions including police brutality in the barrios of Los Angeles set the stage for the "zoot suit" riots. Off-duty sailors considered zoot-suiters fair game for harassment. On a June evening in 1943, around 200 off-duty sailors all jumped into a fleet of taxi cabs and went to the barrio "to teach the Mexicans a lesson." The sailors stripped zoot-suiters of their clothes and attacked any and all Mexican Americans they could find. These assaults went on for seven days until the State Department made a ruling that Los Angeles was off limits to all military personnel.

Another brown-white disturbance, a riot, broke out in September 1970. It involved Mexican Americans and whites in East Los Angeles and resulted in fifty-two injuries, seventy arrests, and extensive property damage.

Also, for two nights in 1984, enraged whites and Hispanics fired guns and tossed rocks and firebombs at each other in Lawrence, Massachusetts—a community 30 miles north of Boston. Besides throwing bricks and bottles at police, rioters overturned and burned three police vehicles and damaged 14 others. Rioters engaged in looting as well.

Still other Hispanic communities have been involved in civil unrest. For example, rioting in Chicago in 1977 involved members of the Puerto Rican community. Long-standing animosity toward police finally boiled over on a hot June evening, resulting in two dead, 108 injured, and 119 arrested.

Asian Americans

Yellow-white conflicts have been frequent in the United States, though less frequent than red-white or black-white conflicts. Sociologist Alphonso Pinkney writes of the violence involving Chinese Americans:

> There were frequent massacres of Chinese railroad and mining workers in the West during the second half of the nineteenth century. For example, a mob of white persons raided the Chinese community in Los Angeles in 1871, killing nineteen presons and leaving fifteen of them suspended from scaffolds to serve as a warning to survivors. And in Rock Springs, Wyoming, during a railroad strike in 1885, white workers stormed the Chinese community and murdered sixteen persons, leaving all their homes burned to the ground.[7]

[‡]Gonzales describes zoot-suiters thus:

"The zoot-suit, popularized by Mexican American youth, was known for its baggy trousers, long draped jacket, and wide-brimmed hat. The zoot-suiters (or *pachucos*) were known for their tattoos, duck-tail haircuts and spoke in their patois. The zoot suiters belonged to palomillas (neighborhood clubs), but the newspapers portrayed the zoot-suit as a badge of crime and gang membership."[6]

Similar things happened from time to time to Japanese-Americans, especially when they were perceived to be an economic threat by white workers and during the internment camp period during World War II.

African Americans

Serious black-white conflicts have occurred quite frequently in American history. Because of the frequency and consequences of much black-white violence, it will be examined in some detail now.

Pre 1960s

Lynching was a common form of racial violence for years. It was used for punishment and for social control to keep blacks from challenging white dominance. Tuskegee Institute reports that between 1882 and 1962, 4,736 Americans were lynched, 73 percent of whom were black. During the 1890s—the heyday of lynching—an average of 111 blacks were lynched every year.

The race riot, however, has been the primary form of black-white violence in the United States. One of the earliest race riots occurred in *Philadelphia* in 1834. Others took place in *New York City* in 1863, *Memphis* in 1866, *Cincinnati* in 1886, *New York City* in 1900, and *Atlanta* in 1906.

Between 1913 and 1963, there were at least 76 significant black-white riots in America. These included conflicts in *Houston* in 1917 (two blacks and seventeen whites dead); *East St. Louis* in 1917 (thirty-five blacks and eight whites dead); *Chicago* in 1919 (twenth-three blacks and fifteen whites dead); *Tulsa* in 1921 (forty blacks and one white dead); *New York* in 1935 (two blacks and one white dead); and *Detroit* in 1943 (twenty-five blacks and nine whites dead).[8]

The race riots of the early 1900s tended to be communal in the truest sense of the word. They involved two communities confronting each other directly. Blacks were asserting new-found pride, and whites were insisting that blacks show respect and keep their distance. The violence mostly involved attacks on *people* not on property.[**]

[**]This type of riot has been termed a *communal* riot. As our survey will reveal, there are other types of race riots as well. They will be elucidated as the survey progresses. The four types of riots can be characterized as follows:

communal riot - attacks on people. Two communities confront each other directly; a kind of pogrom

commodity riot - attacks on the property or symbols of the opponent. Symbols may be law enforcers, firemen. Arson and looting may occur, the latter being a kind of primitive income-redistribution, given the grievance of poverty.

terroristic riot - firebombings, shootouts, sniper attacks

composite riot - a mix of all of the above.[9]

The riots of the next era—the 1960s—tended to feature more attacks on *property* than on people. The riots of this period were initiated by blacks more than whites, though blacks often blamed white police for provoking situations. As will be noted later in the protest part of the "Theories of causation" section, much of the 1960s collective violence was an expression of grievances on the part of black Americans. The grievances focused on discrimination and poverty; and that is why looting and the fire-bombing of stores—seemingly contradictory behaviors—began to happen more often.

Although there was a riot in Harlem in *New York City* in 1964, it was soon eclipsed by the Watts riot. The well-known Watts riot happened late in the summer in *Los Angeles* in 1965, and it raged on for six days. Thousands of blacks took part, looting stores, setting buildings on fire (especially white-owned ones), and overturning and burning cars. While not commonplace, direct physical attacks on whites did occur. Blacks pulled whites from their cars and beat them. They also threw stones at firemen and exchanged gunfire with law-enforcement personnel.

The Watts violence spread over 46.5 square miles and required the intervention of National Guardsmen and the use of temporary curfews and martial law. Thirty blacks and four whites died, including a fireman and two law-enforcers. Injuries totaled 1,032, and 3,927 arrests were made.[10]

After studying the Watts Riot, the McCone Report by the California Governor's Commission concluded that officials were indecisive, especially with respect to calling out the National Guard and declaring a curfew. However, the report stated that while no evidence surfaced that the riot was planned in advance, criminal elements and political agitators did exploit the riotous situation after it started.[11]

The Watts riot received saturation coverage by the mass media, and this marked the beginning of the media's increasing involvement as a causal factor in collective violence, whether in urban disorders, prison riots, or rock-concert melees. Within a few years, parts of many other American cities went up in flames in what seemed a contagion of urban disorder. Among the more serious cases: *Newark* in 1967 (twenty-one blacks and two whites dead) and *Detroit* in 1967 (thirty-three blacks and two whites dead). See Exhibit 1 for the cost consequences for these and other civil disorders.

Some of these racially-based riots seemed to have had a *terroristic* component, that is sniper attacks on police and firefighters and firebombings of certain stores and government buildings. The public safety personnel and the buildings targeted in these attacks symbolized white racial oppression or exploitation to many of the rioters.

Representing a kind of "controlled experimental situation," there was almost no looting or disorderly behavior when a long electrical blackout hit New York City in 1965. There was plenty of opportunity since the city was plunged into total darkness with almost no police presence for hours on end.

During the five years between June of 1963 and June of 1968, over 200,000 people were involved in 239 *violent* race-based conflicts in the United States. These resulted in a total of 190 deaths, eight thousand injuries, and fifty thousand arrests. Significantly, though, during this same period, 1,100,000 people were involved in 310 *nonviolent* race-based conflicts, including among others, clashes over civil rights and integration issues.[12]

1970s

The start of this decade saw much less cataclysmic collective violence than occurred during the 1960s. Perhaps this was because local, state and federal law enforcement officials increased their resources (personnel and equipment) after the 1960s disorders. This increase in social control may have frightened some inner-city residents into "behaving themselves."

There *were* numerous anti-busing riots (e.g., *Boston* in 1975), and racial tensions were never very far below the surface in many areas. For example, white opposition to racial desegregation efforts resulted in a lot of localized outbursts of violence.

Interestingly, in July of 1977—12 years after the placid response to the electrical blackout of 1965—New Yorkers went crazy during a similar blackout. Long-simmering anger finally burst forth; and during a hot, totally dark night of terror, 2,000 stores were looted and almost 4,000 rioters were arrested. Tens of thousands of black residents poured onto the streets in Brooklyn's Bedford-Stuyvesant area, in Manhattan's Harlem and in the South Bronx.

> Roving bands of determined men, women and even little children wrenched steel shutters and grilles from storefronts with crowbars, shattered plate-glass windows, scooped up everything they could carry, and destroyed what they could not. . . The arsonists were as busy as the looters. Firemen fought 1,037 blazes. . . When the firemen showed up, their sirens screaming, the crowds pelted them with rocks and bottles. . . . In all, 59 firemen were injured fighting the fires. . . A number of looters were robbed in turn by other thieves, who clawed and wrenched away their booty.
>
> . . .[G]iven a similar combination of total darkness, blistering heat and simmering anger on the part of an underclass, much the same kind of riotous looting could erupt in almost any other city in the U.S.[13]

This "accidental" civil disorder was clearly an expression of growing economic dissatisfaction, and it clearly had elements of a terroristic type riot.

1980s

The communal type riot seems to have returned in a big way in the 1980s, especially in the various *Miami* riots. To illustrate, the riot in May 1980 was triggered by the acquittal of four police officers who were charged with beating a local black businessman to death. The decision by an all-white jury enraged blacks as a miscarriage of justice.

An African-American social scientist suggested that the riot was directed at people as well as property:

> We have seen horrible things in this community, the bodies in the streets. I've seen and others have seen, the mutilations, and what have you. This riot involves the intentional attempt to kill. In the riots of the '60s—white people were killed because they got in the way; black peo-

ple were killed because they got in the way. But in this situation, the anger is so intense, the feelings are so rampant now, that the attacks as I've seen them have been aimed at white people with intent to do great bodily harm to people. . .

There may be other areas in which black people will compromise. . . but when it comes to the question of justice, there is no room to give. And people feel intensely wounded by the sense that justice has been denied in such an atrocious case as this.[14]

Besides anger about injustice in the courts, an underlying issue in this Miami riot was black resentment about the perceived favorable treatment of the Cuban community. Blacks did not want Cubans to be treated badly; they just wanted the city to give top priority to addressing long-standing black concerns and needs.

Rioting flared again in Miami in 1982 and 1989; and similar situations (alleged police misbehavior) triggered the tumultuous expression of deeply felt resentments. However, this time resentment was expressed against other Hispanic ethnic communities besides Cubans: namely, animosity was expressed against the influx into the area of 100,000 Nicaraguan immigrants and 75,000 Haitian refugees.

And in 1986, three black men inadvertently wandered into a predominantly white, Italian-American section of Queens (called Howard Beach) in *New York City.* A group of white Howard Beach teenagers proceeded to severely beat them; and as one of the black men fled across a highway, he was struck by a car and killed. Racial tensions and episodes like this were not uncommon in the late 1980s as evidenced by problems in *Chicago, Boston,* and *Charleston.*

1990s

In *Washington, D.C.,* trouble between an Hispanic community and a black community reached the boiling point in May of 1991. Angry blacks and Hispanics engaged in a frenzy of violence for two nights, setting fire to vehicles, looting stores, and lobbing Molotov cocktails. (The rioting resulted in 12 injuries, 225 arrests, and $2 million in damage.)

In August of 1991, violence raged for three days between black and Jewish communities in the Crown Heights area of Brooklyn in *New York City.* A report indicated that the black mayor and police commissioner at the time failed to take prompt action to stop the violence, even though they knew it was out of control. A seven-year-old black boy and a 29-year-old Jewish rabbi were killed during the tumult.

The deadliest riot this century

The *Los Angeles* riot in 1992—triggered by the verdict in the first Rodney King beating trial—has provoked some debate. Experts cannot make up their minds about whether it was a communal, commodity or terroristic riot. It most likely was a combination of all three, that is a *composite* riot.

What is clear, however, is that it was the deadliest civil disturbance in America this century. Forty-five people lost their lives, 2,300 were injured, 623 fires were set, and 11,400 people were arrested. Over 1,100 buildings were damaged or destroyed by fire. Less serious rioting occurred in other American cities during the same period, including *San Francisco*, *Berkeley* and *Las Vegas*.

A chronology of the South Central L.A. riot:

After the trial verdict was announced around 5:00 p.m. in the evening on April 29th, the din of horns could be heard blaring in many parts of South Central, L.A. (People were yelling, "Honk for Justice.") Soon, though, the honking escalated to the hurling of rocks and bottles. Many people contend that young gang members were responsible for this. Allegedly, members of the Eight-Trey Gangster Crips went house-to-house after the verdict, exhorting people to "Take it to the streets."

Police reports indicate that a gang member stole some liquor from a Korean-owned store and—in an ensuing fight—hit the owner's son in the head with a bottle. When police arrived, the suspect had gone but a crowd had gathered. Some youths then began throwing rocks and bottles at the police, saying "Cops gonna die tonight. It's Uzi time."

When the police officers were ordered by their lieutenant to retreat, the crowd was elated and energized. Emboldened, members of the crowd attacked a *New York Times* photographer nearby who barely escaped alive. Some people assert this was the flashpoint of three days of frightening chaos and collective violence in L.A.[15] And even though reports of violence began flooding in over police-radios, the lieutenant in charge and other commanders insisted police be passive and stay at a "field command post" away from the escalating violence.

Why such passivity? A possible answer: During the long months leading up to the verdict, the Los Angeles Police Department (L.A.P.D.) brass were determined to be very low key about everything. Various minority politicians had warned the L.A.P.D. against any overt preparation for unrest, and so preparations and riot control training were kept to a minimum. Moreover *if* trouble did break out, minority city councilman Mark Ridley-Thomas warned "A massive show of force would be a mistake." In sum, the L.A.P.D. was fearful of provoking any more public animosity. The police also did not feel inclined to do the hard work that is necessary to prevent trouble because they felt unappreciated in many quarters. "The police feared being criticized for overreacting, and so they underreacted."[16] However, police in other Los Angeles area towns—such as Culver City and Santa Monica—were ready, prepared, and proactive.

Crowds were now looting and still throwing concrete, bricks, and rocks—often at hapless passers-by. A delivery man was pulled from his vehicle and beaten while a bystander yelled "That's how Rodney King felt, white boy." And then at 6:45 p.m., Eight-Trey Gangster Crips youths surrounded Reginald Denny in his 18-wheeler truck, pulled him out, and kicked him mercilessly. One gang member even bashed his head in with a fire-extinguisher, and millions of Americans watched it happening "live" on their TV sets! Luckily for Denny, four good Samaritans—all black—rushed to his aid and got him to a hospital where surgeons barely saved his life.

And *still*, police continued to be under orders not to intervene, and especially vocal in this decision was the police lieutenant who ordered the withdrawal from the liquor-store incident. Why this oddity in organizational decision-making? It happened partly because many of the upper L.A.P.D. brass—including embattled lame-duck police chief Daryl Gates—were away from headquarters for various legitimate reasons when the verdict unexpectedly came down. Suffice it to say, without police presence in the troubled areas, the mob ruled. Los Angeles skies were soon aglow from an orgy of arson fires.

In addition to the incident where African Americans rescued Reginald Denny, other cases of mixed-race behavior—good and bad—make simple generalizations about the South Central riot difficult. (For example, a black man rescued a Japanese motorist who was being attacked, and a Korean shopkeeper shot a black girl). There were also many within-race violent incidents. In one, an Hispanic store owner, who engaged in gunplay with armed Hispanic looters, cried out when he was wounded: "Latinos! My own people!" The race and ethnicity of the scores of people who died during the entire tumult reflect the mixed nature of the violence: 41% African American, 33% Hispanic American, 20% European American, and 5% Asian American.

Finally, at 8 p.m. in the evening—two-and-a-half hours after trouble broke out—waiting police were allowed *back* into the troubled areas that now resembled "war zones." The areas reminded many combat veterans of Vietnam: fires everywhere with columns of smoke rising into the night sky.

Although police numbers had been augmented many-fold over their earlier strength, the police were simply unprepared for the major civil unrest that was unfolding. People were swarming everywhere, and many were looting. There seemed to be too many people to arrest.

The rioting, looting, and arson went on throughout the night Wednesday. One Korean owner of a grocery store fought off looters all night. The fury and frenzy finally peaked late Thursday night, but the disturbance carried on through Friday. The disorder was finally brought under control on Saturday when thousands of National Guard troops brought into South Central used force to effectively impose curfews throughout the area.

After the riot, there was much criticism. It was imputed that black mayor Tom Bradley made incendiary statements on TV after the verdict; and Bradley was accused of not being decisive enough during the trouble. Police chief Gates, naturally, was criticized for restraining the police too long and also for not preparing adequately for all post-verdict contingencies.

Of course, many people criticized the arsonists, especially the few arsonists who torched their own buildings for the insurance proceeds. Many critics lambasted "down and outs" for opportunistic looting. Some looters even dragged big-screen TVs—inch by inch—along the pavement to get the huge units back to their apartments. A few critics suggested that many of the looters were recent immigrants who did not relate or care much about the "not guilty" verdict.

Some observers felt that most of the initial protests and demonstrations were spontaneous expressions of pain and anguish about the verdict but that the fires and looting that came later were not. One long-time South Central inhabitant felt the rioting was done by a small segment of malcontents and that the majority of residents were dismayed and disgusted with their lawlessness.[17] (An almost carnival-like atmosphere prevailed at times in some places.)

FINANCIAL CONSEQUENCES OF COMMUNAL VIOLENCE

Deaths and injuries are far and away the most important consequences of communal violence. In fact, such casualty figures have been emphasized in this survey. However, the economic cost of disorders is important, too. As can be seen from the figures in Exhibit 2, the Los Angeles Watts riot in 1965 was the costliest civil disorder in U.S. history, from a financial point of view.

EXHIBIT 2

Costliest Riots in U.S. History[18]

Locale	Date	Insured Losses* In present Dollars (in millions)
Miami	1980	$103.5
Los Angeles	1965	182.6
Detriot	1967	162.4
Los Angeles	1992	100.0
New York City	1977	90.1
Washington, D.C.	1968	45.3
Newark	1967	58.7
Baltimore	1968	52.6
Chicago	1968	48.4
New York City	1968	15.8
Pittsburgh	1968	7.5

*Estimated

The Los Angles South Central riot in 1992, on the other hand, cost $100 million. Moreover, there are estimates that besides the $100 million in insured losses, the riots cost untold millions more dollars in uninsured losses and overtime costs of police and other peacekeepers. Some experts put the total dollar figure for the South Central riot at $1 billion. The disorder also resulted in 10,000 lost jobs due to damaged businesses and the like. However, some jobs have returned to South Central. For instance, five years after the disorder, a $10 million Superior Warehouse opened—one of five supermarkets to be rebuilt in the area—providing jobs for 150 people.

THEORIES OF CAUSATION

There are a variety of theories about the causes of communal riots, and some of these date back to the start of western civilization and thought.

"Absolute" deprivation

The theory of "absolute" deprivation originates with Plato, who suggested in the *Republic* that extreme poverty could cause violence between aggregates. Aristotle seconded this notion in his *Politics*. Aggregates deprived of all but a modicum of food and shelter—and in present-day terms, employment, education, and health-care as well—are likely to attack their neighbors or anyone else they perceive to be responsible for their deprivation. This is essentially a theory of haves versus have-nots.

Interestingly, data on the standard of living of African Americans during the racial disorders of the 1960s show that *absolute* deprivation did not exist for most black Americans. Other evidence, especially from countries with a good deal of civil disorder, suggest that the theory of absolute deprivation is unsound.[19] In fact, the theory breaks down completely when one considers *absolute-zero* deprivation. People and collectivities with severe deprivation and its accompanying low food intake are usually apathetic and sluggish rather than angry and violent.

"Relative" deprivation

This theory is more sophisticated. It contends that a community is driven to violence not by the absolute amount of deprivation it experiences, but by the amount of deprivation it experiences *relative* to other communities. The standard of living data just mentioned does show blacks were economically deprived relative to whites during the period leading up to and including the early 1960s.[20] Thus, according to relative deprivation theory, blacks in the United States, who are much better off materially than blacks in Africa or peasants in India, may nonetheless be more prone to violence because the proximity of white wealth makes them feel relatively more deprived. The incessant reminders of the mass media in the United States make blacks even more acutely aware of their relative deprivation.

The issue of *inequality* is integral to the theory of relative deprivation. The sharper the perceived inequality between two communities—or between one community and another that serves as a standard of comparison—the greater the likelihood of violent conflict.

The issue of *legitimacy* is also critically important. For instance, one reason peasants in India put up with their lot is that their frame of reference—comprised of religious beliefs, rationalizations for the caste system, and so on—tells them that their deprivation is legitimate. It is part of the grand order of creation. The frame of reference for blacks in America tells them just the opposite. Their deprivation is therefore *perceived* to be illegitimate.

Support for relative deprivation theory comes from the fact that most of the active participants in the racial violence of the 1960s were relatively, rather than absolutely deprived. Indeed, they were somewhat "advantaged" vis-a-vis others rather than being absolutely "disadvantaged." According to the National Advisory Commission on Civil Disorders (the Kerner Commission), most of the participants were *young* (an advantage in a youth-oriented culture), *male* (an advantage in the male-dominated culture of the time), *employed* (an advantage at a time when many people were without jobs), and passably *educated* (an advantage in a technocratic society).[21]

Underclass desperation

Related to the above two notions, this theory receives mixed support. According to William Julius Wilson's analysis, poverty in America may be a permanent condition for many; and members of minority communities seem to be particularly at risk for being part of a permanent underclass.[22] Besides economic hardship, underclass members disproportionately suffer housing, health, education and familial deprivation. Part of the latter problem is highlighted by the huge number of female-headed households in the underclass.

Clearly, some members of the underclass have participated in recent civil disorders such as the South Central disturbance. However, some people question this theory as follows: Was the "unrest" inevitable? Was South Central a community on the verge of exploding because of years of government neglect? Are money and jobs the only variables, or are the social ills of South Central—and much of the rest of America—more complex than this because they include the variables of the deification of consumerism, the breakdown of the family, and the loss of direction and values?[23]

Frustrated expectations

As an adaptation of the well-known frustration-aggression hypothesis, this theory suggests that the frustration of expectations is the mechanism that fuels collective violence. **Frustration** is the blockage of goal-attainment, especially when people are close to reaching a goal. Applied to a communal situation, this theory suggests that people may react violently when they feel an expected goal, say economic advancement, eludes them. Sociologist James C. Davies believes that many black communities in the 1960s engaged in civil disorders because of the downsizing (and even disappearance) of many governmental programs that had been promised during John F. Kennedy's New Frontier and implemented during Lyndon Johnson's Great Society and War on Poverty.[24]

There is considerable evidence to support the notion that the frustration of high expectations can cause communal violence. Much of the race rioting in the 1960s in America occurred in Northern cities (a) which had above average civil rights records, (b) which had taken stands against discrimination, and (c) which had implemented many community relations projects. The hopes and expectations of blacks were high in these cities. When federal aid was cut back to finance the Vietnam War and the space program, black aspirations were terribly frustrated. Also during the 1960s, the passage of the Civil Rights Act and various Supreme Court decisions had raised hopes. When reality eventually failed to measure up, the disillusionment and disappointment were overwhelming.

In Davies' view an important factor in causing communal violence is the frustration which stems from the gap between real and ideal (expected) social conditions. Of course, communal frustration does not always lead to collective aggression and violence. Just as with individuals, frustration may lead instead to apathy, withdrawal, fixation, or rationalization. Drugs, religion, and other modes of coping may also take the place of aggression and violence.

One reason communities in the U.S. have been vulnerable to the frustration of rising-but-disappointed expectations is that Americans have proclaimed America to be the "land of opportunity" and encouraged millions of immigrants over the decades to partake in the dream. While countless people have achieved *individual* economic mobility, others have failed. Also, *collective* upward mobility rates have differed for various racial and ethnic communities.

Institutional racism

After studying 24 of the most destructive civil disorders of the 1960s, Otto Kerner and the Commission on Civil Disorders concluded in 1968 that *institutional* racism was a cause as well as a consequence of the civil unrest of the 1960s. Kerner wrote: "Our nation is moving toward two societies, one black, one white—separate and unequal."[25]

Institutional racism is the process whereby persons are systematically, though often not intentionally, denied the opportunity for full participation in society's formal and informal institutions because of race.

Whether such racism has continued to be a factor in later unrest is not clear. The Voting Rights Act, the Civil Rights Act, and countless government affirmative action programs have clearly changed American society since the indictment handed down by the Kerner Commission in 1968. To use just one measure as a gauge, the Voting Rights Act helped to increase the number of blacks holding elective office in the U.S. from 100 in 1965 to 1,813 in 1980.

The relative quiet after the end of the 1960s may have been due to some of the early gains in black-white relations because of government legislation. However, starting about the same time, black Americans in inner cities—especially in the "rust belt"—inexorably began to lose jobs because America was undergoing a shift from an economy based on manufacturing to one based on service and hi-tech. Add to this the gradual revocation of aid to cities and the progressive dismantling of certain social programs, and one understands some of the desperation and deprivation that characterized certain aspects of the South Central riot in Los Angeles.

The contagion effect and media instigation

Since television started covering civil disorders, there has been a concern that such coverage could instigate copycat disorders. (Comedians have even said that live TV coverage constituted a "home shopping" channel for looters.) This phenomenon is sometimes called the *contagion effect* because its operation is similar to the contagiousness of cold or flu viruses.

The contagion effect has been found to be a factor in prison riots which seem to come in spurts in the U.S. However, there are many fewer variables at play in prison rioting in comparison to communal rioting. Also, prisoners, almost by definition, are resentful about their situation and circumstances.

Research supports the existence of a contagion effect with regard to other kinds of violence: bombings, plane skyjackings, and violent crimes with very distinctive M.O.s (modus operandi). In sum, in a McLuhanesque television age, it is not surprising that reportage of real violence—including riots—can result in a subsequent increase in the chance of the violence being imitated or copied.

Relatedly, some have alleged that the media even instigate communal violence on occasion. A black journalist, in fact, claims that the media's endless re-broadcasting of the 81-second Rodney King tape during the trial was essentially "a long infomercial for violence."[26] A quasi experimental "control" for testing this theory might be the situation after Martin Luther King, Jr. was assassinated in 1968. One might ask why Los Angeles did not erupt in a major civil disorder after the M.L. King assassination when it did after the R. King verdict? One answer: the media did not relentlessly rebroadcast any assassination footage. In some ways, the killing of M.L. King, Jr. was the ultimate injustice, making the Rodney King verdict pale by comparison. In essence, this instigation theory suggests that the endless repetition of the Rodney King tape "radicalized" everyone with a grudge and "agitated" those down on their luck—regardless of whether they were African American or had ever experienced police brutality first hand.

Protest of grievances

This theory suggests that civil disorders are essentially a form of political protest, a way of letting grievances be known. Thus, riots are just the *violent* extreme of a continuum. At the other extreme are *nonviolent* actions (say, assemblages and picketing). In the middle of the continuum is civil disobedience (e.g., demonstrations where traffic, building entrances, or construction equipment is blocked). As noted by distinguished writers such as Thoreau, Gandhi, and M.L. King, Jr., civil *disobedience* may lose its power when it deteriorates into civil *disorder*.

Protests are efforts to make clear people's dissatisfaction with a government, a policy, or a lack of policy, for that matter. Protests can be expressive or instrumental. Scholars generally view riots and civil disorders—especially those which result in injuries, deaths, and damage—as expressive (emotional) and not instrumental (pragmatic).

Concluding remarks

Besides the theories presented here, there are other notions about communal violence that have been put forth. These deal with the following factors, among others:

— outside agitators who stir up trouble and discontent——for political reasons,

— long, hot summers with a lack of anything to do,

— the relative willingness of a majority community to tolerate attacks on itself and not respond with repressive measures, and

— the relative willingness of people in power to share power with those who have less.

Some of these notions might be incorporated into existing, more formal explanations and theories. In any case, there should be further efforts to understand the causes and dynamics of intercommunal riots and civil disorders.

And more importantly, there should be more efforts made to reverse the declining economic prosperity of many minority communities in America. These efforts might eliminate some of the despair and hopelessness that many inner city minorities and recent immigrants feel. These efforts might also go a long way toward lessening the chance of another South Central.

One way to start this process has been suggested by David Hackworth, a much-decorated and esteemed army colonel who grew up in South Central. He recommends we set up "a job training and reconstruction corps to lead our disenchanted youth of all races on a campaign to rebuild themselves, our crumbled roads, swaying bridges, and to tear down America's Third World ghettos and rebuild them into modern cities."[27]

CHAPTER 18—ENDNOTES

[1] Leonard Broom, Charles Bonjean, and Dorothy Broom, *Sociology: A Core Text with Adapted Readings* (Belmont, CA: Wadsworth, 1979), p. 269.

[2] Broom (1990 edition), p. 351.

[3] *Newsweek*, January 27, 1997. Data are for 1995.

[4] Kenneth Monteiro, *Ethnicity and Psychology* (Dubuque, IA: Kendall/Hunt, 1996) and Juan Gonzales, *Racial and Ethnic Groups in America* (Dubuque, IA: Kendall/Hunt, 1990), *passim*.

[5] Baynard Rustin, "Some Lessons from Watts," in S. Endleman, ed., *Violence in the Streets* (Chicago: Quandrangle, 1968), p. 335.

[6] Gonzales (1996 edition), p. 227.

[7] A. Pinkney, *The American Way of Violence* (New York: Random House, 1972), p. 73.

[8] Based on data from Pinkney, 87-93; Leslie et al., *Order and Change* (New York: Oxford, 1973), 471; and Kerner Commission, *Report of the National Advisory Commission on Civil Disorders* (New York: Bantam, 1968), pp. 38, 60.

[9] An adaption of Morris Janowitz's ideas. See his *Social Control of Escalated Riots* (Chicago: University of Chicago Center for Policy Studies).

[10] The McCone Report, issued by the California Governor's Commission (Sacramento, 1966), *passim*.

[11] *Ibid*.

[12] Karl Schonborn, *Dealing with Violence: The Challenge Faced by Police and Other Peacekeepers* (Springfield, IL: Charles C. Thomas, 1975), pp. 112-113.

[13] Anonymous, "Night of Terror," *Time* (July 25, 1977): p. 12.

[14] Marvin Dunn, "Miami Riots," interview, in *MacNeil/Lehrer Report* (May 19, 1980) (New York: Educational Broadcasting Corporation), p. 3 of a transcript of the broadcast.

[15] Chronology based on various accounts, especially: Anonymous, Newsweek (May 18, 1992); David H. Hackworth, *Newsweek* (May 25, 1992); Ralph Kineey Bennet, *Readers Digest* (October 1992); and Karen English, *Newsweek* (May 24, 1993).

[16] Jerome Skolnick (U.C. Berkeley Law professor), quoted in Bennet, p. 80.

[17] English, *passim*.

[18] Source: Property Claim Services

[19]See literature on studies of protests, upheavals, and revolutions (including the American, French, English, and Russian revolutions), especially books by Crane Brinton and Alexis de Tocqueville.

[20]Otto Kerner, *A Report of the National Advisory Commission on Civil Disorders* (New York: Bantam, 1968), *passim*.

[21]*Ibid.*

[22] William Julius Wilson, *The Truly Disadvantaged: The Inner City, the Underclass, and Public Policy* (Chicago: University of Chicago Press, 1987), pp. 3-186.

[23] English, *passim*; Hackworth, *passim*.

[24] J.C. Davies, "Toward a Theory of Revolution," *American Sociological Review* 27, no. 6 (1962), *passim*.

[25] Kerner, p. 1.

[26] Robert Drummand, "The South Central Riot," interview, in *National Public Radio Report* (July 30, 1992), (New York: Educational Broadcasting Corporation), pp. 1-12.

[27] Hackworth, p. 33.

19

TERRORISM—REID

Terrorism is a crime that frequently involves violence. Most terrorism victims are innocent and unsuspecting persons who become the targets of violent attacks, which frequently result in death. Before attempting to define terrorism, however, it is important to look briefly at political crimes.

Since all laws must be interpreted, it could be argued that all law enforcement is political. The term **political crime** is used here to refer to crimes that are considered criminal because they are a threat to the state or its political stability. Political crimes include any crime committed directly against the government, as is the case with many terrorist acts. Examples are treason and sedition.

Treason involves assisting the enemy with information to help overthrow the government to which one owes allegiance. Treason is the only crime defined in the U.S. Constitution, which authorizes Congress to provide punishment for it. Treason convictions carry the punishment of death (a provision that has been questioned by constitutional scholars) or imprisonment for not less than five years and a fine of not less than $10,000. In addition, a person convicted of treason may not hold any office in the U.S. government.[1]

Sedition involves written or oral communication aimed at overthrowing the government by defaming it or by inciting others to become involved in treason or other crimes. Sedition in the form of written expression is called *seditious libel*. The federal criminal code prohibits *seditious conspiracy*.[2] A 1988 Arkansas trial of fourteen defendants, representing only the fourth time in forty years that the federal government has prosecuted for seditious conspiracy, resulted in acquittals.

Actions aimed at changing the social structure may be considered political crimes and may result from violations of statutes designed to preserve that structure or of laws with other purposes (for example, vagrancy) that may be enforced for political reasons (that is, enforced only against minorities, students, or some other targeted group). The student protest movements of the 1960s and 1970s, civil rights violations, and violations of draft laws are examples. In 1989 in the People's Republic of China, thousands of students demonstrated in Beijing's Tiananmen Square. When they refused to disperse, the People's Liberation Army gunned down hundreds (and some say thousands) of the unarmed students with army tanks. Some demonstrators who survived were arrested and executed by firing squads.

Some scholars include in the definition of political crimes such crimes as police brutality and other acts committed by government officials against citizens. This position is emphasized by the radical approach. As Michael J. Lynch and Graeme R. Newman suggest in their discussion of terrorism, the radical approach brings out these issues:

— terrorism is not what it appears to be on the surface,

— terrorism is defined in relation to particular economic, social and historical circumstances—or terrorism is a social construction defined by those with the power to do so in accordance with prevailing structural conditions, and

— the powerful, including the state and other economic and political elite, may, in many instances, also engage in terroristic behavior.

Lynch and Newman note, however, that usually we do not think of the government as engaging in terroristic activities. We do not perceive the state as deviant because of the ability of those in power to define deviancy in a way that avoids inclusion of their own behavior. "In a word, the political and economic elite are, by virtue of their positions and the power associated with those positions, able to structure definitions of deviance and avoid negative labels."[3]

Hate crimes illustrate another form of terrorism that is not covered by most traditional definitions. Targeting of religious, racial, ethnic groups, or disabled persons, as well as increased violence because of gender or sexual orientation, illustrates the types of behavior that fall within the definition of some hate crimes. Such behavior threatens persons not because of who they are as individuals but because of their membership or participation in a group that is being targeted by the terroristic behavior.

DEFINITIONAL ISSUES

Although there is little agreement on a definition of terrorism, most people have a concept of what it means. A broad legal definition is one found in the American Law Institute's Model Penal Code, which defines terrorist threats as follows:

> A person is guilty of a felony if he threatens to commit any crime of violence with purpose to terrorize another or to cause evacuation of a building, place of assembly, or facility of public transportation, or otherwise to cause serious public inconvenience, or in reckless disregard of the risk of causing such terror or inconvenience.[4]

Applied to the political arena, terrorism has been defined simply as "motivated violence for political ends."[5] The Task Force on Disorders and Terrorism of the National Advisory Committee on Criminal Justice Standards defined terrorism as "a tactic or technique by means of which a violent act or the threat thereof is used for the prime purpose of creating overwhelming fear for coercive purposes." Terrorism is a political crime but may be a violent personal crime as well. Acts of terrorists are planned in advance, and to be effective, terrorists must manipulate the community to which the message is addressed. The inculcation of fear is paramount and deliberate; it is the real purpose of the activity, and an audience is important. In this respect, the terror involved in an individual robbery, for example, differs from terrorism. In the latter, the immediate victim is not the important focus; the emphasis is on the larger audience.[6] It is in this respect that terrorism differs significantly from violent personal crimes.

THE CATEGORIES OF TERRORISM

The task force on Disorders and Terrorism divided terrorism into six categories:

1. *Civil disorders:* "a form of collective violence interfering with the peace, security, and normal functioning of the community."

2. *Political terrorism:* "violent criminal behavior designed primarily to generate fear in the community, or a substantial segment of it, for political purposes."

3. *Nonpolitical terrorism:* terrorism that is not aimed at political purposes but that exhibits "conscious design to create and maintain a high degree of fear for coercive purposes, but the end is individual or collective gain rather than the achievement of a political objective."

4. *Quasi-terrorism:* "Those activities incidental to the commission of crimes of violence that are similar in form and method to true terrorism but which nevertheless lack its essential ingredient." It is not the main purpose of the quasi-terrorists "to induce terror in the instant victim," as in the case of true terrorism. Typically, the fleeing felon who takes a hostage is a quasi-terrorist, whose methods are similar to those of the true terrorist but whose purposes are quite different.

5. *Limited political terrorism:* Real political terrorism is characterized by a revolutionary approach; limited political terrorism refers to "acts of terrorism which are committed for ideological or political motives but which are not part of a concerted campaign to capture control of the State."

6. *Official or state terrorism:* referring to "nations whose rule is based upon fear and oppression that reach terrorist proportions."[7]

Terrorism may consist of acts or threats or both. The task force discussed several characteristics that distinguish modern acts of terrorism from classical terrorism in its original form. First, as the result of our technological vulnerability, the potential for harm is greater today than in the past. This development has increased the bargaining power of the modern terrorist, who has been aided by developments in intercontinental travel and mass communication. Television has carried the activities of terrorists to the entire world, giving modern terrorists more power than classical terrorists. Finally, modern terrorists believe that through violence there is hope for their causes.

THE OBJECTIVE, STRATEGY, AND TACTICS

A primary objective of terrorists is to instill fear, to terrorize, and to create violence for the sake of effect. The particular victims may not be important to the cause other than to create the fear toward which the violence is aimed. Instilling fear is not the only objective of terrorists. In addition, they seek to destroy the confidence people have in government.

Terrorist groups have been categorized as *xenofighters*, who are fighting foreigners, or *homofighters*, who are fighting their own people. Often xenofighters are seeking removal of a foreign power or the changing of political boundaries regarding a foreign power. They have such goals as the following:

1. To attract international attention

2. To harm the relations of the target country with other nations

3. To cause insecurity and to damage the economy and public order in the target country

4. To build feelings of distrust and hostility toward the government among the target country's population

5. To cause actual damage to civilians, security forces, and property in the target country.[8]

Homofighters must win the support of their compatriots in their fight to discredit their own government; thus they must adopt policies that do not alienate the citizenry. One approach is the Robin Hood demand, in which terrorists use an acceptable cause to justify their unacceptable tactics. The kidnapping of Patricia Hearst in 1974 is an example. The Symbionese Liberation Army demanded that Hearst's family distribute free food to the needy. Some of the strategies used by homofighters are these:

1. Undermining internal security, public order, and the economy in order to create distrust of the government's ability to maintain control

2. Acquiring popular sympathy and support by positive action

3. Generating popular repulsion from extreme counterterrorist repressive measures

4. Damaging hated foreign interests

5. Harming the international position of the existing regime

6. Causing physical damage and harassing persons and institutions that represent the ruling regime.[9]

THE NATURE AND EXTENT OF TERRORISM

Political terrorist attacks of various types have occurred for centuries. Stewart J. D'Alessio and Lisa Stolzenberg trace the beginning of political terrorists to the Roman imperial period when the Jewish Sicarii, who rejected Roman dominance over Judea, utilized kidnapping and assassination to "incite a Jewish uprising against Rome."[10] Terrorist attacks in large numbers, however, are traced to the mid-1980s.

Top terrorism experts of the State Department reported in 1986 that terrorist attacks, with more than 750 reported worldwide in 1986, representing a 55 percent increase over the previous four years, could be expected to continue. They warned that the slowdown of attacks after the United States bombed Libya on 15 April 1986 should not be taken as indicative of the future. The report indicated that terrorists are adaptable to change and that they can be expected to continue to attack targets designed to kill large numbers of people at a time. As airport security increases, terrorists can be expected to deploy surface-to-air missiles against commercial aircraft.[11]

The report was referring to some of the terrorist attacks of the early 1980s such as the one on the *Achille Lauro*, an Italian cruise ship hijacked on 7 October 1985 with 400 people on board. The hijackers threatened to kill their hostages unless fifty Palestinian prisoners were freed by Israel. The hostages were released later, but one passenger, Leon Klinghoffer, a tourist from New York City, was killed and his body thrown overboard. During the Christmas season of that same year terrorists struck at the Rome, Italy, and Vienna, Austria, airports, throwing hand grenades into the crowds, killing seventeen and wounding one hundred or more. Apparently the attack was aimed at Israelis, but victims were from many countries, illustrating the possibility of death or injury because of international travel.

Terrorist attacks are not new to this or other countries, although today they involve larger numbers of victims; but it was not until 1981 that the U.S. government perceived the threat of terrorism "to be serious enough to warrant classification as a major component of American foreign policy."[12]

Kidnapping and hostage taking are other forms of terrorism that characterized the 1980s. In mid-1985 William Buckley, the Central Intelligence Agency (CIA) station chief in Beirut, Lebanon, was forced from his car and kidnapped by pro-Iranian gunmen. He died in December in a makeshift dungeon where he was held in chains.

Terrorism may affect the lives of many persons as noted in Exhibit 1. Property damage may be extensive as well, and the problems are escalating. In 1996 the Bureau of Alcohol, Tobacco and Firearms (ATF) reported that 994 bombings cost society almost $600 million, which is thirty-five times the amount of damages from 1990 bombings. The number of cases in 1994 was 52.5 percent higher than in 1990. These figures do not include the cost of the 1995 bombing of the federal building in Oklahoma City.[13]

TERRORISM VICTIMS

In one sense all of society is victimized by terrorist acts. The action taken against the victim is coercive, designed to impress others. Terrorism is not a victimless crime. The immediate victims may be involved incidentally, as when they are killed by the randomly placed terrorist's bomb. Or they may be selected with considerable discrimination, as for example, when a prominent politician is assassinated or a businessperson is kidnapped. Terrorism is characterized by gross indifference toward the victims, their dehumanization, and their conversion into mere elements in a deadly power play.

The randomness of victimization by terrorism is indicated by most of the examples discussed in Exhibit 1. The ultimate objective of the terrorist, particularly the political terrorist, is the establishment of a bargaining position; so the victims are unimportant in most cases. Kidnapping and taking hostages are terrorist techniques par excellence for this purpose. The victims are treated largely as objects to be traded for what the terrorist wants: money, release of prisoners, publication of manifestos, escape, and so on. These bargains are extralegal and rest on a recognition of the powers of life and death that the terrorist holds over victims. This aspect raises the most serious social, political, and humanitarian issues for those who must make these awesome decisions affecting the lives and safety of the victims.

Terrorist victimization produces special individual and collective traumas. Many hostages and kidnap victims experience incongruous feelings toward their captors, and the events may constitute a serious challenge to their own value systems. The most striking manifestation of this is the **Stockholm syndrome,** named after an incident that occurred in the Swedish capital in 1973.[14] Stockholm syndrome is an incongruous feeling of empathy toward the hostage takers and a displacement of frustration and aggression on the part of the victims toward authorities.

Another way in which many individuals are victimized by terrorist attacks is in the creation of fear that leads to changes in life-styles. In recent years terrorist incidents have led many Americans to cancel their plans to travel abroad. In 1995 and 1996 they had increased reasons to fear traveling—or just living—in their own country, as noted below.

THE CONTROL OF TERRORISM

When President Reagan returned from the twelfth annual summit of industrial democracies, held in Tokyo in May 1986, he proclaimed the meeting a "triumph in Tokyo" that had produced a "strong measure of allied unity" on economic, agricultural, and antiterrorism issues. Of primary concern here is the response of the seven summit nations to the increased terrorist acts in the year before the meeting. According to Reagan, "We agreed that the time has come to move beyond words and rhetoric. Terrorists and those who support them—especially governments—have been put on notice. It is going to be tougher from now on."

Reagan's comments followed the U.S. air raids on Libya after the Libyan government was accused of sponsoring terrorist attacks on Americans in foreign countries. The U.S. air raid had split her allies; some argued against the raid, whereas Great Britain permitted the use of her bases for launching the attack. *Time* reported that the United States "had crossed a fateful line in the intensifying battle between civilized society and terrorism, with consequences that no one could truly predict." Some who opposed the raids predicted retaliation; supporters argued that terrorist force could be met only with force. Libya's Colonel Mu'ammar Gadhafi, whose living quarters and command center were the focus of the raid, lost an adopted daughter; two sons were injured. Gadhafi called Prime Minister Margaret Thatcher of Great Britain (who gave the United States permission to use Britain's bases and to fly over her country) and President Reagan "child murderers" and vowed to get revenge. Polls taken after the raid indicated that 71 percent of Americans approved the attack, and 56 percent thought that in the long run the air raid would help stop terrorist attacks on Americans. Only 66 percent of the British respondents approved, whereas 84 percent thought the participation of Great Britain would increase the likelihood of terrorist attacks on their country.[15]

What is the most effective way to respond to terrorism? If the government meets the demands of the terrorists, does that concession raise the specter of creating inconvenient or unreasonable precedents for the handling of future incidents? Ted Gurr, author of *Why Men Rebel*, says, "The most fundamental human response to the use of force is counterforce. Force threatens and angers men. Threatened, they try to defend themselves; angered, they want to retaliate."[16]

After terrorist attacks on U.S. planes, skyjacked in large numbers in the 1970s, security measures were required in all U.S. airports and skyjacking decreased. But terrorists are adaptable, as indicated by their planting of bombs *outside* the secure areas of airports. It is obvious that although efforts to secure airports and aircraft have increased, they are not sufficient. During late December 1994 French paramilitary commandos stormed a hijacked airliner in Paris, freeing the 170 hostages who had been held for fifty-four hours. Twenty-five people were injured and the four Islamic militants who hijacked the plane in Algiers were killed instantly. The hijackers had, however, killed three hostages before permission for the plane to be flown to Paris was given.

In the summer of 1995 President Clinton urged Congress to pass his antiterrorism bill. After considerable negotiation the House and Senate passed a bill, and President Clinton signed it shortly before the first anniversary of the Oklahoma City bombing. The Antiterrorism and Effective Death Penalty Act of 1996 does not include some of the provisions President Clinton wanted, such as increased wiretap authority. Some features of the approved bill are that it restricts the legal opportunities for death row and other inmates to appeal their sentences. It makes it more difficult for foreign terrorist groups to raise money in the United States and provides for easier deportation of alien terrorists. It authorizes an expenditure of $1 billion over the next five years for fighting terrorism in the United States. The bill contains provisions for terrorism victims such as mandatory restitution and a provision for them to have access to closed-circuit television to view a trial that has been moved more than 350 miles from the venue in which they were victimized by a terrorist act.[24]

As a result of tragedies in the summer of 1996, Congress considered amending the act passed only a few months earlier. President Clinton and the FBI director urged them to include some of the provisions mentioned above that had been excluded, especially extended wiretapping authority. It appeared that Congress would make at least some changes, but they adjourned at the end of July without doing so. The House overwhelmingly passed a bill, but it did not include the administration's push for extended wiretapping or for requiring manufacturers to mark black and smokeless powder (often used in bombs) with chemical elements that would make the finished product more easily traceable.

Finally, at this writing, investigations were continuing into the 25 June 1996 truck bombing in Saudi Arabia that killed nineteen Americans. The latest suspicion was that the bombing was linked to Iran, but that has not been confirmed.

EXHIBIT 1

Terrorism Case Studies

World Trade Center Bombing

Judge Kevin T. Duffy told one of the four defendants, "You are the biggest hypocrite in the room. . . . What you have done is turn your life into a total lie. . . . You violated the laws not only of man but of God," as he sentenced him to 240 years in prison without possibility of parole. The same sentence was imposed on the other defendants. Unless the laws are changed or these cases are reversed on appeal, Nidal Ayyad, Mahmud Abouhalima, Ahmad Ajaj, and Mohammad Salameh will spend the rest of their lives in prison for convictions on all charges connected with the bombing of the New York City's World Trade Center. The bombing cut a five-story hole in the building and caused six deaths, 1,000 injuries, and a half billion dollars in property damage.[17]

Upon the completion of the trial in the World Trade Center bombing, prosecutors began preparing for another terrorism trial, one that was related but far more complicated. Sheik Omar Abbel-Rahman and his codefendants were accused of plotting and conspiring to bomb the United Nations building and other New York City landmarks. This prosecution was more difficult. The bombings did not occur. The defendants were charged with seditious conspiracy, so prosecutors had to prove an intent to overthrow the government, a more difficult job than proving that they bombed government buildings or tunnels.

In his opening statement in late January 1995 the prosecutor said:

> This is a case about war. The enemy in this war was the United States of America. The battlefield in this war was the streets and buildings and tunnels of New York City. The weapons . . . were car bombs, terrorism, and homemade explosives. The soldiers who fought this war are seated before you in this courtroom.

The prosecutor linked the defendants to the World Trade Center bombing. The first defense attorney referred in his opening statement to her client as a champion of the oppressed, not a terrorist. Her client's name in translation means "the Servant of God," leading her to refer to the case as "The United States v. the Servant of God."[18]

The prosecution rested its case after five months of evidence. During that period one defendant entered a guilty plea, leaving the sheik and ten of his codefendants. A few days after the Oklahoma bombing, discussed below, the judge warned jurors not to link that bombing with this trial. That bombing was "the work of Americans whose grievances have nothing to do with what goes on in this courtroom."[19]

The sheik's defense was overshadowed by the trial and acquittal of O. J. Simpson, with little attention given even to the trial's end that resulted in the sheik's conviction of seditious conspiracy. In January 1996 the fifty-seven-year-old sheik was sentenced to life in prison, and Islamic groups vowed revenge on Americans.[20]

Oklahoma City Bombing

The blast that rocked the Oklahoma City federal building on 19 April 1995 killed close to 170 people (including nineteen children in a day care center), injured many others, and resulted in millions of dollars in property damage. Shortly after the blast Timothy McVeigh was arrested for a traffic violation. Subsequently he was charged with the bombing, along with a second suspect, Terry L. Nichols. A third suspect, Michael Fortier, entered a plea negotiation with federal prosecutors and agreed to testify against Nichols and McVeigh.

Attorneys for the defendants asked for Judge Wayne Alley to recuse himself, arguing that he had a conflict of interest because his chambers were damaged by the blast. The judge refused to do so but was removed by an appelate court, which stated: "A reasonable person, knowing all the relevant facts, would harbor doubts about the judge's impartiality."[21]

In December 1995 the chief judge of the United States Court of Appeals for the Tenth Circuit appointed Judge Richard P. Matsch, the chief judge of the Federal District Court in Colorado, to preside over the bombing case. After hearing arguments on the venue issue, Judge Matsch moved the trial to Denver, Colorado. The trial was expected to begin in the fall of 1996.

The Reign of the Unabomber

He terrorized by mail, sending sixteen letter bombs and eluding law enforcement officials for seventeen years, killing three and injuring twenty-two. In the summer of 1995 he began issuing threats, one of which involved planting a bomb on an airplane in the Los Angeles airport during the Fourth of July holiday period. Authorities increased security, but the Unabomber called off his threat. He communicated that he would stop sending bombs if newspapers would print in full an article he wrote.

In July 1995 editors wrestled with the dilemma; some published part of his essay. *The Washington Post* published the essay, "Against the Future: The Luddities and Their War on the Industrial Revoltuion," in a special eight-page section in September 1995.

The full essay was distributed to professors throughout the country in hopes that one would recognize the writing as that of a former student. The Unabomber claimed that he is trying to save the world from becoming enslaved by technology. His targets were chosen from what he considers technical fields.

In early April 1996 Theordore John Kaczynski, a former University of California-Berkeley math professor, was taken into custody from his one-room mountainshack in Montana. He was held without bail and arraigned on one count of possessing bomb components. It was Theodore's brother David whose information tipped off the FBI. David Kaczynski became suspicious that his brother Theodore might be the Unabomber after reading the Unabomber's articles published in newspapers. He reported this to an attorney who discussed these fears with authorities. The tip led the FBI to the mountain cabin of the person they suspect to be the nation's most-wanted serial killer.

Media reports of the investigative search of the cabin and surrounding area, as well as hotels and bus depots the suspect may have frequented, and persons he may have known, raised the prospect that Kaczynski is the Unabomber. Extensive pretrial publicity surrounded the apprehension of Kaczynski, with several books published within a few months. The author of one stated this important warning:

But we must caution that Mr. Kaczynski is just that—a suspect. According to our system, he and everyone else must be presumed innocent unless—and until—proven guilty in a court of law. Everything that follows should be read in that context.[22]

The Unabomber's trials were not expected to occur until late 1996 or 1997, with numerours issues concerning charges and venues for the trials yet to be decided.

Paris, France, Subway Bombings

Four people died and over sixty were wounded when a crowded commuter train blew up near Notre Dame Cathedral in Paris, France in late July 1995. By late October Paris had endured eight subway bombings. An Algerian terrorist group claimed responsibility for those bombings and stated that they would continue until France changed her policies toward Algeria.

No arrests had been made. The previously open "city of lights" was experiencing increased security, which was said to be taking a psychological toll on many citizens while the "anguish of law enforcement authorities [was] reaching the breaking point."[23]

The tragedies may or may not be the result of terroristic acts. In July 1996, the explosion of TWA Flight 800 shortly after takeoff for Paris, France, from John F. Kennedy Airport in New York City, killed all 230 people aboard. It crashed into the ocean, and many think that it was the result of a bomb. The FBI had not confirmed that as of this writing. A few weeks later a bomb exploded in the Centennial Olympic Park near the site of the 1996 Olympics in Atlanta, Georgia, killing one and injuring several, some critically. This incident was also still under investigation. A security guard had been identified as a suspect, but no arrests had been made.[25]

The root causes of terrorism must be identified and eliminated if the threat of terrorist attacks is to be reduced significantly. Clearly those threats have not been eliminated.

CHAPTER 19—ENDNOTES

[1] For a discussion of the history of the treason statute as well as the constitutionality of the death penalty for treason, see James G. Wilson, "Chaining the Leviathan: The Unconstitutionality of Executing Those Convicted of Treason," *University of Pittsburgh Law Review* 45 (1983): pp. 99-179.

[2] U.S. Code, Title 18, Section 2384 (1996).

[3] Michael J. Lynch and Graeme R. Newman, "The Meaning of Terrorism: Conflicting Views from the Left," *Violence, Aggression and Terrorism* 2, no. 4 (1988): 309.

[4] Model Penal Code, Section 211.3.

[5] Quoted in H. H. A. Cooper, "Terrorism: New Dimensions of Violent Criminality," *Cumberland Law Review* 9 (1978): 370.

[6] National Advisory Committee on Criminal Justice Standards and Goals, *Disorders and Terrorism* (Washington, D. C.: U.S. Government Printing Office, 1976), p. 3.

[7] National Advisory Committee, *Disorders and Terrorism*, pp. 3-7.

[8] Ariel Merari, "A Classification of Terrorist Groups," *Terrorism* 1, no. 2 (1978): 332-347.

[9] Ibid., p. 339.

[10] For a discussion see Stewart J. D'Alessio and Lisa Stolzenberg, "Sicarii and the Rise of Terrorism," *Terrorism* 13 (1990): 329.

[11] U.S. Department of State, *Patterns of Global Terrorism: 1986* (Washington, D. C.: U.S. Government Printing Office, 1988).

[12] Robert H. Kupperman, "Terrorism and Public Policy," in *American Violence and Public Policy: An Update on the National Commission on the Causes and Prevention of Violence*, ed. Lynn A. Curtis (New Haven, Conn.: Yale University Press, 1985), pp. 184, 188.

[13] "Bomb Cases Soar 52.5 Percent since 1990," *USA Today* (6 May 1996), p. 1.

[14] See Frederick J. Hacker, *Crusaders, Criminals, Crazies* (New York: W. W. Norton, 1976), p. 137.

[15] "Hitting the Source: U.S. Bombers Strike at Libya's Author of Terrorism, Dividing Europe and Threatening a Rash of Retaliations," *Time* (28 April 1986), pp. 16-27.

[16] Ted Robert Gurr, *Why Men Rebel* (Princeton, J. J.: Princeton University Press, 1970), p. 232; quoted in Robert G. Bell, "The U.S. Response to Terrorism against International Civil Aviation," in *Contemporary Terrorism: Selected Readings*, ed. John D. Elliott and Leslie K. Gibson (Gaithersburg, Md: International Association of Chiefs of Police, 1978), p. 191.

[17] "Perspectives," *Newsweek* (6 June 1994), p. 15; "Trade Center Bombers Get Prison Terms of 240 Years," *New York Times* (25 May 1994), p. 1.

[18] "Lawyers Open in Bomb Plot Case," *New York Law Journal* (31 January 1995), p. 1.

[19] "Jurors Warned," *Baltimore Sun* (25 April 1995), p. 3.

[20] "Islamic Group Vows Revenge on Americans," *New York Times* (22 January 1996), p. 1B.

[21] "Appeals Court Removes Judge in Oklahoma Bombing Case," *New York Times* (2 December 1995), p. 6.

[22] John Douglas, *Unabomber: On the Trail of America's Most-Wanted Serial Killer* (New York: Pocket Books, 1996), p. vii.

[23] "Paris Strolls Past Tighter Security: Police, Troops Make Checks after Terrorist Bombings," *Washington Post* (28 October 1995), p. 1.

[24] Antiterrorism and Effective Death Penality Act of 1996, 104th Cong., 2d Session, No. 104-518 (1966).

[25] "Bad Weather Foils Divers at Crash Site," *New York Times* (2 August 1996), p. 13; "Jewell Ends Cooperation with FBI," *USA Today* (2 August 1996), p. 3.

CREDITS

Excerpts taken from *Dealing with Violence* by Karl Schonborn. Copyright 1975. Reprinted by permission of Charles C. Thomas, Publisher, Ltd.

Politics: Power and Authority, taken from Henslin, *Sociology: A Down to Earth Approach*. Copyright © 1993. All rights reserved. Reprinted by permission of Allyn and Bacon.

Understanding and Preventing Violence, taken from *National Institute of Justice Research in Brief*, February 1994. Reprinted by permission of the National Academy Press.

Domestic Violence, taken from *Crime & Criminology* by Sue Titus Reid. Copyright 1997. Reproduced with permission of The McGraw-Hill Companies.

Violence, Fear and Firearms, taken from *Crime & Criminology* by Sue Titus Reid. Copyright 1997. Reproduced with permission of The McGraw-Hill Companies.

Gang Delinquency, taken from Clemons Bartollas, *Juvenile Delinquency*, 4th ed. Copyright © 1997. All rights reserved. Reprinted by permission of Allyn and Bacon.

Types of Religious Organizations, taken from Henslin, *Sociology: A Down to Earth Approach*. Copyright © 1993. All rights reserved. Reprinted by permission of Allyn and Bacon.

The FBI, ATF, and Waco, taken from *Crime & Criminology* by Sue Titus Reid. Copyright 1997. Reproduced with permission of The McGraw-Hill Companies.

A Call to Arms, taken from *San Francisco Chronicle*, March 12, 1995. Copyright 1995. Reprinted by permission.

Is Deadly Force Justifiable?, taken from *Newsweek*, June 21, 1993. © 1993, Newsweek, Inc. All rights reserved. Reprinted by permission.

Violence and the Police, taken from *Criminal Justice*, 3/E by Reid, Sue, © 1996. Reprinted by permission of Prentice-Hall, Inc., Upper Saddle River, NJ.

The Control of Policing, taken from *Criminal Justice*, 3/E by Reid, Sue, © 1996. Reprinted by permission of Prentice-Hall, Inc., Upper Saddle River, NJ.

Terrorism, taken from *Crime & Criminology* by Sue Titus Reid. Copyright 1997. Reproduced with permission of The McGraw-Hill Companies.